ECOTOURISM

A Sustainable Option?

Edited by

ERLET CATER
University of Reading, UK

GWEN LOWMAN
Royal Geographical Society, London, UK

Published in association with the
Royal Geographical Society

JOHN WILEY & SONS

Chichester · New York · Brisbane · Toronto · Singapore

Published in 1994 by John Wiley & Sons Ltd,
Baffins Lane, Chichester,
West Sussex PO19 1UD, England
Telephone National Chichester (0243) 779777
International (+44) 243 779777

Reprinted June 1995, December 1995

Other Wiley Editorial Offices

John Wiley & Sons, Inc., 605 Third Avenue,
New York, NY 10158-0012, USA

Jacaranda Wiley Ltd, 33 Park Road, Milton,
Queensland 4064, Australia

John Wiley & Sons (Canada) Ltd, 22 Worcester Road,
Rexdale, Ontario M9W 1L1, Canada

John Wiley & Sons (SEA) Pte Ltd, 37 Jalan Pemimpin #05-04,
Block B, Union Industrial Building, Singapore 2057

Library of Congress Cataloging-in-Publication Data

Ecotourism: a sustainable option?/edited by Erlet Cater and Gwen Lowman.
p. cm.
"Published in association with the Royal Geographical Society."
Includes bibliographical references and index.
ISBN 0-471-94896-9
1. Ecotourism. I. Cater, Erlet. II. Lowman, Gwen. III. Royal
Geographical Society (Great Britain)
G155.A1E285 1994
338.4'791—dc20   94-15985
                                                      CIP

British Library Cataloguing in Publication Data

A catalogue record for this book is available from the British Library

ISBN 0-471-94896-9

Typeset in 10/12pt Times by Dorwyn Ltd, Rowlands Castle, Hants.
Printed and bound in Great Britain by Bookcraft (Bath) Ltd

ECOTOURISM

For John, Carl and Kirsten
E.A.C.

For Tom
G.A.L.

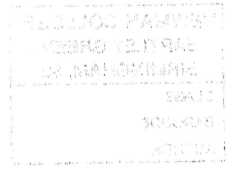

Contents

About the Contributors

Prince Sadruddin Aga Khan is chairman of Alp Action. Since its launch by Prince Sadruddin at the World Economic Forum in Davos in February 1990, Alp Action has contributed to the launch and implementation of many environmental projects with the support of its 25 corporate partners in conservation, which include several major European firms.

Erlet Cater PhD lectures on Third World Development issues in the Geography Department, University of Reading. Her main research interest is tourism in the developing world, focusing in particular on problems and prospects for sustainable ecotourism. She has co-convened two major conferences on tourism at the Royal Geographical Society.

Baroness Lynda Chalker is Minister for Overseas Development in the UK Government. The Rt. Hon. The Baroness Chalker of Wallasey was made Minister of State at the Foreign and Commonwealth Office in January 1986. In June 1987 she was made a Privy Counsellor and in July 1989 she became Minister for Overseas Development. She was made a life peer in April 1992.

Maureen de Coursey has been associated with the Annapurna Conservation Area Project since 1986 as a consultant in conservation education and tourism management. Her current work involves investigating the development potential for non-timber products in the Annapurna region as a means to generate village income and promote biodiversity conservation.

Chandra Gurung PhD has been director of the Annapurna Conservation Area Project, Nepal since 1989. In 1992 he was decorated Gorkha Dachhin Bahu by his Majesty King Birendra of Nepal, and with the order of the Golden Ark by His Royal Highness Prince Bernhard of the Netherlands.

C. Michael Hall PhD is director of the tourism programme in the Faculty of Communication at the University of Canberra. He moved to this position in May 1993 from his post as senior lecturer in the Tourism and Recreation Programme at Massey University, New Zealand.

Derek Hall PhD is principal lecturer in geography and convenor of the Tourism and Leisure Enterprises Unit at the University of Sunderland. He is an ecotourism consultant for the IUCN and the Government of Romania.

Vivian Kinnaird is a lecturer in geography at the University of Sunderland. Her research and teaching interests are in development studies, tourism and gender and development. She is co-editor with Derek Hall of *Tourism: Gender Analysis* (Wiley).

Gwen Lowman is Deputy Editor of the *Geographical Journal*, which is the academic journal of the Royal Geographical Society (RGS). Subsequent to teaching posts in the UK and Germany she trained as a book editor and has worked as a freelance editor of educational and general publications for a number of publishers. She has worked at the RGS since 1986.

Robert Prosser PhD is a lecturer in Recreation and Tourism Studies at the Centre for Urban and Regional Studies, University of Birmingham. He was previously Head of Geography at Newman and Westhill Colleges of Higher Education, Birmingham.

Richard Sisman is chairman and managing director of Green Flag International. He is advisor to the Countryside Commission, the Laona Project (Cyprus), the Malta Minister of Tourism and the Association of Independent Tour Operators.

Bernard Stonehouse PhD is at the Scott-Polar Research Institute, University of Cambridge, where he is head of the Polar Ecology and Management Research Group. An ecologist with over 40 years of experience in the Arctic and Antarctic, he has published several books on polar subjects and has been a guest lecturer on a number of Antarctic cruises. Until 1991 he was editor of *Polar Research* and has received the Polar Medal.

Sir Crispin Tickell is chairman of the Climate Institute of Washington, DC, Earthwatch Europe and the International Institute for Environment and Development. He is Warden of Green College, Oxford. He was formerly British Ambassador to the United Nations and, from 1990 to 1993, was President of the Royal Geographical Society.

David Weaver PhD is an associate professor of geography at Luther College, the University of Regina, Canada. He received his PhD at the University of Western Ontario in 1986 and specialises in alternative tourism and in the spatial and historical development of tourism in the Third World, in particular in the Caribbean.

Pamela Wight is in the Tourism Development Division of the Department of Economic Development and Tourism in Edmonton, Canada. She has been extensively involved in sustainable tourism initiatives, including Tourism in Alberta, which focuses on how to develop sustainable tourism in the state.

Foreword

Ecotourism means many things to many people. In my view it should mean travel to enjoy the world's amazing diversity of natural life and human culture without causing damage to either.

Some ecosystems—or natural habitats—are more vulnerable than others. Such closed island systems as the Galapagos Islands, where Charles Darwin first grasped the principles of evolution, are particularly sensitive. Any outside intruder, whether cats, goats or plants, can soon have disastrous effects on ecosystems which have grown up in isolation. The sensitivity of human cultures is often forgotten. In some places the vestigial remains of old cultures have been put at risk by our enthusiasm for them. At Lascaux in France the Magdalenian cave paintings of 13 000 to 14 000 years ago have become gravely contaminated as a result of visitors, in particular their breath and moisture. In Egypt ancient sites are being destroyed by the constant pounding of visitors' feet. Present day cultures are also at risk: in the Amazon basin the corrosive effects of tourism on indigenous peoples can be clearly seen.

Tourism is one of the world's largest industries. There is nothing like changing places to refresh the mind and put daily life into better perspective. Human curiosity is insatiable. It can bring enormous wealth to the host country, which in some cases can be used to help preserve the natural environment.

The preservation of such environments and cultures is subject to thresholds of numbers and control. Most environments are sufficiently robust to withstand a limited number of visitors provided ground rules are obeyed. In the Galapagos Islands it is forbidden to leave the delineated paths across the islands, or to take advantage of the amazing tameness of birds and animals. Likewise tourists have to learn not to make a mess or to clear it up if they do. Recent visitors to the Himalaya have found a dismaying amount of litter on the lower slopes of Mount Everest and along the Sacred Path.

A vital requirement is that visitors should show respect for both the environment and the people who live in it. Wanton abuse of ecosystems, including the introduction of alien species, can happen too often. Looking at indigenous people as if they were animals in a zoo is an affront to human dignity. We are all different in our appearance and customs, and should glory in our differences rather than subordinate ourselves to some grey middle standard. Tourists should also be obliged to pay for their enjoyment. Day trippers operating from liners in the Caribbean or bus loads of people well furnished with sandwiches are rarely popular.

Above all, the tourist industry has to remember a central precept: do not kill the goose which lays the golden eggs.

Sir Crispin Tickell

Acknowledgements

The customary acknowledgements are doubly valid in the case of this publication. As several of the chapters originate from the proceedings of the conference of the same title held at the Royal Geographical Society, the considerable work put into the preparation for that event by all involved must be gratefully recorded. In particular, Alison Glazebrook, programme co-ordinator for the RGS, organised matters with her customary efficiency. Sir Crispin Tickell and Martin Brackenbury (Thomson Travel) guided the proceedings as chairmen of the two sessions. Valuable contributions, in addition to those published in this text, were made by Geoffrey Lipman (WTTC), Emma Bannister (British Airways), Noel Josephides (AITO), Fergus Keeling, Major Dudley Spain, Bella Bird, Julia Hailes, Dr Roger Millman and Shailendra Thakali. The Director of the RGS, Dr John Hemming, has shown a continued and much valued interest in both the conference and book. At Reading, David Foot and Dr Antoinette Mannion have been generous with their time and advice.

The technical support given to us has been second to none. Sonia Luffrum showed unfailing patience and good humour when faced with typing even the most illegible of drafts, ably assisted by Donna Edwards and Susan Haase. The superb line drawings and tables were produced by Heather Browning and Judith Fox. Erika Meller was responsible for transforming some of these into excellent slides for projection at the conference, and also for producing most of the black and white photographs for the book from a motley assortment of colour photographs and slides.

Keith Madders of the Zimbabwe Trust gave freely of his time and contributed material for Chapter 6, including a set of photographs taken by Steve Thomas. Dr Tödter of CIPRA also met repeated requests for background information on Alpine Conservation for Chapter 7.

We consider ourselves very fortunate to have been able to draw on this wealth of experience from contributors, colleagues and collaborators alike. Such cooperation, together with the support and understanding of our families, has ensured that this publication is essentially a team effort, for which we should like to register our grateful thanks.

SECTION I
ISSUES AND INTERESTS

1

Introduction

ERLET CATER

PROBLEMS OF DEFINITION

No other form of economic activity transects so many sectors, levels and interests as tourism. This book embodies as much of that variation as possible, being based on a conference of the same title convened at the Royal Geographical Society in September 1992. Several of the papers presented at the conference are included as individual chapters, representing a range of interests from tourist boards to conservation organisations, and local communities to central government.

Considering the diversity of interests in tourism, it is not surprising that it is difficult to reach a consensus concerning the definitions that are used and the criteria employed in arriving at those definitions. It seems that the number and variety of interpretations are as broad and disparate as the backgrounds and interests of all those interested and involved in tourism development. As will be highlighted, the dimensions of time and space are further complicating issues. Consequently, even the interpretation of the title of this book can be subject to considerable debate.

Ecotourism: product or principle?

In particular, the term ecotourism is surrounded by confusion (Mowforth, 1992). Is it a form of 'alternative tourism' (furthermore, what is 'alternative tourism'?)? Is it responsible (defined in terms of environmental, socio-cultural, moral or practical terms)? Is it sustainable (however defined)? The list is endless and, it is feared, much of the debate counter-productive. To simplify the issue without, it is hoped, being simplistic, it is perhaps helpful to view 'alternative tourism', [with all its own difficulties of interpretation (Butler, 1992; Pearce, 1992), but generally taken to be alternative to mass tourism], as the generic term. Ecotourism can then be seen as a particular variant of alternative tourism. The attributes of ecological and socio-cultural integrity, responsibility and sustainability are qualities which may, or unfortunately may not, pertain to ecotourism as a product.

Ecotourism: A Sustainable Option? Edited by E. Cater and G. Lowman
© The editors and contributors. Published in 1994 by John Wiley & Sons Ltd

This leads on to the distinction that needs to be made between how eco-tourism has been, is and, it is anticipated, will be interpreted in general and how it should be interpreted in particular. It is necessary to adopt a pragmatic stance and recognise that, inevitably, the widest use (and abuse!) of the term is in the travel and tourism trade, where ecotourism has the dubious distinction of being singled out as the fastest growing sector in the industry. As such, it is identified as a niche or market segment, generally equated with nature or ecologically based tourism. Steele (1993), for example, describes it as 'an economic process where rare and beautiful eco-systems are marketed internationally to attract tourists'. It may also include the cultural attractions of the destination. In Chapter 9, Michael Hall highlights the indivisibility of the cultural and natural landscapes. To the indigenous peoples of the south-west Pacific, the environment is a natural resource and natural landscapes are, in fact, cultural, having evolved over thousands of years of indigenous land management practice.

In practice, ecotourism has often been seized upon by opportunistic tour operators who merely relabel their products as a marketing ploy. Pamela Wight, in Chapter 3 of this book, expresses her concern that there is a proliferation of advertisements in the travel field promoting experiences prefixed with 'eco' aimed at increasing interest and consequent sales. Thus the terms ecotour, ecotravel, ecovacation, eco(ad)ventures, ecocruise, eco-safari and so on are often little more than examples of environmental opportunism. Ecotourism, thus interpreted, may be ecologically based but not ecologically sound.

Before moving on to how 'ecotourism' should be interpreted, it is perhaps also useful to examine its use in both an unhyphenated and hyphenated form. There is no clear direction concerning this issue, but the hyphenated eco-tourism does tend to have a much wider interpretation which embodies environmentally sound practices in tourism in general. Thus 'the decade of the 1990s has been predicted to become the decade of *eco-tourism*, and the travel industry is becoming sensitised to mounting global concern about the social costs and environmental damage created by too much tourism' (Eadington and Smith, 1992). This wider interpretation is evident in Chapter 4, where Dick Sisman is concerned with the coincidence of good business and sound environmental practice in tourism as a whole.

The distinction of how ecotourism is most commonly interpreted as a product and what it should embody as a principle is an important one as it gives rise to many of the points raised in this book. As a resource-based industry it is vital to pay attention to the essential principle outlined in Chapter 5. Equating the natural resource base with the capital stock, and the annual production of the biosphere with the interest, it is essential that only the interest should be used and the capital stock not cut into (Rees, 1990). This concept of conservation and protection thus takes us one step further, arriving at a somewhat broader, but still narrow definition of ecotourism as ecologically sound and requiring a two-way link between itself and nature conservation (Valentine, 1993).

To consider the natural resource base without recognising the inextricable link with the human resource base will, however, compromise sustainability. As the text proceeds and, in particular, as the case studies are raised, it will become increasingly evident that conservation must not, indeed cannot, be divorced from development issues. To satisfy the multitude of interests involved, at present and in the future, ecotourism needs to be sustainable.

Sustainability: rhetoric or reality?

The oft-quoted definition of the Brundtland Commission Report 'development which meets the needs of the present without compromising the ability of future generations to meet their own needs' incorporates the essential principles of intra-generational and inter-generational equity. These principles, however, are taken on board without adequate recognition of the discontinuities involved between the varied interests. The question of 'for whom will ecotourism development be sustainable?' is particularly apposite, owing to the number and diversity of interests involved. What may appear to be sustainable from one point of view is unlikely to be so from another. This conflict will be examined in more detail.

It is, perhaps, no coincidence that much of the debate concerning what constitutes ecotourism has its parallel in the weighty debate surrounding the definition of sustainable development. Both tend to be overworked terms, neatly co-opted by political and business interests to confer an aura of respectability to their activities. In both instances all that may be involved is a re-labelling of the status quo, as Rees (1990) suggests 'a laboured excuse for not departing from continued economic growth'.

Options or dictates?

This preoccupation with growth leads on to the final consideration of the book's title; how far is ecotourism development an option, particularly as far as destinations are concerned? This is especially pertinent to the developing world, where it is evident that little choice can be exercised. The use of the term 'option' is somewhat of a misnomer for two reasons. Firstly, the pattern and organisation of international tourism often mean a degree of loss of sovereignty of destination countries in terms of decision-making. Wilkinson (1989) describes how micro-states, in particular, become targets for exogenous decision-making that is often insensitive to local issues and needs. Even the original emphasis on ecotourism may have arisen from outside, leading to accusations of green imperialism and eco-missionaries (Dowden, 1992), and of eco-colonialism (Cater, 1992) or eco-imperialism as described in Chapter 9. Secondly, the element of choice implied by the use of the term 'option' may not be there; many small developing nations have little other than their natural resource endowment upon which to base their development prospects. The situation is particularly acute in a virtual monoculture situation, such as that described by Weaver in Chapter 10 on the Caribbean island of Dominica. The withdrawal of preferential access to the UK market for the island's banana crop, which constitutes the bulk of its agricultural exports, will have serious repercussions for the Dominican economy. Hence an enhanced emphasis on its promotion as 'nature island' of the Caribbean.

This question of choice also has a vital bearing on the whole question of sustainability for the poorest people, whose very poverty forces them into unsustainable behaviour. As Redclift (1992) suggests, 'poor people often have no choice but to choose immediate economic benefits at the expense of the long term sustainability of their livelihoods' and 'there is no point in appealing, under these circumstances, to idealism or altruism to protect the environment, when the individual and household are forced to behave "selfishly" in their struggle to survive'. Clark (1991) also endorses this view, suggesting that 'there is some poverty level below which sustainability becomes an unaffordable luxury. Vast numbers of impoverished people throughout the world face this dilemma every day of their lives'.

THE RANGE OF INTERESTS

The multitude of interests involved in ecotourism ranges from nature reserves to National Parks, from local tourist boards to government departments, and from tour operators to conservationist organisations. They are expressed at different spatial scales, and vary over time. There has been a conscious attempt in this text to embrace this variation and to consider the problems and prospects for sustainable ecotourism development across these dimensions. The chapters draw from the experience of decision-makers, practitioners, conservationists, consultants and advisers, as well as academics. The geographical coverage of illustrative case material ranges from polar (Chapter 12) through tropical and subtropical (Chapters 9, 10 and 11) to temperate latitudes (Chapters 7 and 8). It encompasses the development spectrum from high income nations (Chapters 7 and 9) through high and lower middle income nations (Chapters 8 and 10) to low income nations (Chapters 5, 6 and 11).

The range of interests involved in ecotourism might be loosely grouped into four categories: tourist guests, tourism organisations, the host population and the natural environment.

Tourists

In Chapter 2, Bob Prosser starts from the demand side of the equation, by examining the characteristics of changing fashions and tastes of tourists and the factors which influence them. These have important repercussions over the temporal and spatial dimensions, as an emulated élite inspires or propagates a fashion which is then adopted by progressively broader sectors of society. It is suggested, therefore, that not only do the numbers arriving at a destination change, but so do the types of tourists, facilitated by the travel and tourism industry. It has been reported that Britain's second biggest tour operators, Airtours, has changed to meet such new demand. It ran a special Cuba programme in the summer of 1994 and also ran regular charter flights for the first time to the Cayman Islands (Barrett, 1993). Meanwhile, the élite move on, driven by a desire for novelty and exclusivity of experience. So-called 'in' destinations include Bhutan and Patagonia. Trailfinders, Britain's biggest specialist ticket agency, selling almost a quarter of a million air seats a year, declares its fastest growing destination to be Vietnam.

Tourism organisations

The interests of tourism organisations are covered specifically in the chapters by Pamela Wight and Dick Sisman. These two chapters, as well as those by Baroness Chalker and Bernard Stonehouse, also cover the all-important regulatory and facilitating roles of government and international agencies as well as of non-governmental organisations (NGOs).

Pamela Wight points to the need for integrity of the tourism product. This brings an implicit advantage not only for the destination but also for the consumer, enabling easy identification of genuine ecotourism suppliers. There is also a benefit for the operator in terms of generating public support, together with increased credibility and market demand for associated products. Dick Sisman also draws attention to these benefits. Using the wider interpretation of ecotourism, he stresses that sound environmental practice not only makes good business sense, but also has relevance because it helps to create a quality product.

It has been suggested by several writers such as de Kadt (1992), and Erlet Cater in this book, that the operation of a free market will not in itself lead to sustainable tourism practice. A more proactive role needs to be taken by the relevant organisations, associations, governments and institutions. Two chapters deal more specifically with this role. Chapter 6, by Baroness Chalker, examines the role of NGOs such as the Campfire Initiative in Zimbabwe and the pump-priming role of official aid agencies, such as Britain's Overseas Development Administration, in facilitating more sustainable tourism practices. The final chapter, by Bernard Stonehouse of the Scott-Polar Research

Institute, includes an examination of the international regulatory role of the
Antarctic Treaty and the need to incorporate tourism in its mandate.

Host populations

The interests of ecotourism destinations are dealt with primarily in the second
half of the book, but the vital need to incorporate the local population in
decision-making and implementation is also referred to in some detail in
Chapters 5 and 6. The moral, conservational, economic and practical reasons
for this are outlined in the former, and Baroness Chalker highlights the ways
that the local population receive direct benefits from the Campfire scheme in
Zimbabwe in the latter. It is vital that these benefits should be direct and not
indirect in the form of handouts or doles, or even the provision of show
factors such as schools or hospitals. Chandra Gurung and Maureen de
Coursey, in Chapter 11, rightly point out that financial patronisation is not a
long-term solution. Indigenous involvement is also dealt with in Chapter 7 by
His Royal Highness Prince Sadruddin Aga Khan, who describes the Hindelang initiative in the Bavarian Alps, integrating the interests of mountain
farmers with those of Alpine tourism.

Michael Hall, in Chapter 9, suggests that the vital recognition of the social
dimension of the relationship between tourism, development and the environment has been absent in ecotourism in the south-west Pacific, thus compromising sustainability. That the interests of the host community, the
environment, tourists and tourism organisations may not always be coincident
is also illustrated by Derek Hall and Vivian Kinnaird in Chapter 8. In much of
Eastern Europe there is a seeming conflict between hunting opportunities
hitherto restricted to the political élite and the requirements of conservationists. If these were to be properly managed in terms of the controlled culling of
wildlife, as suggested for wild boar on the Estonian Baltic island of Sareema
by Pikner (1993), there might be a higher degree of complementarity. The
involvement of the local population in the management of their own wildlife
resources in Zimbabwe is described in Chapter 6.

The natural environment

The final interest is that of the environment, which, if not adequately safe-
guarded, will compromise all the foregoing interests in ecotourism. Tourists,
present and future, will be denied the opportunity of visiting and experiencing
environments different to those of home. The profit-maximising and revenue-
earning aspirations of tourism organisations, private and public, are very
much bound up with satisfying tourist expectations. Host populations will
stand to lose out in two ways. Environmental degradation will affect not only
their immediate prospects, but they will also be denied the potential, not only

for tourism development, but also for development in general, that such environments offered for the future.

The current example of Kenya is a graphic illustration of the economic significance of sound environmental management as the baseline of successful tourism operations. The Kenya Wildlife Service, faced with a projected decline of two per cent in wildlife tourist days between 1990 and 1995, with a corresponding drop in tourism receipts, has instituted reforms for the protection of the environment. It is estimated that such reforms will reverse this projected decline, resulting in an eight per cent increase in wildlife tourist days per annum and amounting to an increase in receipts of US$306 million over the five year period (Table 1.1). These reforms embody 15 strategic elements, which include better coordination of land use, involvement of the local population and integration with other sectors (EIU, 1992).

CONFLICT OR COMPROMISE?

It can be seen, therefore, that the major rôle-players in tourism all have a stake in sustainable tourism and that their present and future interests are in many ways tied to one another and to sound environmental practice. The protection of the environment is an essential part of ecotourism development. Without adequate environmental protection ecotourism development in particular, and development prospects in general, are undermined, compromising the present and future prospects of tourism organisations, tourist guests and host destinations alike.

Given the multitude of interests involved, however, a completely sustainable outcome is likely to remain more of an ideal than a reality. With regard to development in general, the World Bank (1992) emphasises the need to build upon the positive links between development and the environment and

TABLE 1.1. Projected tourism receipts in Kenya with and without the KWS environmental programme. Reproduced by permission from Economist Intelligence Unit (1992)

	1990	1991	1992	1993	1994	1995	Total
KSh mn							
Receipts without project	4320	4234	4149	4066	3985	3905	24 659
Receipts with project	4320	4666	5039	5442	5877	6347	31 691
Increase due to project	—	432	890	1376	1893	2443	7034
$ mn							
Increase due to project	—	19	39	60	82	106	306

to break the negative links. With regard to ecotourism, it is possible to identify four different scenarios which are a reflection of the balance and relative strengths of environmental and developmental interests. (Figure 1.1). The first of these is one where the positive links are immediately evident and mutually beneficial. The remaining three are a reflection of the conflicts that occur and point to the need for compromise resolution to arrive at more sustainable outcomes.

The win–win scenario

This is the situation where the positive links between environment and development result in environmental improvement at the same time as the promotion of income growth. In the field of ecotourism, such situations arise where sound environmental and business practices coincide, described by Dick Sisman in Chapter 4.

The most obvious win–win situation is, perhaps, in the field of energy conservation, a double-edged sword that will reduce the relative consumption of fossil fuels and consequent carbon dioxide emissions and at the same time reduce costs and enhance profits. The more efficient use of fuelwood also has important repercussions for forest conservation and reduction of soil erosion. In Chapter 11, Gurung and de Coursey describe the various measures that are being implemented in the Annapurna Conservation Area Project to promote such practices and the use of alternative energy resources to decrease pressures on the Himalayan forests. As well as the obvious environmental benefits, lodge operators will realise financial savings. There are also important implications for the time budgets of the women and children of the household, who were hitherto forced to forage further and further afield to gather fuel.

Such win–win situations tend to be the exception rather than the rule, however. Set into the overall context of sustainability other considerations, economic and socio-cultural, have to be brought into the decision-making equation. Conflicts will occur between the different interests involved. It is therefore possible to identify three further scenarios in addition to the win–win ccase.

The win–lose scenario

This is represented by the situation where the environment benefits, but where other interests may lose out. Such an example is that of the designation of National Parks and Protected Areas, which aim to fulfil conservational aims and, if properly managed, the expectations of tourists. The local population, however, will lose out if they are denied access to their traditional practices such as nomadic pastoralism, agriculture and the gathering of fuel and building materials, as described in Chapter 5. Hall, in Chapter 9, points to the important requirement of recognising that the environment constitutes an

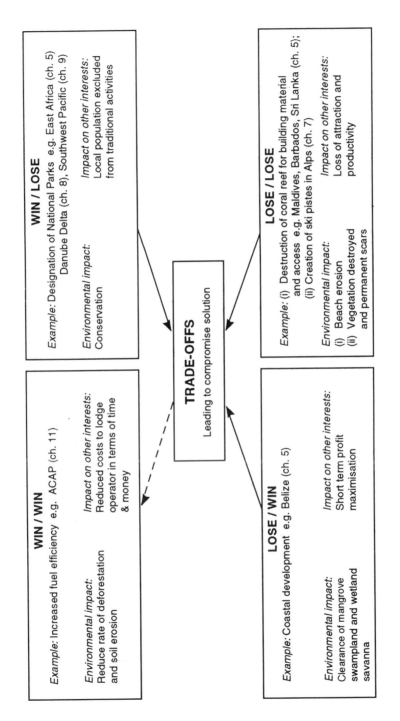

FIGURE 1.1. Examples of mixed outcomes of ecotourism for the environment and development

economic, ecological, social and cultural resource to the indigenous population.

The lose–win scenario

This situation, which occurs when the environment may be downgraded whilst other interests benefit, is a lose–win situation, even if it may only be short-lived. An example of this is the case of coastal tourism development, where the environment is downgraded in the interests of short-term profit maximisation. Chapter 5 describes how coastal development in Belize results in the destruction of two distinctive ecosystems. Of particular consequence is the destruction of the mangrove swampland which fulfils three important functions, acting as a protective barrier against coastal erosion, a filter for off-land sediment and a rich feeding ground for fish. A significant environmental loss, therefore, has resulted from the development of two international hotels in this coastal zone in 1991.

The lose–lose scenario

This is where, resulting from the degradation of the very resources which attracted tourists in the first place, all interests are compromised. Indeed, without proper management this is likely to be the end state of the two previous scenarios.

A prime example is the destruction of offshore coral reefs. This may result from direct physical damage or as a result of increased marine pollution. The former results from blasting to create access channels, such as in Barbados, or to utilise the coral for building material, such as in Sri Lanka, the Maldives and Bali. In the Maldives, a quarter of the coral mined from resort islands is used directly for resort construction (the remainder is used on the capital island of Malé). It will also result from souvenir hunting and careless treatment resulting from the mishandling of boat and scuba equipment, together with direct trampling of the reefs at low tide. Pollution results from the increased turbidity and sewage discharge which arise from the construction phase and ongoing site utilisation, as well as petrol and oil spillage consequent upon boating activities. Destruction of the coral reefs not only has an opportunity cost in terms of the loss of the very resource which attracted tourists in the first place, but also results in the loss of a protective barrier against coastal erosion. Ironically, therefore, it may result in the erosion of the sandy beaches which were also part of the tourism attraction, as has been evidenced along the coasts of Tanzania, Bali and Barbados.

Another lose–lose situation is described in Chapter 7, where His Royal Highness Prince Sadruddin Aga Khan documents how tourism pressures have downgraded the Alpine environment.

It can be seen, therefore, that there are a number of discontinuities which occur between the environment and ecotourism development; what is a win situation for one interest, level or sector is likely to be a loss for another. The complexity of the situation is further compounded, however, by the likelihood that these conflicts will vary over time and space. Mannion (1992) suggests that: 'What is sustainable is sustainable only for one time and for one place'. So, not only must the question be posed of for whom tourism development is sustainable, but also where and when.

Spatial considerations

The spatial scale of most of the chapters in the book is that of the individual nation or groupings of nations. A case study at the regional level, however, is offered by Derek Hall and Vivian Kinnaird in Chapter 8, where they examine the opportunities that ecotourism offers in terms of an ecologically meaningful and economically profitable strategy for the Danube Delta. At a more local scale, Chandra Gurung and Maureen de Coursey give a detailed account of the pioneering work of the Annapurna Conservation Area Project in Nepal. The bottom-up approach of the project (Hough and Sherpa, 1989) is an interesting example of local involvement at all stages in the planning for, and implementation of, more sustainable ecotourism practices. The sound reasons for greater local involvement are raised in Chapter 5. The vexed question of what actually constitutes truly local involvement needs to be raised, however. The interests of a local élite may be as far removed from those of the community as those of foreign entrepreneurs. Hall describes this situation with reference to the so-called 'big men' of the Solomon Islands in Chapter 9.

Spatial considerations must, however, transcend national boundaries. These are at their most obvious when the movement of tourists between origins and destinations and within destinations is considered. An example is that of air travel. Ecotourism constitutes only a small proportion, albeit growing, of such travel, but when it is considered that aircraft emissions are estimated to contribute three per cent to global carbon dioxide concentrations, the significance is undeniable (British Airways, 1993).

What is not so obvious, but still of great importance, is the recognition that tourism in general, and thus ecotourism, is cast in an unequal global context. The requirement for intra-generational equity is, as mentioned earlier, a vital requisite of sustainable development. This wider context, however, has often conveniently been skated over. Redclift (1992), for example, with regard to development in general, cites the 'failure to take adequate account of both international (structural) and cross cultural factors in sustainable development'. Gonsalves (1990) examines the situation with regard to Third World tourism, suggesting that 'it cannot be equated with that of the First World—it is rooted in structural inequalities—locally, nationally, regionally and globally'. He describes how the basis of this inequality is not ecological or cultural, but political and economic and accuses responsible or alternative tourism of being a 'technological intervention'. Structural problems, he suggests, require structural solutions.

The emphasis of this book is very much on international tourism, but the significance of domestic tourism must not be forgotten. Michael Hall, for example, in Chapter 9 describes how domestic tourism bolsters the numbers visiting natural attractions in New Zealand to a total of just under five million visits. Dick Sisman recently described (Sisman, 1993) the burgeoning whale-watching industry, which now attracts an estimated four million domestic and foreign participants world-wide each year. Anfield (1994) gives an account of the pressures on the Peak National Park (UK) with 22 million visitors a year (mainly domestic), the most visited National Park in Europe.

Finally, mention must be made of the role that mass tourism has, and will continue to have, as an economic, social and environmental safety valve. Tourism's forms and practices can be influenced but its volume cannot be curtailed (Jafari, 1989). Where would Europe be without Spain (35 million tourist arrivals in 1992), and where would Spain be without the Costas? As Pearce (1992) asks, how can low key alternative tourism survive without having some other form of tourism to be an alternative to?

Temporal considerations

The time dimension is a final vital consideration in sustainable ecotourism. The present and future requirements of the various interests involved have already been mentioned. Short-term benefits to one interest result in long-term losses for others. They are also likely to result in long-term losses for the same interest. The concept of inter-generational equity is also central to sustainable development, but again conflicts are bound to occur. Already there are signs in Belize that the sustainable ecotourism development that was being strived for is being compromised by the pursuit of immediate economic gain (Chapter 5).

In an industry previously inclined towards sacrificing longer term interests for short-term gain, an about-turn is clearly indicated. Past models of development in general tended to assume that the future will look after itself. The sustainable development approach, however, acknowledges that the ability to do this can be seriously impaired by actions taken now, and that future generations are not likely to be able to choose as freely as those at present. The problem is, however, how to build those future interests into the decision-making equation. The attempted quantification of such future interests is dealt with elsewhere (for example, Costanza, 1991). The precise nature of these interests, however, must remain somewhat of an unknown. Redclift

(1992) poses the essential question as to whether human needs are fixed or static. He suggests that development itself entails the development of 'needs' as well as the means to satisfy them. The situation is therefore dynamic, but once again comes round to the requirement to involve those who best understand their own present needs and can best anticipate those of the future. Thus sustainable ecotourism development might be defined by the people themselves; they need to be both architects and engineers of the concept.

What, then, of the future? As a whole, international tourism arrivals are set to double between 1990 and 2010 from 456 million to 937 million, the growth rate peaking a 4.4% in the year 2000. Although ecotourism will comprise only a small part of that total, it is growing at over double that average growth rate. The clear trend towards more individual travel, away from cheap packages, has been noted in the industry. According to the British Government's International Passenger Survey, the number of British people taking non-package holidays grew from 7.7 million to 13.7 million during the 1980s. The ecotourism component of this figure can only be conjectured, but is likely to be of growing significance.

It has been recognised that ecotourists are typically older than conventional mass tourists (Boo, 1990). A survey conducted of lifestyles in 1993 found that people in the 45–64 year age bracket were more likely than any other age group to have more than one holiday a year. This, together with the characteristics of an ageing population in the more developed world points to the continued growth in the number of ecotourists from that age group. As far as the travelling public as a whole is concerned, the environment is likely to remain high on the tourist agenda. The prospects of pressures from green consumerism to continue unbridled has sometimes been questioned, but it is certain that the near future will bring more regulatory and legislative measures. In addition, Gray (1990) suggests that additional pressures will be brought to bear from 'green' shareholders and 'green' employees.

ACHIEVING A COMPROMISE

In terms of policy implications, individual chapters make various recommendations, but the overall message of the text must be one of a holistic approach integrating the myriad of interests across the dimensions of time and space. It is naive to pretend that this will be easy or that experience can be generalised.

The target of sustainable ecotourism is elusive. To recognise the types of conflict that occur, however, is an essential step towards attaining more, if not completely, sustainable outcomes. Identification of the relative costs and benefits to the various interests should then be possible. To arrive at the most sustainable outcome will inevitably involve trade-offs (Figure 1.1); it is unlikely to be optimal either from the point of view of the environmentalist or the developmentalist. To enable such decisions to be made, however, policy-makers need to be furnished with more detailed information on the extent and nature of such trade-offs. A major problem in the past has been that environmental considerations have not been incorporated in models or meas-urements and thus not in decision-making. The environment was externalised, treated as a 'free' good. This has been more fully documented elsewhere with regard to development in general (Pearce *et al.*, 1989) and to tourism in particular (de Kadt, 1992).

Particularly evident omissions in terms of environmental measurements exist in accountancy procedures. As the environment was not incorporated into accounting frameworks, the resultant picture which was then used as a basis for decision-making was incomplete, helping to contribute towards the negative aspects of the scenarios described earlier. More complete account-ancy procedures must include environmental considerations. One tool for 'green' accounting is that of environmental auditing. Goodall (1992) examines how this technique may be used to monitor how the products and processes of tourism interact with the environment. Such an exercise may be carried out not only at company and organisational levels, but also for individual establishments and destinations.

Such improved procedures will help to break the negative links between ecotourism development and the environment and build on the positive links to enable a move towards a more sustainable win–win situation, if only a small step on the way. Trade-offs between development and environmental quality need to be carefully assessed, taking long-term, uncertain and irreversible impacts into account (World Bank, 1992). To more fully address the needs of the local population, and thus to be more sustainable, a careful balancing of costs and benefits is likely to result in a compromise solution which is site-specific. It will probably be suboptimal from the viewpoints of all concerned but, in the circumstances, will be the most feasible, practicable and, hence, result in more sustainable ecotourism than hitherto.

REFERENCES

Anfield, J., 1994, Sustainable tourism in the nature and National Parks of Europe, *George Wright Forum*, **11**, 1.
Barrett, F., 1993, 'Having a fine time: glad you're not here', *Independent*, 31 January.
Boo, E., 1990, *Ecotourism: the Potentials and Pitfalls*, Vol. 1, World Wildlife Fund, Washington.
British Airways, 1993, *Annual Environmental Report*, British Airways, London.
Butler, R., 1992, Alternative Tourism: the thin edge of the wedge, in Smith, V.L. and Eadington, W.R. (eds) *Tourism Alternatives*, University of Pennsylvania Press, Philadelphia.
Cater, E., 1992, Profits from Paradise, *Geographical*, **64**(3), 16–21.
Clark, C.W., 1991, Economic biases against sustainable development, in Costanza, R. (ed.) *Ecological Economics*, Columbia, New York.

Costanza, R., 1991, *Ecological Economics*, Columbia, New York.
de Kadt, E., 1992, Making the alternative sustainable: lessons from development for tourism, in Smith, V.L. and Eadington, W.R. (eds) *Tourism Alternatives,* University of Pennsylvania Press, Philadelphia.
Dowden, R., 1992, 'Eco-missionaries preach the new gospel in Africa', *Independent,* 3 June.
Eadington, W.R. and Smith, V.L., 1992, The emergence of alternative forms of tourism, in Smith, V.L. and Eadington, W.R. (eds) *Tourism Alternatives,* University of Pennsylvania Press, Philadelphia.
Economist Intelligence Unit, 1992, *The Tourism Industry and the Environment*, E.I.U. Publications, London.
Gonsalves, P., 1990, Responsible tourism, *Tourism Concern Newsletter,* **3**, 17.
Goodall, B., 1992, Environmental auditing for tourism, in Cooper, C.P. and Lockwood, A. (eds) *Progress in Tourism, Recreation and Hospitality Management*, Vol. 4, Belhaven, London.
Gray, R.H., 1990, *The Greening of Accountancy,* Certified Accountants Publications, London.
Hough, J.L. and Sherpa, M.N., 1989, Bottom up vs basic needs: integrating conservation and development in the Annapurna and Michuru mountain conservation areas of Nepal and Malawi, *Ambio,* **18**(8), 434–441.
Jafari, J., 1989, Soft tourism, *Tourism Management,* **9**, 32–34.
Mannion, A., 1992, Sustainable development and biotechnology, *Environmental Conservation,* **19**(1), 297–306.
Mowforth, M., 1992, Eco-tourism: terminology and definitions, *University of Plymouth Research Report.*
Pearce, D., 1992, Alternative tourism: concepts, classifications and questions, in Smith, V.L. and Eadington, W.R. (eds) *Tourism Alternatives,* University of Pennsylvania Press, Philadelphia.
Pearce, D.W., Markandya, A. and Barbier, E.B., 1989, *Blueprint for a Green Economy*, Earthscan, London.
Pikner, T., 1993, Sustainable tourism in Estonian islands in the frame of the association of the islands of the Baltic, paper presented at the *International Conference on Sustainable Tourism in Islands and Small States, November 18–20, Malta.*
Redclift, M., 1992, The meaning of sustainable development, *Geoforum,* **23**(3), 395–403.
Rees, N.E., 1990, The ecology of sustainable development, *The Ecologist,* **20**(1), 18–23.
Sisman, D., 1993, Sustainable tourism as a business concept, paper presented at the *Tools for Sustainable Tourism Conference,* October 6, Royal Geographical Society.
Steele, P., 1993, The economics of eco-tourism, *In Focus,* **9**, 4–6.
Valentine, P.S., 1993, Ecotourism and nature conservation: a definition with some recent developments in Micronesia, *Tourism Management,* **14**(2), 107–115.
Wilkinson, P.F., 1989, Strategies for tourism in island microstates, *Annals of Tourism Research,* **16**(2), 153–177.
World Bank, 1992, *World Development Report,* Oxford University Press, Oxford.

2

Societal Change and the Growth in Alternative Tourism

ROBERT PROSSER

TOURISM AS A GLOBAL INDUSTRY

David Lodge, in his novel *Paradise News*, proclaims tourism half-seriously as the new global religion. Using guidebooks as devotional aids, ever-increasing millions make 'pilgrimages' to a galaxy of holy places—from Disneyland to Delhi, from Cairo to coral reefs, from Harrods to the Himalayas:

> Sitting on a lump of rock beside the Parthenon, watching the tourists milling about, clicking their cameras, talking to each other in umpteen different languages, it suddenly struck me: tourism is the new world religion. Catholics, Protestants, Hindus, Muslims, Buddhists, atheists—the one thing they have in common is they all believe in the importance of seeing the Parthenon. Or the Sistine Chapel, or the Eiffel Tower.
>
> (Lodge, 1992: 76)

What Lodge parodies is, of course, mass package tourism, the extreme form of the travel phenomenon, and 'phenomenon' it is indeed, as it sweeps the world with seemingly unstoppable energy like a tsunami. The numbers and the growth rates are impressive: by the mid-1990s some 500 million travellers will cross international boundaries each year (Table 2.1). In addition, throughout the world, domestic travel is growing as a component of social and economic change. Despite indications of a slowing down, travel and tourism remains, in the 1990s, one of the world's fastest growing industrial sectors (see Figure 2.1), and is poised to become the world leader, with six per cent of global GNP and at least 13 per cent of consumptive expenditure. Equally significant is the realisation that, although over 60 per cent of all travel still occurs between countries of North America and Europe, the highest growth rates are being recorded by newly industrialised countries (NICs) and less developed countries (LDCs) (Table 2.2). It must be remembered too, that demand for, as well as supply of, tourism opportunities is becoming truly

Ecotourism: A Sustainable Option? Edited by E. Cater and G. Lowman
© The editors and contributors. Published in 1994 by John Wiley & Sons Ltd

TABLE 2.1. International tourist arrivals: world
totals (millions). Source: World Tourism Organisation (1991)

Year	Tourist arrivals
1950	25
1960	70
1970	160
1980	290
1990	440
1995 (est)	500

TABLE 2.2. Regional growth rates in tourist arrivals,
1985–90 average annual percentage growth. Source:
World Tourism Organisation (1991)

Region	Tourist arrivals (% growth)
Oceania	10.5
Africa	9.0
Asia	8.5
Americas	7.5
Europe	5.5

global, illustrated vividly by the rapid growth of high-spending tourists from
Japan and the NICs of south-east Asia.

THE ROLE OF TOURISM

Grandiose claims continue to be made for the economic, social and psycho-
logical benefits of tourism, many of which contain a body of truth, e.g. attracting foreign currency, improving world understanding and broadening the
mind. There is no doubt that travel opportunities can enhance the quality of
human experience in spiritual as well as material ways, as witness the section
headings used by a well-known book on tourism (Krippendorf, 1987).

- travel is recuperation and regeneration
- travel is compensation and social integration
- travel is escape
- travel is communication
- travel broadens the mind
- travel is freedom and self-determination
- travel is self-realisation
- travel is happiness

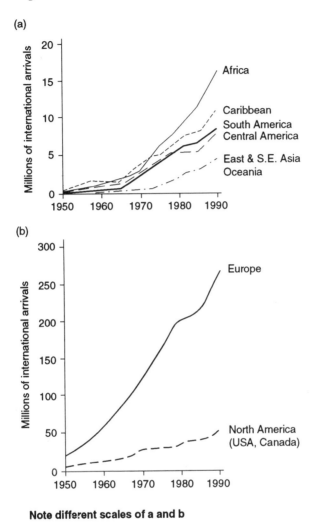

FIGURE 2.1. Growth of world tourism 1950–90. Source: World Tourism Organisation (1991)

Yet a rising chorus of critical comment and analysis surrounds this tourism phenomenon. Writers such as Boorstin (1961) and Fussell (1982) have bemoaned the transition from the qualities of travel to the artificialities of tourism, but only in the 1970s did a broad debate and critique emerge, exemplified by the publication in 1975 of *The Golden Hordes* by Turner and Ash. In this seminal book, Turner and Ash describe tourists as a plague of marauders spreading across the earth. During the 1980s, more carefully argued analyses emerged, such as those of Krippendorf (1987), who describes tourists as 'landscape eaters', Murphy (1985) and Urry (1990). The central concerns persist, however. The issues relating to tourism stem from: (1) the continuing growth of numbers; (2) the increasing ability to penetrate ever more remote locations; and (3) the assumption of the right to do so. In 1992, about 6000 people paid an average of £6000 each to penetrate the fringes of Antarctica through the innovative energies of specialist tour operators (see Chapter 12).

Each component of the tourism system has a distinctive perspective concerning these central themes. Actual and potential tourists, i.e. the demand component, are becoming more questioning in their approach to and selection of travel alternatives. The destinations which supply the attractive resources are attempting to be more cautious in their thrust for tourism wealth. The industry which organises the experiences by linking demand and supply is responding to these shifts in perception, attitude and policy. Yet they all remain locked into the focal dilemma: each component is placing increasing emphasis upon quality while faced with the inexorable growth in quantity. In addition to its sheer scale, the tourism industry has distinctive attributes which make a particular impact upon people and environments. For instance, international tourism behaves as an export industry in that foreign currency is earned for a product, but is distinctive in that the consumption takes place at the point of production: tourists walk into a travel agent in Doncaster, Dortmund or Denver, purchase a Botswana holiday, a proportion of the cost of which is transferred to that country, and ultimately they consume the product in the Chobe National Park and the Okavango Delta.

CHANGING FASHIONS IN DESTINATIONS AND EXPERIENCES

One of the most important characteristics of tourism is that it is, in essence, a fashion industry. The complex two-way relationships between demand and supply are based upon the dynamics of people's perceptions, expectations, attitudes and values. Participation in tourism is, therefore, subject to powerful cultural filters which may change over time. For example, the Japanese are well-known for their strongly developed work ethic, but this is changing, both organically in the ways people think, and as an element of public policy, where the government is emphasising the benefits of the leisure ethic. One result is the explosion in the Japanese demand for tourism experiences. For instance, succeeding the well-publicised 'sex tourism' packages to Bangkok for business executives, there is the rapidly growing Australian tour itinerary: Cairns/Barrier Reef – Ayers Rock – Sydney, which is causing concern over its carrying capacity, impacts and quality of experience.

As tourism is influenced strongly by fashion and the related concepts of status and image, tourist demand is notoriously fickle. Societies which generate tourists change their motivations, expectations and demands. The interests and reasons for travel often change, and, even where they remain essentially the same, the fashion filter enters the equation. Thus, despite health warnings, getting a tan is still central to many people's expectations of a holiday, but just any suntan is not enough—it is where you get it: not Margate, not even Marbella, but Mauritius! Yet this obsession with bronzing, with its connotations of health, sexuality and status, dates back only to the Côte d'Azur lifestyle of the leisured classes of the 1920s. Perhaps by the millennium natural skin tones will be the fashion, precipitated by the concern with skin cancer. In consequence, the demand–supply relationships in tourism are peculiarly dynamic, and many experiences and destinations pass through a product cycle.

Tourism as an exploitative industry—the product cycle

In the terms of this paradigm, tourism becomes an exploitative process, comparable with the extraction of a primary resource such as timber or iron ore.

The model shown in Figure 2.2, adapted from Butler's original formulation (1980), summarises the evolution of this cycle: a destination is discovered, i.e. its resources are perceived to be valuable/attractive—they are made increasingly available—demand grows and the destination booms—the resource becomes maximally exploited—the resource/product becomes less competitive/attractive/valuable—the destination declines and may even die as the demand disappears or the resource is exhausted. Contemplation of this scenario leads to the key question: is there life after tourism?

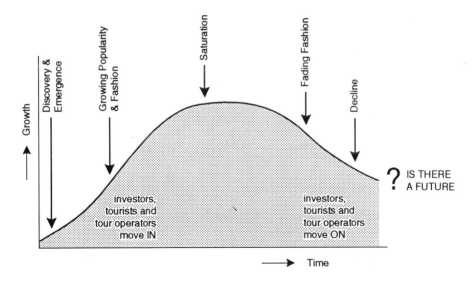

FIGURE 2.2. Tourism: the product cycle

Three energisers of this product cycle are the concepts of conspicuous consumption, successive class intervention and the pleasure periphery.

Consumption

All tourism involves consumption, but the element of conspicuousness enters along with the fashion, status and image dimensions of tourism: consumption must be seen and displayed, via suntan, photos, dinner party anecdotes, artifacts, etc. Psychologically too, there are satisfactions connected with such conspicuousness related to self-esteem, ego and image. The seeking out of new places and experiences is part of this consumption for exhibition. For example, an article in *Time* magazine in 1989, extolling the virtues of a new exclusive resort in Hawaii, uses the title—'Wait till we tell the folks back home!' Such élites seek exclusivity and novelty, and move on once a destination no longer offers a perception of exclusivity or novelty.

> There are not many places left on this earth that still confer bragging rights now that Kathmandu has as many package tours as Atlantic City and darkest Africa is bright with flashbulbs. So just in time comes the spanking new Hyatt Regency Waikoloa on the Big Island of Hawaii. . . . there's an ego boost in going home saying 'We took a helicopter to a remote spot and had a picnic just for two'. Can't you imagine that kind of story in the Des Moines bridge circle?
>
> (*Time* 27 February 1989)

Class intervention

The concept of successive class intervention states that, over time, a particular mode of consumption, fashion or lifestyle will spread downwards through the socio-economic class structure of a society. An admired élite inspires or propagates a fashion which is then aspired to by progressively broader sections of society, who as they become able, attempt to emulate the behaviour and style of the perceived élites. This introduces a fresh dimension to the product cycle model: as the cycle evolves, not only do numbers arriving at a destination change, but so do the types of tourists, facilitated by the travel and tourism industry. This is accompanied by a progressive metamorphosis of the destination environment.

The pleasure periphery

As this process continues, the discoverer and élite groups, driven by the desire for novelty, uniqueness and exclusivity of experience, seek out fresh destinations and move on, potentially triggering the product cycle all over again. It is this constant search, again enthusiastically encouraged by the tourism industry, which drives the pleasure periphery rippling outwards over time from tourist-generating regions to envelop ever new destinations (Figure 2.3). The

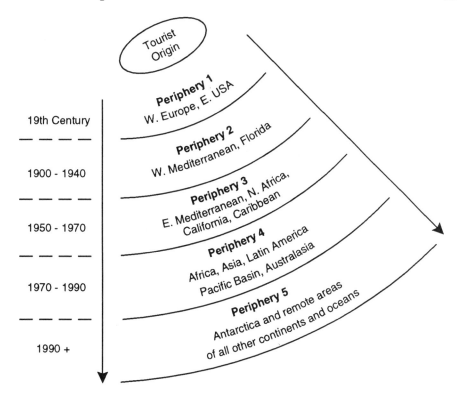

FIGURE 2.3. Tidal wave of the pleasure periphery

motivational and organisational energies which drive this élite tidal wave are vividly illustrated in the text from a 1990 brochure of a specialist company marketing exclusive cruises:

> With discovery as their guiding star, the great explorers ventured forth from the familiar to lands that were little more than whispered tales and outlines on map. The adventure continued today on Society Expeditions' 1990 voyages to Antarctica, the Arctic, South America, the South Pacific, Indonesia and Australia.
>
> The bold programme of expedition cruising will take you far away from the beaten tourist tracks, and, like all great discoverers, you won't just pass by, but will land and explore these destinations that most people miss. None of this would be possible without their two specially designed expedition ships—*Society Explorer* and *World Discoverer*.
>
> Yet *Society Explorer* and *World Discoverer* offer yacht-like comfort all but unknown on larger vessels.
>
> To add to the comfort, you will share the ship with, at most, 139 other expeditioners.
>
> Moreover these voyages are designed to feed the mind as well as the body.
>
> (Society Expeditions, 1990)

Temporal and spatial variations in the product cycle

It must not be assumed that the product cycle model in all its phases is applicable to all destinations, and certainly, the time-scale varies widely.

For many British seaside resorts, the passage of the cycle lasted at least a century. Resorts such as Brighton and Scarborough emerged as élite destinations in the first half of the nineteenth century, were booming as classic 'bucket-and-spade' resorts by the 1920s, and since the 1950s have been struggling to respond to the changes in fashion and demand. Other resorts, such as Blackpool and Margate, originated after 1850 as working class 'mass' resorts, access to which was made possible by the coming of cheap rail fares and the progressive socio-economic transformation of the urban population. In such cases, the successive class intervention energy radiates from the generic idea of a holiday, not from the specific destination which enjoyed no élite phase. By contrast, the cycle appears to have surged through the Spanish 'Costas' in barely 40 years, with bookings down by at least two per cent between 1990 and 1992.

The cycle is less easily applicable to planned resort developments such as those of the Languedoc–Roussillon coast of southern France. As a component of French regional planning policy, the six developments (*unités touristiques*) have been built since 1970 with a capacity of 350 000 visitors. From the start, the tourism environment has been planned to provide spatially segregated opportunities across the experience spectrum, from exclusive apartments with private yacht moorings to mass tent campsites, albeit with few large package holiday hotels, reflecting the forecast of a shift in demand away from a homogeneous product.

Where the product cycle does evolve at least in part, there is no doubt that there is a progressive and eventually total transformation of the human and natural environment in the destination region. The tourism system changes in all its elements—tourists, organisation, impacts, experiences—across the economic, socio-cultural and environmental dimensions. This transformation is encapsulated in Figure 2.4. This product cycle model may also be used to locate a given destination at a moment in time, enabling a forecast of what the future may hold, and hence provide a basis for planning and management.

Figure 2.5 gives examples of how this works: Alaska is about to emerge from the discovery and élite stage into a phase of rapid growth, which will have serious consequences for (a) the fragile attractive resources and (b) the quality of the wilderness experience which is the prime attraction.

Northern Queensland, with its tropical climate, rainforests and above all the Great Barrier Reef, has entered an explosive growth phase accelerated by the upgrading of Cairns airport, and the combination of massive investment and the coming of package tourism—for example, investment and tours from Japan.

Type	Explorers *discover a destination*	Off-beat Adventurer *penetrate a region*	Elite *wealthy status conscious groups arrive on expensive tours*	Early Mass *middle income groups on organised hotel or villa rental packages and tours*	Mass Package *tourists on fully standardised packages*
Number	Very few	Small numbers	Limited numbers	Steady flow	Massive numbers
Expectation and Impacts	Accept local conditions	Revel in local conditions	*Either* demand Western amenities *or* "rough it in comfort"	Look for Western amenities	Expect Western amenities
Example	Scientists and travel writers	Student back-packers	Social elites	Professional families	Wide range of social groups

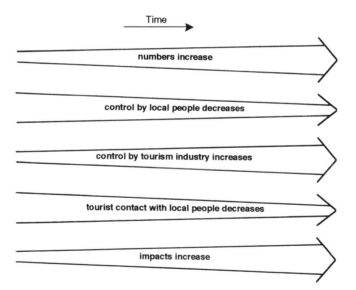

Time →

numbers increase

control by local people decreases

control by tourism industry increases

tourist contact with local people decreases

impacts increase

FIGURE 2.4.   Change in tourist types over time

The carrying capacity of the fragile ecosystems, which are the key resources, is already being threatened. Southern California and Florida appear to be reaching their saturation and even stagnation phase. They retain their enormous popularity as domestic and international tourist destinations, but

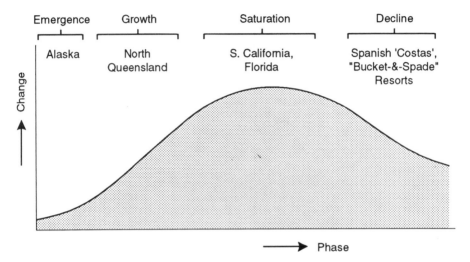

FIGURE 2.5.   Product cycle: examples in the early 1990s

their entire coastline and key attractive resources are now developed, except where given protected status or used as military bases. Both these destinations figure significantly in European mass tourism operators' portfolios, and while élite enclaves survive, for example, Palm Beach and La Jolla, there is much evidence of the 'trend-setters' having moved on. For instance, in society magazines it is becoming more prestigious to be recorded as having vacationed in Santa Fe, New Mexico, than in La Jolla, California. As outlined above, many British resorts and the Spanish 'Costas' are fighting to avoid slipping down the slope of decline as fashion shifts, and an increasingly sophisticated customer market seeks out trendier destinations and different experiences offered to them by the industry.

The vulnerability of tourist destinations

Destinations which rely heavily upon tourism have become fully aware of their vulnerability. They witness what is happening to their society and their environment and are increasingly asking the question 'What if the tourists stop coming?' Even those who oppose tourism acknowledge the economic benefits it may bring, although the lure of wealth and foreign exchange has all too often proved deceptive, as significant proportions of tourist spending leak out of the destination region.

The vulnerability of destinations may be expressed too, in their status within the tourism industry. Global tourism has been described as economic colonialism, with the economically powerful countries of the North exploiting

the attractive resources of the dependent South. Investment sources, expertise and controlling organisations, together with the bulk of the demand, still
remain firmly within the domain of the more developed countries; for example, eight of the largest hotel chains in the world are USA-based. For a
tour operator or investment company, the issue is based simply upon the
sales–profits equation:

> The value in understanding the nature of the product life cycle is in its relationship
> with marketing strategy. It will alert the company to the need for positive action at
> the so-called threshold point, where some change to strategy will be essential. . . .
> As sales peak and falter, the company has to look at the relative merits of revitalis-
> ing the product, allowing it to decline slowly, or killing it off and planning a
> replacement.
>
> (Holloway and Plant, 1992)

Faced with such cool decision-making by external agencies, a crucial issue for
a tourism destination is to attempt to gain as much control of the product and
the progress of the product cycle as possible.

It needs to be emphasised that the charges extend beyond economic exploitation to social and environmental exploitation. As tourism proceeds from the
initial discovery stage towards mass tourism, so there is progressive community displacement, societal dislocation and cultural transformation (Ryan,
1991). Village farmland is appropriated, there is inter-generational stress as
younger groups succumb to the 'demonstration effect' of tourist material
wealth and behaviour, intra-family stress as the male–female role balance
shifts, and community disharmony as religious ceremonies and artforms are
commercialised. Doxey (1975) has constructed his 'index of tourist irritation'
to mirror this progressive change in perception, attitude and response by the
destination population (Figure 2.6). Such impacts have raised questions about
the ethics of tourism, especially when there is a wide cultural gap between
hosts and guests (Prosser, 1992).

Concern over the environmental impacts of tourism has grown alongside
the emergence of the global environmental movement (McCormick, 1992),
and as all components in the tourism system—tourists, destinations,
operators—acknowledge their reliance upon finite and vulnerable environmental resources (Ryan, 1991). Yet with all this experience and realisation,
changing attitudes and policies is not easy, as a 1993 report on Goa by the
pressure group Tourism Concern suggests (Table 2.3).

The changing nature of demand

There is little doubt that the character of demand will continue to shift and
that the industry and destinations will respond to, and indeed, help to mould
such shifts. Any strategies to avoid the errors of the past, and to break away

1. Euphoria

- Enthusiasm for tourist development
- Mutual feeling of satisfaction
- Opportunities for local participation
- Flows of money and interesting contacts

2. Apathy

- Industry expands
- Tourists taken for granted
- More interest in profit making
- Personal contact becomes more formal

3. Irritation

- Industry nearing saturation point
- Expansion of facilities required
- Encroachment into local way of life

4. Antagonism

- Irritations become more overt
- The tourist is seen as the harbinger of all that is bad
- Mutual politeness gives way to antagonism

5. Final level

- Environment has changed irreversibly
- The resource base has changed and the type of tourist has also changed
- If the destination is large enough to cope with mass tourism it will continue to thrive

T I M E

FIGURE 2.6.   Doxey's index of tourist irritation. After Doxey (1975)

from the exploitative paradigm, must take into account the likely trends. Schwaninger (1989) forecasts the following

- demand will continue to grow and to become increasingly differentiated
- there will be greater market specialisation and segmentation—a stronger emphasis upon more active pastimes at the expense of passive vacations
- packaged holidays will be customised to accommodate greater individual freedom via a modular product design

Reflection upon such a differentiated, personalised, active tourism scenario forces the realisation that resource and facility demands may be even more penetrative than existing mainstream enclave mass tourism.

TABLE 2.3. The conflicting views. Reproduced by permission from Tourism Concern (1993)

The place	The image (what the brochures say)	The criticisms (what local people say)
Taj and Fort Aguada holiday complexes	'Relaxed . . . laid back . . . beautifully and peacefully positioned' (Inspirations India)	Local people denied beach access and access to water pipeline
Leela Beach Hotel	'Walk about in the extensive grounds and the predominant noise is birdsong' (Inspirations)	Refuses to rent out coconut trees to tappers, damages trees, illegal walls built, villagers displaced from land, beach access denied
Cidade de Goa Hotel	'Lovely, beachside setting . . . comfort, elegance and friendly service' (Cosmos)	Beach access denied by wall, sewage dumped, court orders taken out against it
Dona Sylvia Hotel	'Excellent location . . . alongside a wonderful beach' (Sunworld)	Illegal fence built, dunes damaged to give guests seaview

THE SEARCH FOR SUSTAINABILITY

The foregoing discussion has established the context and background to the strong surge of concern energising the search for a fundamental shift from an exploitative to a sustainable approach to tourism development.

The driving forces of social change

Four forces of social change are driving this search for sustainability: (1) dissatisfaction with existing products; (2) growing environmental awareness and cultural sensitivity; (3) realisation by destination regions of the precious resources they possess, both human and natural, and their vulnerability; and (4) changing attitudes of developers and tour operators.

The potential for sustainability in tourism lies within the principles of sustainable development. Hence, any tourism policy should reflect 'concern for the environment and provision of an economic resource base for future generations', with the concept of sustainability depending upon 'the persistence or desirability of a system's productivity under known or possible conditions, and on consumption not exceeding resources' (Curry and Morvaridi, 1992: 131). Sustainable tourism therefore seeks to sustain the quantity, quality and productivity of both human and natural resource systems over time, while respecting and accommodating the dynamics of such systems.

This search for the 'holy grail' of sustainability has spawned an expanding set of subspecies of tourism with meaningful and at times pious labels—soft, green, responsible, harmonious, quality, gentle, eco, progressive, sensitive, community, appropriate—all assembled under the generic title of 'alternative tourism'. Cazes (1986) suggests that this form of tourism can be identified, measured and assessed in terms of a set of dynamic values, processes and forms. The values, as perceived by the demand component, are based upon dissatisfaction with existing products and heightened environmental awareness, resulting in a 'search for spontaneity, enhanced interpersonal relations, creativity, authenticity, solidarity, and social and ecological harmony' (Pearce, 1989: 101).

The need for changing attitudes

A more sustainable approach requires shifts in social and individual attitudes within all three components of the tourism system.

Attitudes of tourists

Concerning the demand component, there is much talk of the need for increased awareness, responsibility and sensitivity in the selection process and the consumptive behaviour of tourists. Despite such rhetoric, and even the good intentions of a 'green fringe' of tourists, engendering the required fundamental shift of attitude, expectation and behaviour by the huge, amorphous and variegated mass of the tourist body seems likely to prove a difficult task:

> When on holiday . . . we may give little thought to whether such behaviour is socially or environmentally acceptable in our chosen destination, and indeed, if we are aware, we may rationalise that we have paid and they have taken our money, so we are entitled to enjoy our holidays as we wish.
>
> This scenario encapsulates one of the central dilemmas of tourism: is it, by definition, a selfish and self-indulgent experience? If so, then is it realistic to expect significant change to be energised from the demand end of the system?
>
> (Prosser, 1992: 39)

The tourism experience is here and now, whether we are the 'discoverers' and 'explorers', the reverent admirers of Luxor, or the lager louts of Magaluf. How many tourists have expressed a desire to visit a destination before it is spoiled? Despite heightened awareness, sharpened sensitivity, responsible behaviour, etc., tourists still move on to new destinations and experiences, believing it is not them but others who create the problems. The attitudes remain élitist and the perspectives essentially short term. A group of 139 'discoverers' arriving twice a season is thought to be a sustainable option, but little thought is given to 139 travellers arriving each week—or even 1390 tourists! Trekking tourists in the Nepalese Himalaya would almost without exception declare themselves to be eco-conscious or green, yet they too are pushing against the carrying capacity and hence the sustainability of the regional environment. The wood demanded and the biodegradable litter created by the several hundreds of the 1950s were sustainable within the system's productivity, but the demands and refuse of the many thousands in the 1990s are not (Chapter 11).

The response of destination areas

The twin issues of numbers and time-scale become even more starkly profiled when the supply of opportunities component at tourist destinations is considered. If there is to be an effective transformation from an exploitative to a sustainable mode, then destinations must adopt longer term perspectives. Thinking and policy need to shift from political and economic time-scales to ecological and social, from the next election or budget to reproductive and regenerative cycles, and to the pace of social processes.

Such statements have a logical and righteous ring to them, and, it can be argued, could only be written by a comfortable academic in the developed world. The proposed transformation from short-term to longer term perspectives may be less justifiable or realistic when viewed from an LDC (less developed country).

Annual population growth rates exceeding two or even three per cent, persistently low incomes and national product growth rates, foreign exchange shortages and widespread need for improved dietary intake, combine to focus government and community attention upon immediate ameliorative measures rather than more gradual, balanced and potentially sustainable programmes and options. Countries such as Belize or Botswana realise that they have resources highly valued by modern tourists and are understandably tempted to maximise short-term economic gains, yet both are making efforts to control the direction and scale of tourism within sustainable limits. Theirs is a classic dilemma—the demand for authentic experiences of coral reefs, rainforests, wildlife and exotic cultures is growing rapidly, but the carrying capacity of these attractive resources is finite. In consequence, optimising the returns while protecting the resource base requires a delicate balance.

The processes by which alternative tourism can develop involve significant contributions by the destination population at all four stages of development—initiation and planning, construction and implementation, running and management, monitoring and modification. The outcome being therefore a much fairer balance of the ensuing benefits between the external entrepreneurs and agencies, and the local communities and regions. The physical, spatial and social forms of the tourism must be compatible and integrated with the human and natural environments of the destination, e.g. the adoption of local architectural styles and scales, local designers and workers at all levels and the use of local materials. This latter requirement must have the added proviso that it does not involve the destruction of the environment. In the Maldives, where no other local materials are available, coral has been extracted, resulting in widespread reef destruction.

The responsibilities of the tourism industry

The pressures for development are exacerbated when the third component of the tourist system is added to the equation, namely the tourism industry. There is no question that, despite the overtly élitist messages transmitted through much of the marketing hype, the travel and tourism industry has been a major force in the egalitarian process, bringing tourism opportunities to a broadening range of social groups and to a growing number of societies. Yet in the private commercial sector the underlying credo is growth which, in the harshly competitive world of tourism, translates into profits, returns on investment and market share. To survive and prosper, a company must attract more people into going to more destinations at the most profitable price the market will stand. Where the company is external to the destination being used, this also means reducing the costs to the operator and hence the benefits to the destination as much as possible, e.g. negotiating the lowest accommodation rates. Furthermore, as tourism is driven, in part at least, by the forces of fashion, status and image, developers and tour operators are not simply responsive, but are initiatory in aggressively seeking out new destinations and experiences to gain a competitive edge. From this perspective too, there is an inevitable drive by external investors and operators to retain as much control as possible over the tourism environment, while dangling the potential benefits in front of local communities and national governments.

Breaking out of such an exploitative culture, based upon an economic rather than an environmental balance sheet, is clearly not an easy translocation. Yet the industry claims to be making efforts to achieve this shift towards a sustainable approach which balances profitability with sensitivity and responsibility. The industry, 'sensitive to criticism that it is . . . destroying the very world it encourages us to see, is desperately trying to appear ecologically responsible' (Wickers, 1992). This applies to all sectors of the industry, from specialist operators to mainstream transnational companies. Study groups have been set up to seek out ways of implementing more sustainable tourism strategies and forms of tourism. The efforts have been given government agency support—for example, the 1991 publication *The Green Light: A Guide to Sustainable Tourism* by the English Tourist Board.

Not all of those who study the travel and tourism industry are convinced of the sincerity or altruism of these efforts. Pressure groups such as Tourism

Concern perceive the shifts as a marketing ploy: tour operators are reacting to the changing demands, attitudes and expectations among customers by marketing their green credentials. Wickers sums up this viewpoint in the phraseology of journalism: 'Much of the noise is marketing babble—another front on which to fight the competition—and many companies are simply slapping the green label on any destination where nature is more rampant than concrete' (Wickers, 1992).

Such viewpoints may seem a wearily cynical reaction to what to others appear sincere efforts on the part of many tourists, destinations and operators to work towards some form of sustainability. Nonetheless, there is some truth in the criticisms that sustainable forms of tourism such as ecotourism, which can prove effective as small-scale projects, fail to face the issue of the continuing growth of numbers. This is what Wheeller (1992) sees as 'the diametrically opposed and widening divergence that exists between the slow, steady, selfless, cosy, back to nature, sustainable, eco-friendly, controlled small-scale solution to tourism problems and the realities of globally, a capitalist society with inbuilt growth dynamics'.

Basic principles for sustainable tourism

The key attractive resources of that form of alternative tourism known as ecotourism are natural or semi-natural systems, and so sustainable ecotourism must be based upon the principles of ecosystem structures and functions. This is true even if the attraction is a single species, such as mountain gorillas in Burundi or Howler monkeys in Belize, for they can exist only if the ecosystem which is their habitat remains. An equally important understanding is that the ultimate protectors must be the local human communities, for there are few ecotourism destinations which are not the domain of long-established societies who perceive the plants and wildlife and the space they occupy in quite a different way from the incoming tourists. Thus, although mountain gorillas are put at risk of disease and stress by the proximity of tourists, they are under greater threat from poaching, deforestation and wars involving regional populations.

A first step, therefore, is education, i.e. modifying the perceptions of local communities, especially the leaders, to show that conservation of the environment on which ecotourism must be based can be (a) economically valuable and (b) integrated into their way of life.

The fundamentals become the readiness and enthusiasm of local and regional populations, the development of skills and resources to control the tourism projects, a steady rate of growth, and a scale and style of development appropriate to both the destination environment and the expected experiences of the tourists. For instance, in the field of safari tourism, the lessons from Kenya seem to be that the resource base and hence the tourism will be sustainable in the longer term, only if (a) tourist numbers and distribution are controlled and (b) local populations take responsibility for the conservation of their wildlife and the management of tourism. Other African countries which are currently expanding their tourism capacity, e.g. Zambia and Botswana, are attempting to follow such principles.

Irrespective of the scenario envisaged, principles such as those set out by Phillips (1988) for rural tourism seem appropriate as base measures for effective, sustainable tourism

- the tourist experiences should draw upon the character of the environment, its aesthetics, culture, vegetation and wildlife
- the tourism development should assist conservation, supplement local people's incomes, bring new use and value to historic structures and enhance reclamation of derelict land
- planning, design and siting of tourist developments should be compatible with and, if possible, enhance the local landscape
- control of tourism should remain as far as possible in local hands; this control and the ensuing benefits should be spread through the community and, equally, those who do benefit should contribute to environmental conservation and enhancement
- tourism investment should support the local economy and encourage a steady dispersal of activity, so avoiding congestion and minimising impacts
- the tourism industry should actively assist the understanding of both the local populations and the tourists—information, interpretation, education

CONCLUSIONS

Of course, *any* influx of tourists creates some impact and change, but natural and human systems are dynamic, with inbuilt mechanisms to absorb impact and make adjustments, i.e. negative feedback. Equally, all systems have finite limits of tolerance to the pace and extent of change before key thresholds are crossed and positive feedback takes over. A crucial issue for ecotourism becomes, therefore, controlling any development within the adaptation thresholds of the local environment. This means that tourism will be only one element in the local economy, possibly not even a dominant element. Perhaps it will be used as a product only in the earlier phases of development, and phased out later as the income gained from it is invested to improve agriculture and to diversify the economy. Thus, tourism would then be seen as an exploitable resource and product within a broader, longer term strategy of sustainability. Such a view of tourism enables it to be both exploitative and sustainable—it serves its economic and social purpose within a destination without destroying the natural and human resource base. So, should the tourists move on to the new fashion frontier, or should the local populations decide to move the tourists on, then there will be life after tourism.

REFERENCES

Boorstin, D.J., 1961, *The Image—a Guide to Pseudo-events in America*, Harper & Row, New York.

Butler, R., 1980, The concept of a tourism area cycle of evolution, *Canadian Geographer*, **24**, 5–12.

Cazes, G., 1986, Le Tourisme alternatif: réflexion sur un concept ambigu, *Problems of Tourism/Problemy Turistiky*, **10**(3), 18–24.

Curry, S. and Morvaridi, B., 1992, Sustainable tourism: illustrations from Kenya, Nepal and Jamaica, in Cooper, C.P. and Lockwood, A. (eds) *Progress in Tourism, Recreation and Hospitality Management*, Belhaven, London.

Doxey, G.V., 1975, A causation theory of visitor–resident irritants: methodology and research influence, *Proceedings of the Travel Research Associates 6th Annual Conference*, San Diego, California, pp. 195–198.

English Tourist Board, Countryside Commission, Rural Development Commission, 1991, *The Green Light, a Guide to Sustainable Tourism*, English Tourist Board, London.

Fussell, P., 1982, *Abroad: British Literary Traveling Between the Wars*, OUP, New York.

Holloway, J.C. and Plant, R.V., 1992, *Marketing for Tourism*, Pitman, London.

Krippendorf, J., 1987, *The Holiday Makers,* Heinemann, London.

Lodge, D., 1992, *Paradise News,* Penguin, London.

McCormick, J., 1992, *The Global Environmental Movement*, Belhaven, London.

Murphy, P., 1985, *Tourism—a Community Approach*, Methuen, New York.

Pearce, D., 1989, *Tourist Development*, Longman, Harlow.

Phillips, A., 1988, The countryside as a leisure product. *Proceedings of the Conference on Rural Tourism*, English Tourist Board, London.

Prosser, R., 1992, The ethics of tourism, in Cooper, D.E. and Palmer, J.A. (eds) *The Environment in Question,* Routledge, London.

Ryan, C., 1991, *Recreational Tourism*, Routledge, London.

Schwaninger, M., 1989, Trends in leisure and tourism for 2000–2010, in Witt, S.F. and Moutinho, L. (eds) *Tourism Marketing and Management Handbook*, Prentice Hall, Hemel Hempstead.

Society Expeditions, 1990, Invitation to a world of discovery, *World*, London.

Tourism Concern, 1993, *Sweet Poison*, Press release, 26 January.

Turner, L. and Ash, J., 1975, *The Golden Hordes,* Constable, London.

Urry, J., 1990, *The Tourist Gaze: Leisure and Travel in Contemporary Societies*, Sage, London.

Wheeller, B., 1992, Alternative tourism—a deceptive ploy, in Cooper, C.P. and Lockwood, A. (eds) *Progress in Tourism, Recreation and Hospitality Management*, Belhaven, London.

Wickers, D., 1992, Whither Green? *Sunday Times,* 5 January.

World Tourism Organisation (WTO), 1991, *Yearbook of Tourism Statistics*, Vols 1 and 2, WTO, Madrid.

3

Environmentally Responsible Marketing of Tourism

P. WIGHT

PRINCIPLES OF ECOTOURISM

The Canadian Environmental Advisory Council (CEAC) has documented the characteristics of 'modern ecotourism' (1991) and held a National Workshop on Ecotourism, which brought together a broad range of stake-holders from across the country, including governments, academia, operators and conservation groups. As a participant in the workshop, this author prefers the definition which emerged in that consensus-oriented milieu: 'Ecotourism is an enlightening nature travel experience that contributes to conservation of the ecosystem while respecting the integrity of host communities' (Scace *et al.*, 1992: 14). This chapter will explore ecotourism's marketing and conservation perspectives within the context of a need for responsible and ethical ecotourism industry activities, to sustain both the industry and the resource over the long term.

There seem to be two prevailing views of ecotourism: one envisages that public interest in the environment may be used to market a product; the other sees that this same interest may be used to conserve the resources upon which this product is based. These views need not be mutually exclusive, and may very well be complementary. What is required is an effective integration of both views, so that both the industry and the resource may be sustained over the long term. Fundamental to a sustainable industry is the acceptance of the key principles underlying the concept of ecotourism

- it should not degrade the resource and should be developed in an environmentally sound manner
- it should provide long-term benefits to the resource, to the local community and industry (benefits may be conservation, scientific, social, cultural, or economic)
- it should provide first-hand, participatory and enlightening experiences

Ecotourism: A Sustainable Option? Edited by E. Cater and G. Lowman
© The editors and contributors. Published in 1994 by John Wiley & Sons Ltd

- it should involve education among all parties—local communities, government, non-governmental organisations, industry and tourists (before, during and after the trip)
- it should encourage all-party recognition of the intrinsic values of the resource
- it should involve acceptance of the resource on its own terms, and in recognition of its limits, which involves supply-oriented management
- it should promote understanding and involve partnerships between many players, which could include government, non-governmental organisations, industry, scientists and locals (both before and during operations)
- it should promote moral and ethical responsibilities and behaviour towards the natural and cultural environment by all players

These principles, although challenging, are already exhibited in some ecotourism operations, for example those documented in the casebook of best practices in sustainable tourism which was developed from the GLOBE '92 Conference Tourism Stream (Hawkes and Williams, 1993).

GREENING OF THE MARKET

There is no question that the marketplace is becoming 'greener', or more environmentally sensitive, both in terms of awareness and in the desire to contribute through its efforts towards a more sensitive approach to numerous activities and purchases. New consumers are beginning to translate their convictions into action. Eighty-five per cent of the industrialised world's citizens believe that the environment is the number one public issue (Carson and Moulden, 1991), whereas over 76 per cent of Americans consider themselves environmentalists (Burr, 1991) and a 1991 Angus Reid poll found that 76 per cent of Canadians believe that environmental protection should remain a government priority during a recession, even if it means a lower economic recovery (Wright, 1991). 'Green' political parties are a fact around the world.

Certain individuals with entrenched attitudes, particularly in the business community, persist in using the word 'environmentalist' as a disparaging term, (e.g. 'Environmentalists are the types who eat granola and aren't fast-food customers, but there they are, standing on the side lines . . . with distortion of the truth' (John Icke, President of Lily Cups Inc., in Bailey, 1992). However, that attitude is receding. Environmentalism takes a very different form from that of two decades ago. Many environmental advocates are working *with* business and the consumer, and business is beginning to recognise the value of cooperation in achieving its goals. In ecotourism, for example, there can be considerable actual and potential economic value, if properly developed and managed. Benefits can include (Ziffer, 1989; Boo, 1990; Lindberg, 1991)

- economic diversification, particularly in rural, peripheral and non-industrialised regions
- long-term economic stability
- the tendency for higher dollar expenditures and length of stay by ecotourists
- demand for local goods and services which benefit local economies
- infrastructure development
- an increase in foreign exchange earnings

This 'greening' of the marketplace should not be taken as some sort of fad, or 'fashionable interest in environmental interests' (Lane, 1990). There is growing 'grassroots' opposition to irresponsible environmental behaviour, and the marketplace is advocating environmental sensitivity and a 'walk lightly' approach to our travels on this earth. In tourism terms there is considerable collective power resting within the hands of the individual tourist, regarding their impact on the places visited, the nature of the tour operation and the attitudes which they take with them on return home (Grotta, 1990; Salazar *et al.*, 1991). The collective interests of this marketplace have the potential to be constructively used or abused.

ECO-EXPLOITATION: USING MARKET INTEREST TO SELL

In *Green is Gold*, Carson and Moulden (1991) present a step by step plan to businesses interested in 'greening' their operation, tapping into the changing marketplace and marketing their newly 'green' company products and services. However, they emphasise the importance of credibility, and warn of the detrimental effects of 'environmental opportunism'.

A US Travel Data Centre survey (Travel Industry Association of America, 1992: 43) has found that travellers, on average, would spend 8.5 per cent more for travel services and products provided by environmentally responsible suppliers (including transportation, accommodation, food services, attractions and sight-seeing tours). The survey reveals that 43 million US travellers could take an ecotourism trip in the next three years.

In the last few years ecotourism has become a buzz word to sell a variety of products. In some ways this resembles the tendency of manufacturers to label numerous products as 'green' or 'ecologically friendly'. The problem has been that the consumers did not know what they were getting, nor its impact on the environment and did not know how the product differed from others, if, indeed, there was any difference. There is no question that 'green' sells. Almost any terms prefixed with 'eco' will increase interest and sales. Thus, in the last few years there has been a proliferation of advertisements in the travel field with references such as ecotour, ecotravel, ecovacation, ecologically sensitive adventures, eco(ad)ventures, ecocruise, ecosafari, eco-expedition and, of course, ecotourism.

James Sanno, Chief Executive Officer of Inner Asia Expeditions, points out the danger of misrepresentation: 'Ecotourism is a fashionable marketing ploy right now. It's often misunderstood, but more often it's exploited. Consumers need to be protected from that. 'Eco' has become just about as ambiguous as the term 'natural' (Masterton, 1991). It is abuse of this potential to market, or ecoexploitation, which presents a problem. Ray Ashton, ecotourism consultant and biologist, feels that ecotourism is a buzz word which is not understood. 'People [i.e. operators] have not changed their itineraries, they just use the word for marketing purposes' (Ignacio, 1990).

The substantial lack of understanding of conservation objectives is evident in some products marketed as ecotourism. For example, one lodge in Belize, complete with the modern comforts of electricity and a bar, is actually situated in the heart of a Mayan plaza leading to ceremonial temples and centres. Visitors are actively encouraged to climb in the ruins (*Belize Currents,* 1990). Some products are completely unrelated to ecotourism, yet this label is being used to sell them. A recent glaring example appeared in an advertisement recruiting sales agents for investors in a property in the Caribbean. This property consists of 240 hectares with a proposed international hotel, 18-hole championship golf course, marina, and 'the most perfect beach frontage imaginable'. The property is billed as a 'tropical paradise', located in 'the Eco Tourism market of the future', with 'precious wild life, the world's second largest living barrier reef and a climate that will encourage both residential and tourist investments'. The advertisement concludes 'your customers will want to buy—"Eco Tourism" means it will remain exclusive'! (*Globe and Mail,* 1991).

Cohen (1989) argues that the trekkers of northern Thailand are victims of similar rhetoric in advertising where hill-tribes are presented as 'primitive and remote'. Thai villagers, too, can be victims. Dearden (1989) indicates that trekking can itself influence the nature of the Thai hill-tribes in terms of dress, consumer goods, village life and resident expectations. This type of transformation is echoed in the Amazon, where tourism 'has swept away the Indians' traditional hunter-gatherer way of life and turned them into souvenir hawkers' (Atwood, 1990). The advertising rhetoric may succeed until the discrepancy between 'sell' and reality becomes apparent.

The word ecotourism is often tacked onto promotional materials (usually for 'exotic' or remote destinations) for a package which is essentially a form of tour and observation, with no explanation of how the tour differs from other scenic tours. Indeed, the tour may simply be yesterday's trip repackaged. In addition, as Kelman (1991) bluntly puts it, 'a tour advertised as environmentally friendly can be just as suspect as many of the products tarted up with green packaging at your grocery store'.

Few tour operators have a financial investment (e.g. accommodation) in the host destination. This means that their vested interest in the long-term sustainability of the destination product is low (Ryan, 1991). Yet, paradoxically, these very operators have the potential to significantly influence tourist numbers and behaviour in the destination, and so have a pivotal role in developing a sustainable industry. Individual operators are only part of the problem; they have little control over their competitors' operations and marketing for the same destination, particularly when these competitors may be located in different countries. In addition, host governments may be oriented toward 'develop and market' objectives, rather than balancing these with conservation objectives. Thus it is little wonder that Lillywhite and Lillywhite (1991) characterise ecotourism as demand-driven, and contrast 'low impact tourism' as supply-driven. But, in fact, as outlined in the principles, it is critical for ecotourism that it has a *supply*-managed orientation.

Ensuring that the values and principles inherent in ecotourism are incorporated into ecotourism products and activities is the challenge for marketers who wish to tap consumer interest in ecotourism. The development of formal or informal agreements or partnerships regarding both marketing and development of the ecotourism destination would considerably advance all parties' interests.

CONSERVATION: USING MARKET INTEREST TO CONSERVE

It has long been recognised that tourism has the potential to act as a force to conserve natural resources (Budowski, 1976). However, to date, most of the effort has been towards advancing the economic objectives of tourism, rather than conservation objectives. Numerous workers have reiterated the need to integrate conservation with tourism development (Romeril, 1985; Wight, 1988; McNeely and Thorsell, 1989).

Conservation groups have not only advocated this tourism–conservation relationship, but have become involved in partnerships with industry to realise mutual benefits (e.g. the World Wildlife Fund, Conservation International, Rainforest Action Network). These partnerships take many forms

- donation of a portion of tour fees to local groups for resource conservation or local development initiatives
- education about the value of the resource
- opportunities to observe or participate in a scientific activity
- involvement of locals in the provision of support services or products
- involvement of locals in explanation of cultural activities or their relationship with the natural resources
- promotion of a tourist and/or operator code of ethics for responsible travel

It is increasingly evident that the types of values espoused by conservation groups and others are appearing in tour operator advertisements. There is a movement from mere eco-sell towards value-driven perspectives. As an example, in one 'ecotourism' advertising insert developed by Co-op America (1991), approximately half the advertisements contained phrases which have been classified in Figure 3.1. They show a spectrum of marketing language, ranging from eco-sell to values-oriented.

Ziffer (1989) divides suppliers of the ecotourism product by their level of involvement with host country concerns and issues and by whether or not they are in the for-profit or not-for-profit sector. Figure 3.2 represents an adaptation of Ziffer's segmentation and shows the sectors, their motivations, degree of local involvement and level of impact upon the ecotourism resources. This model is a simplification as there may, in reality, be a dynamic overlap in the motivations and activities of the sectors. Nevertheless, it illustrates the tendencies, which could be confirmed by examining such criteria as group size, pre/during trip information, infrastructure ownership and degree of local staff or management.

The spectrum of marketing language (Figure 3.1) ranges from eco-sell to values-oriented perspectives and tends to parallel the range of motivations of stake-holders involved in supplying the ecotourism product (Figure 3.2). Although the exploitative and sell-oriented motivations of some ecotour operators clearly need to be modified, their varied perspectives and motivations need not remain in opposition. There is a need to integrate them advantageously, using responsible marketing as part of an economically sound, responsible travel experience, which benefits local communities and conserves and respects the resource base.

RESPONSIBLE MARKETING

Romeril (1985) pointed out that the tourist industry is a complex and multifacted one, resulting in difficulty in ensuring that environmental awareness *with accompanying responsible actions*, percolates to all its sectors. It makes sense to use the fact that 'green sells' for marketing purposes, but only when the product labelling conforms with both consumer expectations and with industry standards. For example, Sobek Expeditions has been marketing various types of adventure tours for many years, but in 1990, Sobek labelled a group of tours as 'environmental adventures', and referred to these as ecotourism. However, this was no mere repackaging: trips include experts, learning experiences, highlighting of poor environmental practices, local revenues, a travel code of ethics and a portion of proceeds going to local conservation groups. This contribution is no token amount, ranging from 6.7 per cent to 10.9 per cent of the total trip costs (Sobek, 1990). As a Sobek spokesperson said, 'people don't want to be fooled anymore'. The answer is to begin with

NONSPECIFIC, SELL-ORIENTED PHRASES

Eco-Sell Oriented
- we just offer the best, most affordable and largest variety of "classic and unusual" eco-tourism one can find, anywhere
- rain forest ecology tours
- budget travel to "untouristed" destinations
- areas generally neglected by the teeming tourist masses
- destinations untouched by mass tourism
- off the beaten track

Generic Language
- environmental awareness, self-discovery and personal exchange with exotic cultures or enchanted adventures to classic destinations
- ecologically sensitive
- cross cultural focus
- environmentally friendly
- sensitive to both the physical environment and to local culture
- spirited adventures for the responsible traveller
- sustainable ecological development
- people-conscious nature tours
- nature travel

Science / Conservation Oriented
- one week volunteer work
- visit the world's natural environments while you help preserve them Trip proceeds support environmental and cultural preservation
- some trips involve travellers in conservation projects
- scientific expeditions
- restoration projects
- tours support jungle conservation and Peruvian children's foundation

Explanatory / Values Oriented
- small groups (8-10)
- maximum group size 12
- worker owned transport companies
- locally owned hotels
- gives 1% of profits to peace and environmental groups
- newsletters prior to departure and lectures throughout tour
- women and indigenously owned business
- supporting local economic development
- your guide is a naturalist, tour parties are small

SPECIFIC, VALUES-ORIENTED PHRASES

FIGURE 3.1.   Spectrum of language used to market ecotourism

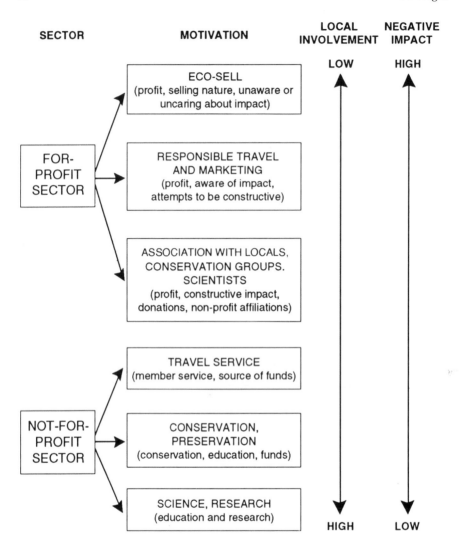

FIGURE 3.2. Segmentation model of ecotourism supplier, motivation and impact.
Adapted from Ziffer (1989)

'our own companies, making the changes that need to be made so we can have
a conscious, responsible and believable product to sell to our clients' (Jarvie,
1992).

In a survey of US travellers, almost one-third of respondents said that a
company's sense of environmental responsibility was an important factor in
selecting travel suppliers. Of travellers likely to take an ecotourism trip in the

next three years, the percentage rose to 43 per cent; less than one per cent of respondents believe this factor was not at all important (Travel Industry Association of America, 1992: 41). Ecotourists bring certain expectations about their experiences, which are in part shaped by marketing. The degree to which these expectations are met will determine whether or not the destination is ultimately regarded as a viable and worthwhile ecotourism destination (Fennell and Smale, 1992: 30).

If properly managed, resource conservation and tourism development can be compatible and complementary. They can benefit greatly from each other and they should be marketing partners (Kelly, 1989; Wight interviewed in Fediow, 1988). There has been no consistent approach, however, to environmental marketing practices. Some firms may neglect their environmental activities, while others may exploit environmental marketing. Meagher (1991), through the environmental action model (Figure 3.3), illustrates the fact that firms may be inactive, active or proactive towards environmental marketing or environmental improvements. In the environmental action model, firms are classified as inactive when they tend not to see the benefits of allocating any resources toward environmental activities; they have a low level of commitment to both environmental improvement and to environmental marketing. Those that see some benefits may have medium levels of commitment in either regard, and are said to be active. Those that clearly see the benefits of environmental action and demonstrate high levels of commitment to environmental marketing and improvement are classified as proactive. The balance of commitment to both environmental improvement and environmental marketing has been examined in consumer literature relative to such firms as McDonalds or Procter and Gamble (Meagher, 1991). This type of analysis can be adapted to ecotourism, and related to the conservation or eco-sell perspectives already discussed.

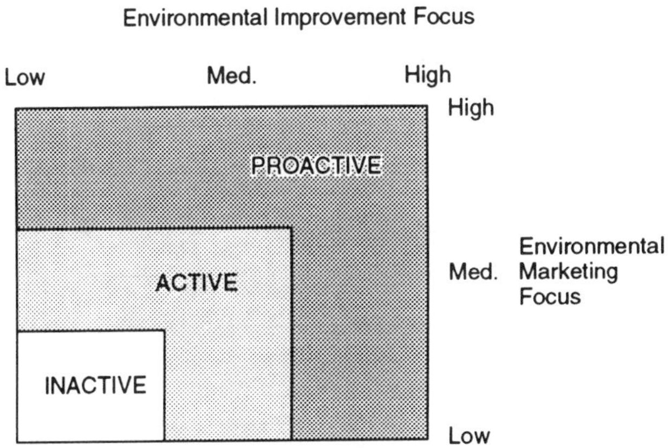

FIGURE 3.3.   Environmental action model. Adapted from Meagher (1991)

The degree to which any firm takes environmentally responsible action or engages in environmental marketing can be shown by its position on Figure 3.4. Firms can take up three positions: balance, eco-exploitation or neglect. Some operators have produced superficial, often short-term changes in their products and calculated shifts in their advertising strategy in an attempt to package 'business as usual'. This has been characterised elsewhere as 'light green' (Plant and Plant, 1991) and has been discussed as eco-exploitation here. In the positioning model, this position of eco-exploitation is shown where marketing activities are not balanced by a 'deep green' commitment. For example, operator A (Figure 3.4) may repackage the tours of a previous year to include eco-sell phrases (such as those which appear on Figure 3.1) without consideration of resource characteristics, local community benefits, environmental ethics or a long-term perspective: it is exploiting consumers' interest in ecotourism experiences. On the other hand, operators may be committed to environmentally responsible action, but fail to market these efforts and the legitimate instinctiveness of their products. For example, operator B may be oriented principally to resource conservation, local education and development, while providing participatory travel experiences to assist in fund-raising. However, it may fail to provide the potential traveller with the reasons for the higher cost of its packages, access limits, tourist activity restraints and the benefits which its package provides to the local resource and community. It is occupying a position of marketing neglect.

Both eco-exploitation and neglect are more vulnerable positions on the model and are unlikely to remain sustainable. There is a third position,

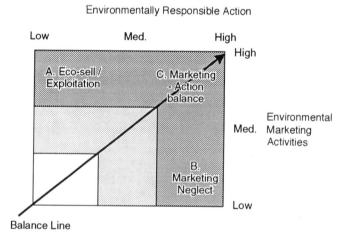

FIGURE 3.4.   Positioning for environmental activities and marketing. Adapted from Meagher (1991)

however, that of balance between commitment to environmentally responsible action and to environmental marketing, as shown by operator C. In this position, not only is ecotourism 'sold' to consumers, but the product is developed sensitively, with regard to its long-term future, and consumers are aware (both before purchase and during the trip) of the genuine concern for the resources involved. This position should involve more than the idea of balance, which implies compromise and trade-offs. It should involve the complementary integration of economic goals and environmentally responsible or conservation goals. When properly integrated, each set of goals can further the success of the other. This position is not only desirable in the short term, but is most likely to remain sustainable in the long term.

The English Tourist Board (1991) points out that any 'green' marketing must be genuine and based on a carefully developed environmental policy. It suggests to organisations

- be honest and substantiate your environmental claims
- identify your product's environmental benefits
- undertake product–market matching
- present details of the environment surrounding your operation
- use recycled paper for all printed materials
- consider developing environmental promotions

PRODUCT, PERFORMANCE STANDARDS AND EVALUATION

The term 'ecotourism' must be viewed with caution until a majority of stakeholders agree upon the definition, or the components which should be present, or perhaps until there are guidelines or other mechanisms in place to indicate standards. Such guidelines have been developed elsewhere. In May 1991, Canadian Consumer and Corporate Affairs published *Guiding Principles for Environmental Labelling and Advertising,* produced by a working group composed of both government and industry representatives. Any company not adhering to them runs the risk of charges of misleading advertising. Vague statements such as 'environmentally friendly' or 'green' are described as meaningless, and environmental claims that are ambiguous, incomplete or misleading are discouraged (Isaacs, 1991). There would be value both to the resource base and to the prospective visitor if such guidelines were to be developed and adopted for ecotourism by industry and governments.

Rich (1991) maintains that well-intentioned guides or outfitters who desire to offer an ethically rewarding experience are unlikely to be able to stay in business if regulations are not used to enforce appropriate standards, limits and competition. However, others consider that voluntary guidelines can be an effective first step. The 40th Annual Pacific Asia Travel Association (PATA) Conference in 1991 addressed the theme *Enrich the Environment.* One conference resolution was that PATA would adopt the Blue Flag model of performance standards and incentives to identify, preserve and market PATA destinations in terms of all aspects of environmental sustainability. Although a creditable step, a more comprehensive approach, appropriate for ecotourism operators in particular, and for all tourism operators in general, would be the Green Flag approach. Green Flag International (GFI) is a not-for-profit company formed in response to the growing demand for conservation advice from tour operators and the travelling public (see Chapter 4). GFI's primary aim is to 'work in partnership with the tourism industry to make improvements to the environment worldwide' (Wood and House, 1991). Through a rating scheme it environmentally audits holidays, tour operators and resorts. Each is analysed in detail according to the following sustainable tourism criteria

- consideration given to landscape, wildlife and cultural heritage
- efficiency
- waste disposal and recycling
- interaction with local communities in terms of goods and services
- sympathetic building and architecture

In Europe, the Association of Independent Tour Operators (AITO) has taken a joint initiative with GFI to promote sustainable tourism. The chairman of AITO has realised the link between environment and economy: 'the more far-sighted of AITO's members have begun to realise that it is time . . . to protect the product on which our businesses depend . . . if we do not help conserve the very places which our clients clamour to see then, in five years' time, we shall have no clients at all . . . those dream locations will have been ruined' (Wood and House, 1991).

In other sectors there has been considerable controversy concerning 'green product' endorsements, most notably Pollution Probe's endorsement of Loblaw's 'green products'. Pollution Probe's motivation was understandable: support and encouragement to industry in developing environmentally sound products; the need for such products in major stores; the educational benefits of endorsement; and funds for environmental groups. But questions arose about whether or not environmental groups should endorse products and receive money, what environmental criteria were applied, the nature of the product testing and publicising of results (Gallon, 1992). Such questions may be equally valid when raised in the context of ecotourism. Donation of funds to local conservation groups or activities may be seen as a fee for endorsement and, although worthwhile, may not go far enough. The Green Flag approach introduces independent product and performance testing, evaluation and accountability for 'green' claims. The industry, conservation groups and government must act responsibly in promoting green consumerism as public trust, like the sensitive spaces of the earth, is fragile.

ETHICS-BASED PERSPECTIVE

Consumers are switching allegiances, challenging traditional ethics and actively seeking out products that are perceived to fulfil their needs, even if more costly. They do not just look at the price of a product, they ask if there is an environmental or a moral issue involved. Tourists, as consumers, are asking similar questions, seeking creative travel alternatives and are willing to pay extra to obtain the travel experience they desire (Millman, 1989). With respect to such larger issues as threatened species and habitat, it is not only environmentalists who are concerned, but a large segment of the population (Fifth Institute Conference on Natural Resources Law, 1991). This concern is reflected in the rapidly growing interest in ecotourism and the desire to have an enlightening travel experience which incorporates a genuine sensitivity to the resources upon which it is based. A US survey found that 45 per cent of US travellers felt that travel suppliers do not provide enough environmental protection training and support to employees. In addition, a majority of respondents felt that travel suppliers did not educate their customers enough on environmental awareness and protection during trips (Travel Industry Association of America, 1992: 43). Clearly, there is a demand in the tourism marketplace for a range of environmentally sensitive products, programmes and education.

Many industries have seen an acceleration in the development of explicit codes incorporating environmental principles or responsible behaviour. In Canada, industry associations related to petroleum products, chemicals, pulp and paper and plastics, to name but a few, have developed codes or programmes to integrate environmental stewardship into the way they conduct business. In part, this is driven by the recognition that consumers of the 1990s will increasingly demand products which provide convenience and comfort, and which do so in a way that does not undermine environmental security (Dickson, 1989). Of course, the development of codes does not necessarily translate into effective implementation as yet, although Brooks (1991) points out that the issue of whether codes are actually effective, or merely window-dressing, is no longer relevant, as most codes have recently become part of the legal framework of well-managed companies. Codes appear to represent the cutting edge of a shift in corporate direction and industry awareness.

The tourism industry has also been moving in the direction of ethical principles, although in an *ad hoc* manner. A number of policies, codes or principles oriented towards natural or cultural resources have been drafted by governments, associations and operators, including the following: National Audubon Society; Sobek International; Australian Tourism Industry Association; American Society of Travel Agents; Center for Responsible Tourism (California); Alliance Internationale de Tourisme; ITT Sheraton Corporation; Field Studies Council (UK); Ecumenical Coalition on Third World Tourism

(Thailand); Countryside Commission (UK); Canadian Pacific Hotels and Resort; Thomsons Holidays (UK); Pacific Asia Travel Association; World Travel and Tourism Council; Ramada International Hotels and Resorts; Centre for Advancement of Responsive Travel (UK); New Zealand Tourist Industry Federation; Commercial Tour Operators in Gwaii Haanas/South Moresby (BC); Annapurna Conservation Area Project (Nepal); International Association of Antarctica Tour Operators; and British Columbia Wildlife Watch.

Tourism codes have tended to be focused on either the biophysical (e.g. National Audubon Society) or the cultural resources (e.g. the Ecumenical Coalition on Third World Tourism). Many have tended to mix codes of ethics (more general and value-based) with codes of practice (more specific guidelines). Many of these codes of ethics have been developed only for the traveller, but all players in the tourism industry need to take a share of the responsibility for ethical activity—tourists, the industry, host communities, governments and non-government organisations. In Canada, a national cooperative initiative has resulted in the development of a comprehensive *Code of Ethics and Guidelines for Sustainable Tourism* (Tourism Industry Association of Canada and National Round Table on the Environment and the Economy, 1992). The codes are for tourists as well as the industry and there are guidelines for the industry overall, as well as detailed guidelines directed towards tourism industry associations, food services, tour operators, accommodation and ministries of tourism. An iterative process of consultation, input and refinement among the many stake-holders in the tourism industry was used to ensure that guidelines were not only comprehensive, but also appropriate for all sectors of the industry. The CEAC study, *Ecotourism in Canada,* has, as a subset of these codes, proposed a code of ecotourism ethics for Canada (Scace *et al.*, 1992: 30).

From an individual ecotourism operator's perspective, there are immediate benefits in adopting and implementing such codes: the generation of public support; increased credibility; easy identification of 'genuine' ecotourism suppliers by both the public and others in the industry; and increased market demand for the associated products. But besides this, an ethics-oriented perspective increases the sustainability of both the resource and the industry, integrating economic, social and conservation objectives.

CONCLUSIONS

There is a range of players involved in ecotourism, with varying perspectives and values. The marketing activities of these players reflect their motivations and can be exploitative of the resource base through eco-sell, or can neglect to market their operation's commitment to environmentally responsible activities. However, they need not act as two forces pulling in fundamentally opposite directions. There is a need for more of a balance between conservation and profit-making perspectives. Through complementary integration, the two perspectives can reinforce and strengthen each other over the longer term. This requires

- a strategic and proactive approach
- better understanding of the linkage and potentially symbiotic relationship between conservation and marketing
- reconciling environmental or 'green' marketing, with industry commitment to environmentally responsible action
- taking a supply management perspective which acknowledges resource values and accepts resource constraints and limits, as well as seizing resource-based opportunities
- development of understanding and partnerships between host communities, governments, non-governmental organisations and the industry
- greater discrimination in client selection through identification of market segments which better match the range of ecotourism products
- development of formal or informal product and performance standards
- promotion and acceptance of a tourist and operator code of ethics, and guidelines for responsible travel practices and behaviour

Acceptance of these concepts provides a positive response to the challenge of incorporating the values and principles underlying ecotourism into both the product and the marketing activities. This increases consumer trust, demand for and satisfaction with the product. In addition, it conserves the resources upon which the product is based, which in turn increases the sustainability of both the resource base and the ecotourism industry.

NOTE

This chapter, now expanded and updated, first appeared as 'Ecotourism: ethics or eco-sell?' in the *Journal of Travel Research*, **31** (3): 3–9. This journal is jointly published by the Business Research Division, University of Colorado at Boulder, and the Travel and Tourism Research Association.

REFERENCES

Atwood, R., 1990, Tourist trade transforms Amazon jungle village, *Chronicle-Herald-Mail-Star*, June 23, D5.
Bailey, I., 1992, Lily cups takes on environmental critics, *The Edmonton Journal*, January 3, B8.
Belize Currents, 1990, Advertisement, Summer, 24.
Boo, E., 1990, *Ecotourism: the Potentials and Pitfalls*, 2 Vols, World Wildlife Fund, Washington.
Brooks, L.J., 1991, Codes of conduct for business: are they effective, or just window dressing? *Canadian Public Administration*, **34**(1), 171–176.

Budowski, G., 1976, Tourism and environmental conservation: conflict, coexistence or symbiosis? *Environmental Conservation,* **3**(1), 27–31.

Burr, P., 1991, Tourism and the environment—partners, not adversaries, in *Tourism: Building Credibility for a Credible Industry, Travel and Tourism Research Association Twenty-second Annual Conference Proceedings, Long Beach, Ca, USA, 9–13 June 1991,* TTRA, Wheat Ridge, Colorado, 59–62.

Canadian Environmental Advisory Council, 1991, *A Protected Areas Vision for Canada,* Supply and Services Canada, Ottawa.

Carson, P. and Moulden, J., 1991, *Green is Gold: Business Talking to Business About the Environmental Revolution,* Harperbusiness, Toronto.

Cohen, E., 1989, Primitive and remote: hill tribe trekking in Thailand, *Annals of Tourism Research,* **16**, 30–61.

Co-op America, 1991, *Ecotourism,* Advertising Supplement, June.

Dearden, P., 1989, Tourism in developing societies: some observations on trekking in the highlands of north Thailand, *World Leisure and Recreation,* **31**(4), 40–47.

Dickson, C., 1989, We're all in this together, *Inside Guide,* **3**(5), 70.

English Tourist Board, Countryside Commission, Rural Development Commission, 1991, *The Green Light, a Guide to Sustainable Tourism,* English Tourist Board, London.

Fediow, S., 1988, The second century: let's not kill the goose that laid the golden egg, *Environment Views,* **11**(2), 5–7.

Fennell, D.A. and Smale, B.J.A., 1992, Ecotourism and natural resource protection: implications of an alternative form of tourism for host nations, *Tourism Recreation Research,* **17**(1), 21–32.

Fifth Institute Conference on Natural Resources Law, 1991, *Resources: The Newsletter of the Canadian Institute of Resources Law,* **34**, 1.

Gallon, G., 1992, The green product endorsement controversy, *Alternatives,* **18**(3), 16–25.

Globe and Mail, 1991, Advertisement, April 12, B18, Toronto.

Grotta, S., 1990, The ecotourist as ambassador, in Kusler, J.A. (ed.) *Ecotourism and Resource Conservation, Selected Papers from the 1st International Symposium: Ecotourism, Merida, Mexico, 17–19 April 1990,* 99–108.

Hawkes, S. and Williams, P. (eds), 1993, *The Greening of Tourism—From Principles to Practice, GLOBE '92 Tourism Stream: Case Book of Best Practice in Sustainable Tourism,* Centre for Tourism Policy and Research, Simon Fraser University with Tourism Canada, Industry, Science and Technology Canada, Burnaby, British Columbia.

Ignacio, G., 1990, Ecotourism spawns new breed of adventure tours, *Tour and Travel News,* February 5, 24–25.

Isaacs, C., 1991, Green marketing directory: additions and developments, in Rhind, I. (ed.) *The Canadian Green Marketing Alert,* **1**(1), 3–4.

Jarvie, L., 1992, Responsible marketing of adventure travel and ecotourism, in *Proceedings of the 1991 World Congress on Adventure Travel and Ecotourism,* The Adventure Travel Society, Englewood, Colorado, 68–69.

Kelly, F.J., 1989, Developing marketing partnerships, in Bureau of Economic and Business Research, *Tourism Research: Globalization, the Pacific Rim and Beyond, Travel and Tourism Research Association Twentieth Anniversary Conference, Honolulu, Hawaii, 11–15 June, 1989,* TTRA, Wheat Ridge, Colorado, 231–242.

Kelman, S., 1991, The eco stampede, *Report on Business Magazine,* (May), 71–72.

Lane, B., 1990, Developing sustainable rural tourism, paper presented at the *Irish National Planning Conference: Planning and Tourism in Harmony, Newmarket, Ireland, April 1990.*

Lillywhite, M. and Lillywhite, L., 1991, Low impact tourism, in Hawkins, D.E. and Ritchie, J.R.B. (eds) *World Travel and Tourism Review: Indicators, Trends and Forecasts*, Vol. 1, CAB International, Wallingford.

Lindberg, K., 1991, *Policies for Maximizing Nature Tourism's Ecological and Economic Benefits*, World Resources Institute, Washington.

Masterton, A.M., 1991, Ecotourism: an economic issue, *Tour and Travel News*, **24**, 1, 51, 52.

McNeely, J.A. and Thorsell, J.W., 1989, Jungles, mountains and islands: how tourism can help conserve the natural heritage, *World Leisure and Recreation*, **31**(4), 29–39.

Meagher, M., 1991, Canadian environmental marketing programs: how to walk the balance line in making good environment into good business, in Rhind, I. (ed.) *The Canadian Green Marketing Alert*, **1**(1), 7–10.

Millman, R., 1989, Pleasure seeking v the 'greening' of world tourism, *Tourism Management*, **10**(4), 275–278.

Plant, C. and Plant, J. (eds), 1991, *Green Business: Hope or Hoax?* New Society Publishers, Gabriola Island, British Columbia.

Romeril, M., 1985, Tourism and the environment—towards a symbiotic relationship, *International Journal of Environmental Studies*, **25**, 215–218.

Rich, J., 1991, Ecotourism—sales slogan or ethical entrepreneurism? in *Proceedings of the 1991 World Congress on Adventure Travel and Ecotourism*, The Adventure Travel Society, Englewood, 37–39.

Ryan, C., 1991, Tourism and marketing—a symbiotic relationship? *Tourism Management*, **12**, 101–111.

Salazar, M., Palmer, P., Barthel, W. and Reed, R., 1991, Local participation in ecotourism development, Talamanca, Costa Rica: opportunities and obstacles, in Kusler, J.A. (ed.), *Ecotourism and Resource Conservation, Selected Papers from the 1st International Symposium: Ecotourism, Merida, Mexico, 17–19 April 1991*, 371–381.

Scace, R.C., Grifone, E. and Usher, R., 1992, *Ecotourism in Canada*, Canadian Environmental Advisory Council, Supply and Services Canada, Ottawa.

Sobek, 1990, *Sobek's Exceptional Adventures*, Sobek Expeditions, Angels Camp.

Tourism Industry Association of Canada and National Round Table on the Environment and the Economy, 1992, *Code of Ethics and Guidelines for Sustainable Tourism*, Tourism Industry Association of Canada, Ottawa.

Travel Industry Association of America, 1992, *Tourism and the Environment*, Travel Industry Association of America, Washington.

Wight, P., 1988, *Tourism in Alberta*, a discussion paper prepared for the Alberta Conservation Strategy Project, Environmental Council of Alberta, Edmonton.

Wood, K. and House, S., 1991, *The Good Tourist: a Worldwide Guide for the Green Traveller*, Mandarin, London.

Wright, W.J., 1991, The Angus Reid report: the environment and 'green' products in recessionary times, in Rhind, I. (ed.) *The Canadian Green Marketing Alert*, **1**(1), 4–7.

Ziffer, K., 1989, *Ecotourism: the Uneasy Alliance*, Conservation International, Ernst and Young, Washington.

4

Tourism: Environmental Relevance

Richard Sisman

THE NEED FOR SOLUTION-DRIVEN INITIATIVES

The following contribution to the debate about a more sustainable future for the tourism industry has to be seen in the context of the much wider changes considered to be desirable in the way in which environmental issues will be dealt with over the coming years. It is necessary for the reader to understand the philosophy of change which underpins this chapter and how this philosophy shapes both a personal contribution to sustainability and the way in which Green Flag International (GFI) operates.

Green Flag International is a not-for-profit environmental organisation operating entirely within the field of tourism and travel. It is a new breed environmental group, its success dependent not on peer pressure or organisational strength, but on the open door to industry that now exists in response to the major changes which have been brought about as a result of the growing awareness of damaging environmental impacts throughout the world.

What is a new breed environmental group? Essentially, for reasons that will be developed further in this chapter, there is a need for environmental groups to dispense with the cumbersome trappings of corporate goals and organisational objectives. The current environmental need is for initiatives which are totally solution-driven. The rate and pace of change in society, throughout the world in general and in the field of environmental action in particular, is such that the need is to 'best guess' such changes and to help influence and direct them in a way which proves the best available environmental solution. Currently, this is not happening to anything like the degree that it might.

The proliferation of environmental agencies

One significant reason for the lack of environmental action is that, unfortunately, the main change so far resulting from growing environmental awareness has not been an improvement in the activities of society as a whole, but a growth in the size of environmental organisations. Many voluntary agencies,

Ecotourism: A Sustainable Option? Edited by E. Cater and G. Lowman
© The editors and contributors. Published in 1994 by John Wiley & Sons Ltd

consultancies and government-funded bodies have grown in size to become large businesses with high central costs and large numbers of staff. Generous government support through grants and core funding, support from concerned members of the public, business sponsorship and the costs associated with environmental legislation and fund-raising have between them helped to create a major expansion in environmental agencies in the government, private and voluntary sectors. For example, the UK market for environmental consultancy work now exceeds £400 million per annum and £30 000 million world-wide. Estimates for the turn of the century put these figures at £1000 million and £50 000 million, respectively. High central costs are now a feature of our environmental movement and fund-raising becomes ever more important. This has led to the undesirable development of 'ambulance chasing', i.e. the use of disasters as springboards to appeal for the funding of organisational costs.

This is not a healthy phase of development. The environmental bonus, which has been so hard-won over a long period of time, should be directed into action by industry, governments and society as a whole, with small, lean environmental groups acting in an enabling capacity. Organisational growth is a feature of the 1970s and 1980s, not the 1990s when, particularly during a recessionary period, it is counter to the prevailing mood of the nation. Large environmental organisations, in common with their counterparts in business, find it difficult to focus debate. They also, as a result of their need to retain an identity to protect existence, tend to internalise policies within unnecessary corporate goals. In addition, the growth in information technology is enabling an explosion in home-based self-employment and access to information. Together with a general rejection of the down side of home to work-station travel time, which can be so wasteful of the working day, this is leading to a welcome weakening in organisational structures throughout the nation as a whole.

The networking role of Green Flag International

During the late 1980s the need for a much more loosely structured environmental movement with close, contractual links with government and industries was personally envisaged. GFI was therefore created and formed on the basis of a 'network'. It has no centrally funded staff and no organisational goals. It does not depend upon growth for survival, it is not subject to 'charity fatigue', i.e. the ups and downs of fund-raising, and it is amorphous in shape and form. Each of its increasing number of projects and initiatives are established as separate cost centres managed by one of its 20 plus advisers, each of whom is selected on the basis of specialist knowledge. These advisers are drawn from people with considerable experience within the environmental field, in many cases those who have made the transition from an organisation base to more entrepreneurial lifestyles.

In this way GFI can run with the demand and the opportunities it creates within the tourism industry and it is not constrained by the burden of corporate planning or programmes based upon a set number of staff or a set budget. It can also fulfil objectives without public sector financial support, avoiding becoming grant-led. This is a problem which has bedevilled so many voluntary groups whose main role now seems to be in fulfilling governmental objectives, simply because they need the money to meet staff costs.

ENVIRONMENTAL RELEVANCE—A WORKING PARTNERSHIP

What follows is based entirely upon a personal view that environmental action should be much more responsive to opportunism, to the highs and lows of the business cycle and to the relevance to society as a whole. It is essentially a summary of how a personal philosophy has been put into practice and it is for the reader to decide how it fits into their personal expectations of the environmental movement. Hopefully, above all, it will point to a way forward which will set a new relationship between tourism and the environment.

Sustainability in practice

Just as Lord's is the home of cricket and Westminster is the home of democracy, tourism seems to have become the home of the generic term. The press gave us mass tourism, to describe all that is seen as bad, and niche tourism to describe opportunities for higher profits. Environmentalists gave us ecotourism and agro-tourism as examples of acceptable tourism. The latest emergent theme is that of sustainable tourism which, as far as can be personally gathered, has emerged simply because all forms of development and activity are now preceded by the term sustainable to describe some form of utopian change in how the world should operate and to provide an undefined benchmark of acceptability.

Generic terms are useful but a little like the blindfolded man trying to describe the elephant (for those who remember Kipling's *Just So Stories*); it depends upon which bit that you touch that describes the beast. So sustainability means different things to different people, and it is surprising, post-Brundtland and post-Rio, just how many organisations have suddenly 'discovered' that their policies can be made to 'fit' the concept of sustainability simply by deciding their own benchmark.

So what does sustainability mean in practice and how is it best achieved in reality rather than in debate or marketing terms? This overview is based upon personal experience and knowledge rather than academic research, and upon a pragmatic approach rather than idealism. Indeed, experience and pragmatism are the fundamentals upon which GFI was founded and presented to the tourism industry. The concept of sustainability must include a working partnership that blends good environmental practice and profitable business for mutual long-term advantages. As others have different views about sustainability, a personally preferred term is that of 'environmental relevance' to describe this relationship.

ENVIRONMENTAL GROUPS—A CHANGING ROLE

Green Flag International was launched just three years ago to a cautious, but receptive, industry whose main links with environmental groups at that time consisted of reading in the press about campaigns to save this or that, or in being asked to contribute towards 'good environmental causes'. There seemed to be a complete lack of any environmental policy or direction within the industry. Extensive criticism appeared on a regular basis in the press with, for example, articles headed 'Tourism, the Enchanted Nightmare' and 'Tourism, the Destroyer'. The problems were well articulated but no-one was offering solutions.

Integrating environmental action into business practice

This lack of action was, perhaps, because mainstream environmental groups were, and many still are, concentrating upon the residual problems of development rather than upon playing a part in helping to create the wider changes in society that would address the actual causes of the problems. Environmentalism should be much more integrated into society as a whole, not an adjunct to it. Environmental issues must be viewed in the context of a much wider partnership with society, not a sectoral extra. Environmental relevance will not be achieved through a system of separate services operated by special interest groups. There are far too many environmental policies, charters and standards prepared by environmental groups for others to implement. They generally smack of 'nanny knows best' and often fail because they lack an understanding of the true nature of business.

Environmental policy-makers seeking to develop a sustainable agenda need to work more closely with major business partners and developers and to take into account the wider interests of the vast majority of the population. There are, as yet, few cases where good environmental practice has been integrated with good business practice to create a stronger and more balanced industry. That is the key to environmental relevance and what GFI is attempting to achieve with the tourism industry.

Green Flag International's philosophy of integrating environmental action into business, with which people in the cut and thrust of the tourism industry can readily identify, has seen membership grow from its 19 founders to over 60 (Figure 4.1). This membership includes market leaders, many of whom influence the shape and direction of tourism world-wide. GFI is recognised as an environmental service belonging to the industry rather than a separate

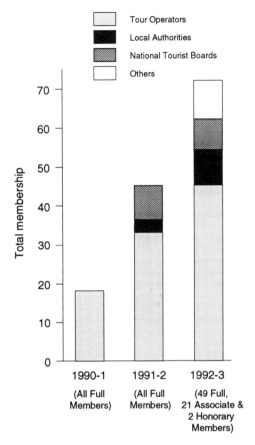

FIGURE 4.1. Membership of Green Flag International, 1990–3

environmental organisation. It is non-profit-making, it has no staff, no spon-sorship and few direct resources, and yet its networking approach is beginning to achieve results.

It is felt that the initial successes with the business community, tour oper-ators, the travel press and many travellers is based upon GFI's ability to match environmental improvements with a realistic approach to business de-mands, a formula strongly recommended for consideration by other environ-mental groups. If environmental issues are to achieve a mainstream relevance, environmental groups in the public and private sector will need to develop new agendas or their interests may well become marginalised, particularly in the field of societal change.

The reason for this is simple: the major environmental groups in the public and voluntary sector in the UK have developed on the basis of élitism and thematic or primacy interests. In many cases the themes are a matter of historical accident—for example, the special interests of their founders, or, in the case of the public sector, the whim of a government minister. Many of the ideals formulated in the post-war era seem out of place in the 1990s. Sustainable environmental agendas must develop as a part of society as a whole, integrated with the highs and lows of the business cycle and recognising other societal pressures and priorities. In the past environmental groups have developed standards for others to follow, but environmental relevance is much more of a partnership; it will not be achieved through either environmental or business primacy, but is a balance of interests.

The current challenge

The challenge at this moment in time is not to try to stop the inevitability of development and change; it is to match a good bottom line with a good environmental policy. This is the real challenge of the 1990s. Vital policies are those which have a relevance to society as a whole, not to a narrow band of middle-class, mobile, mainly rural, relatively wealthy and often vocal supporters. Although there is great personal respect for those who founded and made strong the environmental movement in the UK, it is felt that some would now recognise that there is a need for a realignment of the environmental movement to reflect the society of the 1990s.

Society is not yet ready to make those much tougher long-term changes that many other environmental organisations feel are necessary and which formulate the policies of the mid- to dark greens. In a sense, progress is analogous to driving a car: currently stuck in first gear, there is the opportunity of changing to second, but fifth gear is a long way off. So the immediate future of sustainable tourism is clear. The quest to create a firmer bonding between good business and good environmental practice needs to be continued. The more experience gained of this, the better we become at achieving it. Some mistakes may be made and questioned, but this is understandable as there is a generation of problems to overcome.

It is unnecessary to dwell upon why, in the past, society has so miserably failed the environment, or to comment upon the undoubted environmental problems associated with tourism development *per se*. The current problems rest with ourselves and our forbears; society in general is guilty of treating natural resources as free or cheap goods. Successive national and international governments, through political weakness, inadequate laws and planning controls and the dogmatic encouragement of market forces, have also failed the environment.

Indeed, the earth's collective ills are now such that many will only start to be addressed through rigorous policies at the international level, with a positive acceptance of the principle that the polluter pays. The crazy legacy of commercial advantage through environmental despoilation which has applied in tourism as well as other industries must be banished forever.

THE CONTRIBUTION OF GOVERNMENTS

There are, of course, some immediate steps that individual governments can take to contribute to sustainability, not only in the field of new laws and regulations, but through their massive spending programmes and through the role of their agencies. For example, how many government agencies have a positive policy to buy from companies with sound environmental polices? Yet such action is expected of the private sector and the public.

The UK Government's launch of *'Green Light: a Guide to Sustainable Tourism'* (English Tourist Board, 1991) is a good example of collective environmental wisdom which, to quote, 'aims to enable all of those involved in running a tourism business to forge a new way forward that combines economic prosperity with sound environmental stewardship'. These are excellent sentiments but, as yet, are without the foundation of any direct action by the government or its agencies to develop such policies in-house.

Environmental relevance also requires a close working relationship between government agencies and business. The environmental civil servant should, like the conservation officer in the voluntary sector, become a part of a wider network, cross-fertilising environmental action throughout society rather than seeking to deliver corporate goals set by their organisation. The stated government policy on tourism (Department of the Environment, 1992), is that 'the tourism industry should flourish in response to the market, while respecting the environment which attracts visitors but also has far wider and enduring value'. If only those choosing such fine words were more active in directly influencing the market!

THE ROLE OF THE TOURISM INDUSTRY

Having rewritten the role of the environmentalist and the role of government, it may be thought that the role of the tourism industry should be rewritten. The true irony for the deep green, and the point missed by many, is that this is not necessary. Tourism represents a fleeting moment in time, holidays last on average a few days and tour operator programmes for just a few months. Each is re-created annually or even more often. Tourism is therefore extremely malleable; it can absorb good environmental practice in its stride. Tour operators will respond to the environmental policies set for them in the countries which their clients visit. What they need are unambiguous policies and consistent interpretation. The fact that tourism's legacy is one of damage to the environment is a reflection of historical failure rather than an expression of future intent.

An agenda for change

Indeed, GFI receives far more encouragement from within the tourism industry than it does from the government or environmental sector. The 130 member strong Association of Independent Tour Operators (AITO), in particular, sees the work of GFI as central to its interests. Not only do AITO members recognise that a good environment is good for business, but that it also has a role in creating a 'quality' product. The best hotel in the world will lose its appeal if it is surrounded by squalor, litter and environmental degradation.

As Noel Josephides, the highly respected Chairman of AITO, states 'I consider environmental issues and their application to the holiday industry to be the most serious challenge that AITO and our sector as a whole has to face. Many current tour operating practices will have to change if we are to protect the host countries' environment. Short term views linked to filling aircraft and fulfilling city analysts' expectations of rapid growth cannot be compatible with balanced, sustainable tourism'.

In terms of helping to create such an agenda for change, the following priorities for the environmental movement can be identified:

1. Help to create an internally helpful and not externally critical information base. Negative campaigning is generally ineffectual, particularly when it is based upon a worst case scenario.
2. Demonstrate that good environmental performance can generate a return on investment of time and money. The new generation of environmental economics needs to be employed so that estimates of what the environment is really worth can be arrived at.
3. Help to stimulate public demand for change. This is woefully underdeveloped in the UK. It must also be recognised that preaching to the converted is increasingly wasteful of time and resources. Just like policemen, environmentalists spend far too much time in the company of other environmentalists.
4. Create a working relationship, or relevance, between environmental action and business. There is no valid reason for any industry to support initiatives unless they and their clients have relevance to it.
5. Engender confidence in the advice given. Scare tactics and extrapolated claims must be tempered with realism.
6. Tourism, like other industry, needs a lead by influential people inside and outside the industry. In all walks of life there are leaders and followers. Quality leaders, sharing the same views, and respected within the tourism industry, need to be identified and assisted.
7. Seek to ensure that tourism is developed upon the basis of equitable and fair national and international policies. Such policies must not give the exploiter commercial advantage, as has been the case in the past.

THE PRACTICAL ROLE OF GREEN FLAG INTERNATIONAL

The practical work of GFI manifests itself in a number of ways. The main practical task is to develop environmental improvement projects at tourism destinations that reflect the concept of environmental relevance to our partners. Each project has to have a combination of the following: a net environmental gain; direct relevance to our funding partner and their clients; the creation of awareness or education; and universal application within its costs and benefits on a non-élitist basis.

The basic requirements of environmental relevance

Essentially, environmental relevance in tourism has three key ingredients: (1) destination management in its widest sense—this must include people and culture as well as habitat; (2) industry action should become more environmentally friendly; and (3) training of the industry and informing the traveller.

These three ingredients form the basics required to create workable models or methodologies for the development of projects that include local people and local authorities (giving them local acceptance), local companies and hoteliers who recognise that a damaged environment is bad for business, tour operators with similar concerns and, of course, the tourists. By involving all of the interested parties, projects and policies of environmental enhancement and protection will start from a robust base.

Partners in environmental relevance

The partnership approach of GFI has helped to create a number of projects at destinations, including: working with Countrywide Holidays to establish financial support for practical environmental projects in UK National Parks; work in Crete, sponsored by the Travel Club of Upminster and Simply Travel, to establish a programme of environmental improvements and countryside management; an environmental plan for Malta, leading to an island clean-up campaign; and the development of a green tourism project in the former East Germany, sponsored by Moswin Tours (GFI, 1992). A number of other studies at destinations have been carried out and environmental and green tourism strategies have been prepared with the assistance of tour operators and others. These await implementation.

Green Flag International has also agreed to provide information to travel agents for display in their shops and for distribution with travel documents. Some operators, such as Sunvil, already distribute environmental information with their tickets. Conferences are run which provide an industry meeting place for the development of sustainable and green tourism initiatives. Assistance is given in the development and promotion of environmentally friendly holiday products. Working jointly with Southampton University, an EU-funded project aims to provide remote environmental training for tourism companies. This will get environmental information right into the heart of the industry.

FUTURE PROJECTS

Many problems are still to be faced. The creation of a more sustainable tourism industry is an uphill task. Perhaps surprisingly, the main hurdle is not perceived to be the business side of tourism. The ability of the industry to change should not be of great concern. It is the very nature of business to respond to change. Those that don't do not survive.

Green Flag International can do its best to ensure that such changes are made on the basis of the best information available. Projects can be instigated which will stand the test of time owing to their robust construction. What cannot be achieved alone is the creation of pressures for change from within the government, from within the mass of environmental organisations working at the periphery, or, most importantly, from within the minds of the tourists themselves. There is nothing more daunting than to be told by the Chief Executive of Thomas Cook that there is little public demand from the British holidaymaker for green or sustainable holidays. How can one deal with such a simple statement of fact?

Environmental relevance can only be ultimately achieved if we are successful in winning the minds of the vast majority of the population. That is the major challenge facing the environmental movement over the next few years. Clearly, tourism industry leaders feel that there has been such a failure to make sufficient progress in this direction for them to respond in a meaningful way. This is sad and reinforces a view of the need for a re-thinking and realignment of the environmentalists' role.

The one message that should be taken to heart by all is that the way forward for the creation of environmental relevance involves a collective approach to the environment as yet unseen in the UK. It needs the self-discipline of all to temper sectoral environmental interests and to adopt policies which integrate environmentalism into the needs and demands of society as a whole. It is only through collective and sustained action that a strong enough case will be developed so that, in a few years time, travel agents will sell only green or sustainable holidays because that is what the public wants and demands.

REFERENCES

Department of Environment, 1992, *Policy Planning Guidelines 21*, HMSO, London.

English Tourist Board, Countryside Commission, Rural Development Commission, 1991, *The Green Light, A Guide to Sustainable Tourism*, English Tourist Board, London.

Green Flag International, 1992, *Rural Tourism and the Eastern Erzgebirge: a Case Study in the Potential for Sustainable Rural Development in Part of the Former German Democratic Republic*, Green Flag International, Cambridge.

5

Ecotourism in the Third World—Problems and Prospects for Sustainability

ERLET CATER

THE INCREASING EMPHASIS ON ECOTOURISM IN THE THIRD WORLD

The development of ecotourism in the Third World appeals to destination areas, tourism enterprises and tourists alike. Its increasing popularity is highlighted by the proliferation of specialist tour operators offering experiences that range from trekking in the Himalaya to gorilla watching in Central Africa. Several destinations have hosted international ecotourism conferences, attracting a large number of delegates from a wide geographical range. The Caribbean has already fielded its fourth annual conference, with its venue in Bonaire, NA. This level of interest is the result of a number of reasons.

Comparative advantage

The less developed world has an undeniable comparative advantage in terms of the variety and extent of unspoiled natural environments. These range from tropical rainforests to savanna grasslands and secluded beaches fringed by coral reefs. Outstanding scenic attractions include spectacular waterfalls and the world's highest mountains. In addition, such countries offer the prospect of viewing unique flora and fauna in their original habitat. Ecotourism offers tourism companies and destination areas the opportunity of capitalising on this comparative advantage. Amongst the last havens of unspoiled nature, these destinations also hold considerable appeal for the ecotourist.

It is difficult to place a financial value on these natural attractions. Attempts to do so have ranged from estimates of the amount that visitors are willing to pay to visit a tropical rainforest in Costa Rica (Tobias and Mendelsohn, 1991) to attributing a financial value to wildlife in East Africa. In the latter case, about 650 000 people visit the National Parks and Protected Areas of Kenya

Ecotourism: A Sustainable Option? Edited by E. Cater and G. Lowman
© The editors and contributors. Published in 1994 by John Wiley & Sons Ltd

each year, spending about US$350 million. In terms of tourist expenditures, Olindo (1991) estimates that on this basis an elephant is worth about US$14 375 a year, or US $900 000 over the course of its life. The significance of ecotourism in terms of tourism revenue to certain individual Third World nations is obvious when prime ecotourism destinations are examined. Table 5.1 shows how the increasing popularity of ecotourism is evidenced by the growth in receipts (over tenfold in the case of Belize) over the last decade. These receipts are of increasing significance to export earnings and gross domestic product (Table 5.2).

Most Third World countries are characterised by severe balance of payments difficulties. The development of ecotourism, therefore, provides an opportunity to capitalise on bountiful natural attractions. For the ecotourist, such destinations provide a unique experience of natural environments which

TABLE 5.1.   Growth in tourism to selected destinations. Source: World Tourism Organisation (1986; 1992)

	Tourist arrivals (thousands)		Tourism receipts (US$ millions)	
	1981	1990	1981	1990
Belize	93	222	8	91
Costa Rica	333	435	94	275
Ecuador	245	332	131	193
Dominica	16	45	2	25
Kenya	373	801	175	443
Botswana	227	844	22	65
Madagascar	12	53	5	43
Maldives	60	195	15	85

TABLE 5.2.   Significance of tourism receipts to selected ecotourism destinations. Sources: World Tourism Organisation (1986; 1992), World Bank (1983; 1992), and IMF (1992)

	Tourism receipts as a percentage of export earnings		Tourism receipts as a percentage of Gross Domestic Product	
	1981	1990	1981	1990
Belize	7.8	42.3	4.5	24.8
Costa Rica	9.7	18.9	3.6	4.8
Ecuador	5.1	7.1	1.0	1.8
Dominica	11.6	n.a.	3.4	n.a.
Kenya	15.3	42.9	2.5	5.9
Madagascar	1.5	12.8	0.2	1.6

contrast with those of their home latitudes. The prestige element of being at the vanguard of tourist visitation is also undeniable as previously isolated areas are opened up. Just recently the Indian Government has announced a partial lifting of the restrictions on the north-eastern state of Arunchal Pradesh (*Geographical*, 1993) and other 'prestige' ecotourism destinations listed recently include Patagonia and Madagascar (*Independent*, 1993). Tourism operators have not been slow to recognise the potential of the fastest growing segment of the tourism industry, in its entirety now the single most important item in international trade (WTTC, 1992). Not only has there been an increase in small, specialist tour operators in recent years, but the larger operators have not been slow to appeal to the ever increasing number of ecotourists. Thomas Cook's Faraway Collection, for example, suggests a visit to the primeval rainforest of Bako National Park, Sarawak.

Local involvement

Viewed as a form of alternative tourism, the emphasis in ecotourism development should be on small-scale, locally owned activities (Weaver, 1991). This has three important repercussions for beleaguered Third World economies. Firstly, the facilities in terms of infrastructure and superstructure are simpler and less expensive than those demanded by conventional mass tourism, and are consequently less of a drain on the limited financial investment available. As such, ecotourism development may well prove a viable alternative in cases where funds for large-scale tourism development are not available (Sherman and Dixon, 1991). Secondly, locally owned and operated businesses are not enmeshed in the need to conform to the corporate Western identity of the multinational tourism concerns, and, therefore, can have a much higher input of local products, materials and labour. This not only has greater multiplier effects throughout the local economy, but also reduces import leakages and the remittances from expatriate labour which result from large-scale, foreign-owned, operations. Thirdly, the profits made should accrue locally instead of flowing back to the parent country. In the capital-scarce situation of most Third World countries, this is a particularly attractive prospect.

Environmental sensitivity

People have become increasingly aware of the adverse socio-cultural and environmental impacts of uncontrolled mass tourism. The very incorporation of 'eco' in its title suggests that ecotourism should be an ecologically responsible form of tourism. Indeed, if it does not comply with this requirement, then the natural attractions upon which it is based will suffer degradation to the point at which tourists will cease to arrive. The scale of such ecotourism activities implies that comparatively low numbers of tourists will arrive and that supporting facilities can be kept to a minimum and will be less intrusive.

It is vital to remember that any human activity dependent on the consumptive use of ecological resources, such as ecotourism, cannot be sustained indefinitely unless an important principle underpins its organisation. The resources may be regarded as the capital stock. If this is cut into, as opposed to only utilising the annual production of the biosphere (the 'interest'), then sustainability will be compromised (Rees, 1990). Ecotourism, with its connotations of sound environmental management and consequent maintenance of environmental capital, should, in theory, provide a viable economic alternative to exploitation of the environment.

It is not surprising, because of these factors, that Third World destinations have turned increasingly towards ecotourism as an apparent way out of their classic impasse: the need to earn foreign exchange without, at the same time, destroying their environmental resource base and thus compromising sustainability. It is, however, necessary to determine if ecotourism development in the Third World is a truly sustainable option. This requires focusing on the different interests involved at various spatial and temporal levels.

A SUSTAINABLE ALTERNATIVE FOR THE HOST POPULATION?

Ideally, the smaller scale, dispersed nature of ecotourism development, with less sophisticated demands, should enable a much higher degree of local participation than conventional mass tourism, with the involvement of local and family-based enterprises, both directly and indirectly. This, however, may be prejudiced by several factors.

The international organisation of ecotourism

Although the emphasis may be on a smaller scale, ecotourists originate from the more developed countries (MDCs) and consequently their tour, travel and accommodation needs are largely coordinated by firms based in those countries. Whilst ecotourists may be affluent [a study by Wilson, cited by Whelan (1991) of US travellers to Ecuador found that a quarter of the group earned over US$90 000 a year in family income], much of their expenditure is not made at the destination end. Consequently, ecotourism must share many of the same characteristics as conventional tourism in terms of leakages. Britton (1982) estimates that the proportion of a total inclusive tour price that is retained locally drops to only 22–25 per cent if both the airline and hotel used are foreign-owned. Furthermore, it has been pointed out that the true wilderness tourist is a poor economic bet, because in the wilderness there is nothing to spend money on! (Butler, 1991).

Foreign investment in ecotourism

This is not a surprising feature of tourism development of whatever type in the capital-scarce situation of Third World economies. As the fastest growing sector in the tourism industry, ecotourism is an attractive investment proposition and is becoming big business. Estimates of its relative significance in terms of global tourism expenditure vary considerably. The Economist Intelligence Unit (EIU) estimated the world-wide ecotourism market at $10 billion in 1989 (EIU, 1992), whereas a study by the Canadian Wildlife Service suggests that as much as $200 billion in total was spent on ecotourism activities globally in 1990 (Ceballos Lascurain, 1992).

Ecotourism is becoming the most significant tourism market segment for many Third World destinations. Overall, a World Wide Fund for Nature (WWF) study estimates that of $55 billion earned by tourism for developing countries in 1988, about $12 billion was the result of ecotourism (EIU, 1992). The figures are even more striking for certain countries which are primarily ecotourism destinations (Table 5.1). In Costa Rica 40 per cent of visitors came to the country for nature-directed activities (Rovinski, 1991). Ecuador, in particular the Galapagos islands, earned US$193 million in tourism receipts in 1990.

Investment in the development of ecotourism in the developing world appears to be a lucrative proposition. Foreign developers, based in the MDCs, have become increasingly involved in countries such as Belize. Of 350 delegates to the first Caribbean conference on ecotourism held in Belize in 1991, only 15–20 per cent could be said to have had no declared financial interest in the development of ecotourism (Figure 5.1). It is estimated that at least one-half were either US-based or expatriates (Figure 5.2). Expatriate involvement in the Belizean tourism industry is such that 65 per cent of the members of the US Aid-initiated Belize Tourism Industry Association are expatriates (Munt, 1993). The location of an English-speaking country, promoting itself as an ecotourism destination, on the doorstep of the USA is bound to prove a mecca for the American ecotourist. Over 40 per cent of tourists visiting come from the USA. Tourists to Belize from North America increased from 30 000 in 1984 to 90 000 in 1990. Inevitable pressures have been generated, to the extent that in May 1992 a scheme was exposed, amidst great controversy, to develop 3000 hectares on the prime tourism resort of Ambergris Caye by US-based developers. The proposed luxury resort included a hotel of international class, a golf course and a marina (Munt, 1993).

Inflationary pressure on local economies

Largely as a result of foreign involvement, prices of land, property and sometimes even local produce are driven relentlessly upward, often beyond the reach of the local population. In Belize, the degree of foreign interest in buying

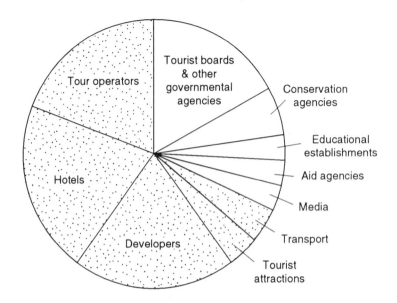

FIGURE 5.1.   Distribution of the 1991 Caribbean Ecotourism Conference delegates by
affiliation

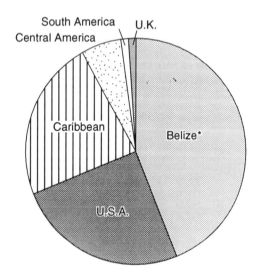

* A significant proportion of delegates registering from
  Belize were expatriate Americans

FIGURE 5.2.   Distribution of the 1991 Caribbean Ecotourism Conference delegates by
origin

land in a relatively unspoiled destination only two hours flying time from Miami, New Orleans and Houston is such that a two-bedroom villa in a coastal location on the prime resort island of Ambergris Caye commanded a price of US$135 000 in 1992. Foreign land-holdings in Belize are, in theory, restricted to 2000 m² in urban areas and 40 500 m² in rural areas. The cumulative effect, however, is such that it has been estimated that 90 per cent of all coastal development in Belize is now foreign-owned (Cater, 1992). The fact that such land has been sold freehold indicates probable permanent alienation from Belizean nationals. It also implies an opportunity cost in terms of benefits that might have otherwise accrued under alternative use of that land (Sherman and Dixon, 1991).

Loss of sovereignty also implies a loss of control in decision-making. Wilkinson (1989) describes how microstates have become targets for exogenous decision-making, which is often insensitive to local issues and needs.

Local participation

The degree of truly local participation is often limited not only in terms of ownership and control, but also in terms of enjoyment of the natural attraction. The cost of even a locally based day trip, for example US$100 for a day trip to Crooked Tree Sanctuary in Belize, precludes the participation of the average low income resident.

SUSTAINING VISITOR ATTRACTION

The financial significance of ecotourism to many Third World economies is evident in Table 5.2. For this contribution towards the national income to be sustained, it is vital to maintain visitor satisfaction. There are a number of factors which militate against this requirement, given the number of tourists arriving, their distribution at the destination, and their characteristics.

Rapid growth in ecotourist arrivals

An examination of the rate of growth in tourist arrivals to selected ecotourism destinations (Table 5.1) reveals how all have approximately doubled the number of visitor arrivals over the past decade. A gradualist approach towards tourism planning, to allow for adjustment, has been advocated for some time (de Kadt, 1979). In contrast, the problems of managing a rapid rate of growth are considerable. More significant and lasting changes are inevitable.

Concentration at prime sites

Much attention has been drawn to the development of tourism enclaves within destinations (Jenkins, 1982). Indeed, the positive aspect of this phenomenon is that the adverse effects of tourism development are usually confined to clearly defined areas. In terms of prime ecotourism sites, however, concentrated visitation may well result in an unacceptable level of degradation. At the Hol Chan Marine Reserve in Belize, snorkellers and divers are amply warned of the consequences of irresponsible behaviour, such as the careless handling of scuba equipment (Figure 5.3). The pressure of numbers is such, though, that the coral reef is showing signs of black band disease, a killer alga which attacks broken coral. Furthermore, visitors tend to be concentrated in time as well as space owing to the marked seasonality of tourism to largely tropical destinations. Vegetation cover destroyed in the dry season, the peak period, leaves fragile soils exposed to the erosive powers of tropical downpours in the wet season. The Amboseli National Part in Kenya has suffered from the excessive pressures of the 220 000 visitors it receives annually to the extent that it was withdrawn from the itineraries of some tour operators in 1992. Widespread flooding in February 1993, which left 80 per cent of the game-viewing tracks under water, resulted in the temporary closure of the park.

Characteristics of ecotourists

There is an inherent risk in assuming that the ecotourist is automatically an environmentally sensitive breed. Although small, specialist, guided groups of

FIGURE 5.3.   Advice for coral reef diving practice, San Pedro, Ambergris Caye, Belize
(John Cater)

ecotourists may attempt to conform to this identity, the net has now been cast sufficiently wide to include less responsible behaviour. Amongst those loosely defined as ecotourists will be those visiting a destination for a few days, unlikely ever to return. This can be referred to as 'this year the Galapagos, next year Antarctica' syndrome. It has been suggested that such tourists are unlikely to pay regard to the long-term repercussions of their activities, particularly as they may consider that they have a right to use the resource in light of the significant outlay they will have made for the experience (Butler, 1991).

ECOTOURISM AND THE ENVIRONMENT: A SYMBIOTIC OR DESTRUCTIVE RELATIONSHIP?

Budowski (1976) suggested that the relationship between nature tourism and conservation may be mutually beneficial. However, unless the requirement of safeguarding the environment is met, ecotourism is in danger of being a self-destructive process, destroying the very resources upon which it is based. Furthermore, the present and future needs of the host population will be prejudiced and future generations of tourists will be denied the opportunity to experience environments very different to those in which they reside. As the interface between ecotourism and the environment is even closer than that of conventional tourism with its surroundings, it is probably not surprising to discover that a symbiotic relationship remains something of an ideal rather than a reality. This occurs for several reasons.

The widening locus of international tourism

The emphasis in ecotourism is on visiting unspoiled natural environments. Previously remote areas, with delicately balanced socio-cultural and physical regimes, are consequently increasingly drawn into the locus of international tourism. These vulnerable locations are thus particularly susceptible to environmental degradation and socio-cultural disruption.

The inevitability of environmental impact

It is impossible that ecotourism, based on natural attractions, will not result in some environmental impact. Even the most environmentally conscientious tourist will have some degree of impact, however small. In aggregate, such impacts become all the more significant, particularly when such activities are inevitably concentrated in time and space (Butler, 1991).

The designation of protected areas

The creation of National Parks and Wildlife Reserves may well satisfy the viewing needs of tourists and, if properly managed, the requirements of conservationists. Frequently, however, the local population is excluded from traditional activities such as nomadic pastoralism, cultivation and gathering of fuel and building materials. As such, they cannot be regarded as truly sustainable constructs because they pay little regard to the needs of the host population in either the short or long term. 'It is not the rural poor who will gain most from the design of national parks, but the rich consumer in the industrialised North with leisure and wealth to be a tourist in the Third World' (Cartwright, 1989).

The supreme irony is that, by ignoring the needs of the local population, the conservational objectives of protected areas may themselves be compromised. Widespread resentment exists amongst the Maasai nomadic pastoralists over their inadequately compensated displacement from traditional grazing lands through the creation of National Parks in Kenya. Wildlife in the Amboseli National Park has been killed by Maasai warriors to emphasise their dissatisfaction (Lindsay, 1987). Experience elsewhere shows that once the local population has become fully integrated in tourism projects, and benefits directly from them, infringements such as indiscriminate tree-felling (Sagarmatha National Park, Nepal) and poaching of wildlife (Zimbabwe) reduce markedly.

Infrastructural and service requirements of ecotourism

Ecotourists originate largely from the MDCs. Destinations are therefore forced to cater for Western tastes and needs. In the Nepalese Himalaya, trekking lodges offer almost impossibly extensive menus, which place excessive pressures on scarce wood fuel and the cook's time as demands are juggled for dishes as diverse as pizzas and rosti. Extra porters ply the trails laden with crates of beer (Figure 5.4), trays of eggs and toilet rolls. In Belize, coastal development involves the clearance of mangrove swampland and subsequent drainage and infilling using topsoil literally shaved off the wetland savanna a few kilometres inland. This involves the destruction of two distinctive ecosystems. Ironically, the international standard Biltmore Plaza hotel, the venue of the 1991 Caribbean Ecotourism Conference, was built on land reclaimed in this way (Figure 5.5).

The cost of environmental management

The low level of development of Third World nations may preclude them from being able to afford environmental protection measures that prevent, ameliorate or restore degradation. It is also patently unfair that these countries should bear the costs of such measures, the need for which arises from the fact that ecotourism to Third World countries is essentially exploiting their environmental carrying capacity. Any efforts made by these destinations, such as the Annapurna Conservation Area Project in Nepal (Chapter 11), should receive the unqualified support of the tourism industry.

FIGURE 5.4. Porter laden with crates of beer below Deorali, Annapurna District, Nepal (John Cater)

FIGURE 5.5. Biltmore Plaza Hotel, Belize City, built on reclaimed mangrove swampland (Erlet Cater)

POLICY IMPLICATIONS

The foregoing discussion indicates that there are inherent dangers in regarding ecotourism in the Third World as some sort of miracle hybrid, bringing bountiful returns without any adverse impacts. It is essential to recognise some basic truths. There is no example of tourist use that is completely without impact. If protection and preservation of the environment in an untouched form is the primary goal, then there should be no tourism development at all (Butler, 1991). Even a small-scale development such as that at Canaima, in southern Venezuela, owned and operated by the state domestic airline Avensa, has had a very evident impact in terms of the construction of a purpose-built airstrip and village to house employees working at the hotel complex (Figure 5.6). Indeed, unless properly managed, ecotourism may result in worse impacts than those of mass tourism to clearly defined and confined resorts. It is often undeveloped areas, all the more vulnerable to disruption and degradation, that are being drawn into the international tourism circuit. The multitude of interests scattered at the local scale may penetrate the socio-cultural and environmental fabric more deeply than conventional tourism and will probably be more difficult to control.

This should not, however, be taken against ecotourism development in the Third World. It must be remembered that sustainable development includes the human dimension; the basic needs of the local population must be satis-

FIGURE 5.6.   Tourist resort at Canaima, Venezuela (Erlet Cater)

fied. Absolute restriction may be a necessity in some instances, for example the heavily protected core areas of Biosphere Reserves (Batisse, 1982). Equally, whilst visitation levels must never exceed the carrying capacity of a locality, restriction is not a truly sustainable option if it results in local populations being denied the development potential that exists. In most cases the solution will be a compromise: neither strictly conservationist, nor completely meeting development needs.

For the reasons outlined in the introduction to this book, ecotourism is here to stay, it is set to grow and will undoubtedly be of increasing significance to developing nations. What is important, therefore, is to point to the particular responsibilities of the three main role players in international tourism: the tourists, the tourism enterprises and the destination areas in achieving sustainable outcomes.

Role of the tourists

Doubt has already been cast on the sustainability of the behaviour and attitudes of individual tourists (Butler, 1991), intentional or otherwise. Unless these change, the cumulative effects of successive waves of ecotourists visiting a destination may progressively downgrade the distinctive characteristics which constitute its fundamental attraction and so compromise sustainability. Sustainable ecotourism offers tourists the prospect of a guaranteed level of satisfaction whenever a destination is visited. This is a vital consideration if it is to continue to attract tourists.

Tourists should become aware of the damaging potential of their stay in Third World destinations. This will require, in many instances, considerable changes in attitudes and behaviour so that indigenous cultures and environments are respected. Often tourists visiting less developed regions must be prepared to forego accustomed standards of comfort and convenience. Properly handled, this should, in fact, prove part of the attraction of the ecotourism experience (Ruschmann, 1992).

The tourists need to be properly informed about the characteristics of their destination and how to behave to reduce the impact of their stay. This is primarily the responsibility of the tourism industry. Certain tour operators, for example World Expeditions, do advise their clients along these lines. Non-governmental organisations, e.g. Tourism Concern in the UK and Equations in India, have made a significant contribution towards raising the level of public awareness. Destinations can reinforce this awareness by advising on ecotourism etiquette once the tourists arrive, for example via the minimum impact code printed on lodge menus in the Annapurna Conservation Area of Nepal (Chapter 11).

Thus the cornerstone to more sustainable behaviour on the part of ecotourists is a greater understanding, via the dissemination of information, on how to behave in the context they are visiting.

Role of tourism enterprises

The onus of responsibility for more sustainable ecotourism development tends to fall on ecotourism enterprises which deliver the end-product to the consumers, i.e. the tourists. Although profit maximisation remains the prime concern of such companies, it has been suggested that historical levels of profit are not compatible with sustainable development. Resource-based companies (which, indeed, includes all tourism enterprises) should be required to demonstrate adequate maintenance of the resource base before declaring a dividend (Rees, 1990). There is an increasing recognition in the trade that maintenance of the resource base is at any rate the baseline of successful operations (Chapter 4). More complete tourism accountancy procedures (Goodall, 1992) would involve the concept of environmental auditing to identify why, where and how tourism products, activities and processes are damaging the environment. It is one thing to identify these factors, another to take action. Whether or not this happens will depend on how the competitive situation of the firm is changed and the organisation's stance on environmental protection (Gray, 1990). In some instances firms may be required to comply with the requirement for more sustainable practices initiated by the host government.

Role of destination areas

To ensure sustainable ecotourism development the governments of Third World destinations need: (a) to intervene in the market; (b) to oversee integration in planning and implementation; and (c) to encourage local involvement.

Intervention

A proactive stance is thus necessary to maximise the benefits and minimise the adverse effects of ecotourism. Allowing the free play of market forces is not conducive to sustainable outcomes. Inevitably, the carrying capacity of destinations will be exceeded as environmental costs continue to be externalised. As a result, there is a need to force tourism companies to internalise these externalities by building in appropriate cost and price signals, via legislation, together with incentives and disincentives such as appropriate taxation measures (de Kadt, 1992). A problem here, however, is that often such destinations are competing with one another and are wary of frightening-off badly needed foreign investment. Indeed, the opposite approach has been for destinations to offer firms attractive tax holidays and other incentives to encourage domestic and foreign investment. Sri Lanka, for example, extended an interest-free loan programme for resort properties and reduced business turnover tax from 20 to only one per cent during the 1980s.

Countries that have attempted extra fiscal measures have sometimes been forced to step down by the threat that companies will divert their interests elsewhere; for example, a proposal that a $50 per head cruise passenger tax should be levied in the Caribbean has met with such threats from US cruise lines. It would appear, therefore, that Cohen's appraisal of the bargaining power of the unspoiled nature of developing nations remains somewhat optimistic. He suggested that, as unspoiled nature becomes rarer and competition for it stiffer, developing nations are better placed to impose the terms of its exploitation on the developed nations who seek it (Cohen, 1978). Written in the aftermath of the mid-1970s oil crisis, the analogy is obvious. The collective muscle of a coordinated region-wide policy has yet to be exerted in the field of ecotourism, however.

The simplest way to raise funds for sustainable management is to introduce user fees. Although many countries already charge entry to National Parks, others, for example Dominica, have yet to do so. There is no reason why foreign visitors, who are essentially exploiting the carrying capacity of the unspoilt destination, should be effectively subsidised in this way. Sherman and Dixon (1991) suggest that even a relatively high fee of US$10 a day would be insignificant in relation to the overall cost of international travel. Two important principles need to be adopted, however. Firstly, the fees levied should be channelled back into ensuring sustainable ecotourism development, for example via environmental protection, local training, grants and incentives towards greater local involvement. Secondly, a lower charge should apply to locals. The Galapagos Islands National Park, for instance, charges international visitors higher fees than Ecuadorian citizens and does not charge local residents at all (Boo, 1990).

Integration

There is no other economic activity that cuts across so many sectors, levels and interests as tourism. There is a vital need, therefore, to integrate planning for ecotourism with national development plans in general and sectoral targets in particular. Ecotourism activities will concern many government ministries, for example environment, agriculture, forestry, parks, education, transportation and public works (Boo, 1991). The need for horizontal integration between these ministries is evident. Vertical integration is also necessary to coordinate interests from the local, through regional, to national levels. It is also necessary to recognise the mutually dependent interests of the public and private sectors in tourism (Holder, 1992). The private sector is dependent on the government because, in its broadest sense, the country is the ecotourism product. Ultimately, however, the services which the tourism enterprises need the government to provide must be paid for by them via taxation. Holder suggests that it is in the government's interests to create the conditions and business environment within which private business can make a reasonable profit. A final element of integration is required to accommodate the time dimension. Too often long-term interests are sacrificed for short-term gain. This is particularly evident in the case of the less developed countries (LDCs) where populations are forced to commit 'ecocide' in the long term to ensure short-term survival. As Blaikie (1985) suggests, environmental degradation is a result of underdevelopment, a symptom of underdevelopment and a cause of underdevelopment.

Involvement

A final general principle to ensure the sustainability of ecotourism develop-ment on the part of destination areas, but perhaps the most vital, is to increase truly local involvement. As de Kadt (1992) points out, the distributional as-pects of tourism development have been all too frequently ignored. It is naive to advocate local ownership versus foreign ownership without recognising that the interests of a local élite are often more intimately bound with those of a foreign élite than their co-residents.

The conflicts are particularly evident in the case of ecotourism develop-ment, where not only may the local population be denied any direct benefits, but may also be actively disadvantaged. They may well be physically excluded from the very resources on which they depend for their basic needs. The classic example of the Maasai pastoralists of Kenya and Tanzania has already been cited. In Belize, traditional *milpa* slash and burn cultivators are con-sidered a threat to ecotourism (Cater, 1992). It is essential, therefore, that local communities are involved directly with ecotourism development. This involvement must not only be in the form of hand-outs or doles, or even the provision of schools, hospitals and social services financed from tourism rev-enue, handsome show factors that these may be. If the traditional means of economic livelihood is being removed from a community, it must be replaced by an alternative.

There are sound reasons for local involvement other than a moral obliga-tion to incorporate the people whom the projects affect. In terms of conserv-ing the natural and socio-cultural resource base, the time perspective of the local population is longer than that of outside entrepreneurs concerned with early profits (Chambers, 1988). They are also more likely to ensure that traditions and lifestyles will be respected. Their cooperation is also a vital factor in reducing infringements of conservation regulations such as poaching and indiscriminate tree-felling. There are also sound practical reasons in terms of utilising local labour. Drake (1991) points to the limited capacity of local and national governments and agencies to effectively manage the grow-ing number of projects unless their functions are decentralised and commu-nities involved. The Annapurna Conservation Area Project is a good example of community involvement (Chapter 11).

Such an involvement must also extent beyond economic survival, environmental conservation and socio-cultural integrity, to allow appreciation by the community of their own natural resources. They must not be excluded physically, for example by coastal development effectively isolating beaches in Barbados, or financially. It is essential to reduce inflationary pressures on land and property and avoid their permanent alienation from the indigenous population through foreign ownership. The very least that is required is that if such transfer has to occur it should be no more than leasehold. To ensure that locals can also afford to participate in the enjoyment of their own ecotourism resources, parks could charge differential, reduced rates for locals (Sherman and Dixon, 1991).

This outline of the essential principles for sustainable ecotourism development in the Third World reflects a central message of collective responsibility and a holistic approach involving governments, tourists, tourism enterprises and destination areas alike. It is also vital to remember that tourism is only a process cast within a markedly inequitable structure, both internationally and intranationally. This has vital implications for sustainability. In their desperate attempts to ensure survival in the short term, the poor are forced to compromise their longer term interests. The poorest countries are the least capable of withstanding the adverse impacts on their potential for sustainability, yet these are the very nations most in need of sustainable tourism development.

REFERENCES

Batisse, M., 1982, 'The biosphere reserve: a tool for environmental conservation and management, *Environmental Conservation*, **9**, 101–111.
Blaikie, P., 1985, *The Political Economy of Soil Erosion in Developing Countries*, Longman, London.
Boo, E., 1990, *Ecotourism: the Potentials and Pitfalls*, Vol. 1, World Wildlife Fund, Washington.
Boo, E., 1991, Making ecotourism sustainable: recommendations for planning, development and management, in Whelan, T. (ed.) *Nature Tourism*, Island Press, Washington, 187–199.
Britton, S., 1982, International tourism and multinational corporations in the Pacific: the case of Fiji, in Taylor, M. and Thrift, N.J. (eds) *The Geography of Multinationals*, Croom Helm, London, 252–274.
Budowski, G., 1976, Tourism and conservation: conflict, coexistence or symbiosis, *Environmental Conservation*, **3**, 27–31.
Butler, R.W., 1991, Tourism, environment and sustainable development, *Environmental Conservation*, **18**, 201–209.
Cartwright, J., 1989, Conserving nature, decreasing debt, *Third World Quarterly*, **11**, 114–127.
Cater, E., 1992, Profits from paradise, *Geographical*, **64**(3), 16–21.
Ceballos Lascurain, H., 1992, Tourists for conservation, *People and the Planet*, **1**(3), 28–30.
Chambers, R., 1988, Sustainable rural livelihoods: a key strategy for people, environment and development, in Conroy, C. and Litvinoff, M. (eds) *The Greening of Aid: Sustainable Livelihoods in Practice*, Earthscan, London, 1–17.

Cohen, E., 1978, The impact of tourism on the physical environment, *Annals of Tourism Research*, **5**, 215–237.

de Kadt, E. (ed.), 1979, *Tourism: Passport to Development*, Oxford University Press, New York.

de Kadt, E., 1992, Making the alternative sustainable: lessons from development for tourism, in Smith, V.L. and Eadington, W.R. (eds) *Tourism Alternatives,* University of Pennsylvania Press, Philadelphia, 47–75.

Drake, S.P., 1991, Local participation in ecotourism projects, in Whelan, T. (ed.) *Nature Tourism*, Island Press, Washington, 132–156.

Economist Intelligence Unit, 1992, *The Tourism Industry and the Environment*, E.I.U. Publications, London.

Geographical, 1993, Secret state opens up, *Geographical*, **65**(2), 7.

Goodall, B., 1992, Environmental auditing for tourism, in Cooper, C.P. and Lockwood, A. (eds) *Progress in Tourism, Recreation and Hospitality Management*, Vol. 4, Belhaven, London, 60–74.

Gray, R.H., 1990, *The Greening of Accountancy: the Profession After Pearce*, Certified Accountants Publications, London.

Holder, J.S., 1992, The need for public–private sector cooperation in tourism, *Tourism Management*, June, 157–162.

Independent, 1993, Having a fine time: glad you're not here, 31 January, 3.

International Monetary Fund, 1992, *International Financial Statistics Yearbook,* International Monetary Fund, Washington.

Jenkins, C.L., 1982, The effects of scale in tourism projects in developing countries, *Annals of Tourism Research,* **9**, 229–249.

Lindsay, K., 1987, Integrating parks and pastoralists, in Anderson, D. and Grove, R. (eds) *Conservation in Africa: People, Policies and Practice,* Cambridge University Press, Cambridge, 149–167.

Munt, I., 1993, Ecotourism gone awry, *Report on the Americas,* **26**(4), 8–10.

Olindo, P., 1991, The old man of nature tourism: Kenya, in Whelan, T. (ed.) *Nature Tourism,* Island Press, Washington, 23–38.

Rees, N.E., 1990, The ecology of sustainable development, *The Ecologist*, **20**(1), 18–23.

Rovinski, Y., 1991, Private reserves, parks and ecotourism in Costa Rica, in Whelan, T. (ed.) *Nature Tourism,* Island Press, Washington, 39–57.

Ruschmann, D., 1992, Ecological tourism in Brazil, *Tourism Management*, March, 125–128.

Sherman, P.B. and Dixon, V.A., 1991, The economics of nature tourism: determining if it pays, in Whelan, T. (ed.) *Nature Tourism*, Island Press, Washington, 89–131.

Tobias, D. and Mendelsohn, R., 1991, Valuing ecotourism in a tropical rain forest reserve, *Ambio,* **20**, 91–93.

Weaver, D., 1991, Alternative to mass tourism in Dominica, *Annals of Tourism Research*, **18**, 414–432.

Whelan, T., 1991, Ecotourism and its role in sustainable development, in Whelan, T. (ed.) *Nature Tourism*, Island Press, Washington, 3–22.

Wilkinson, P.F., 1989, Strategies for tourism in island microstates, *Annals of Tourism Research*, **16**, 153–177.

World Bank, 1983; 1992, *World Development Report*, Oxford University Press, Oxford.

World Tourism Organisation (WTO), 1986; 1992, *Yearbook of Tourism Statistics*, WTO, Madrid.

World Travel and Tourism Council (WTTC), 1992, *World Travel and Tourism Environment Review,* WTTC, Brussels.

6

Ecotourism: on the Trail of Destruction or Sustainability? A Minister's View

THE RT. HON. BARONESS CHALKER, MINISTER FOR
OVERSEAS DEVELOPMENT

INTRODUCTION

Tourism is a major global industry. It is one in which we all participate directly or indirectly. Britain is a major tourism destination with about 18 million visitors a year. In 1991 over 30 million Britons travelled abroad.

Tourism inevitably has a price. It can generate great wealth for both developing and developed countries. But it also has the potential to damage and destroy the very resources on which it depends. An essential message, therefore, is that all tourism, not just ecotourism, should be sustainable.

Like other sectors of development, tourism must be seen in the context of a collective, global agenda on sustainable development. The United Nations Conference on Environment and Development (UNCED) set that agenda.

UNCED

UNCED was a global landmark. At the conference the leaders of the world established the eco-agenda for the 21st century. Its implementation will be a formidable, but vital, task.

Shortly after UNCED the British Prime Minister set out his plan for follow-up action. His lead was subsequently broadly endorsed by our EU and G7 partners. The plan he set out covered UNCED's all-embracing agenda for development and the environment. Some elements of that agenda have a particular bearing on tourism.

Climate Change Convention

The Climate Change Convention is the first international treaty to recognise global warming as a threat to the planet.

Ecotourism: A Sustainable Option? Edited by E. Cater and G. Lowman
© The editors and contributors. Published in 1994 by John Wiley & Sons Ltd

The Convention provides the framework for all signatories to plan and implement their own actions. Both developed and developing countries will undertake real measures to tackle the threat we jointly face. Britain, like other developed countries who ratify the Convention, would be committed to take actions aimed at returning emissions of CO_2 and other greenhouse gases to their 1990 levels in the year 2000.

The link between success in tackling climate change and the tourism industry is clear. At its most fundamental, if sea levels rise as expected, some of the world's most beautiful centres for tourism—the Maldives, for example—will be inundated. There could also be drastic changes to reefs around the world. Without this natural protection many of the world's coastal areas, where many tourist resorts are centred, could be seriously affected. Climate change may also affect those very features of a region that are central to its tourism potential.

Biodiversity Convention

The same link applies to the conservation of biodiversity. Imagine the impact on the tourism industry if the current pace of wildlife and habitat destruction continues. As the poet Hopkins said, 'After-comers cannot guess the beauty been'.

The Biodiversity Convention sets out a framework for further global action to identify, conserve and protect the world's biological resources at genetic, species and ecosystem level. The government sees a special role for the UK in helping this exchange of skills and knowledge. Britain, under the Darwin Initiative for the survival of species, launched by the Prime Minister at UNCED, will take this process forward, drawing on this country's considerable scientific and commercial expertise in conservation and the understanding of biodiversity and natural habitats. The Overseas Development Administration (ODA) is already working with developing countries to study their natural resources and biodiversity. Funding of biodiversity-related projects to help these countries meet the aims of the Convention will continue.

One example of such cooperation is in Kenya. Tourism is vital to Kenya's development, providing 37 per cent of its foreign exchange. In recent years there has been a precipitous decline in Kenya's wildlife in the country's system of National Parks and Reserves. The Government of Kenya urgently wants this situation reversed. They are working to establish a sound foundation to preserve the country's biodiversity, conserve its natural resources and promote tourism in a sustainable manner. The British Government is helping by giving £12 million within a large multidonor project to improve the management of the Kenya Wildlife Service. Benefits of the project will be shared with the mainly poor local communities through community wildlife services and through a process of conservation awareness education.

This is a clear example of linkages between tourism, the environment and development.

Another example is in Brazil. Britain is providing £1.6 million towards the safeguarding of the extraordinary biodiversity of an area of seasonally flooded forest in the western Amazon. In the longer term, such areas could be prime destinations for ecotourists, in a controlled manner that brings real benefits to the local economy.

Agenda 21

This was the most wide-ranging initiative to be launched at Rio. It sets out a strategy for environmentally responsible development into the next century. It includes action to combat poverty, to support environmental health, to protect natural habitats and biodiversity, to combat land degradation and place agriculture on a sustainable path, to prioritise family planning and to improve education services, particularly for women and girls.

Britain will mobilise its Aid programme in support of the goals of Agenda 21. Substantial resources are to be made available to assist forestry conservation, biodiversity, energy efficiency, population planning and sustainable agriculture. This agenda is not entirely new to the ODA. Sustainable development is already a central theme of the Aid programme, but it has given renewed focus to our work.

UNCED has served to underline the need for global cooperation and partnership. This increasingly applies to tourism as greater mobility allows greater numbers of people to travel further and wider.

TOURISM

The tourism industry is one of the world's most important sectors of economic development, for both developing and developed countries. A recent survey by the World Travel and Tourism Council showed tourism to be one of the world's largest industries. Within that industry, ecotourism is the fastest growing sector.

The figures are astounding. The industry employs over 112 million people world-wide; it is said to invest over US$350 billion per year in new facilities and capital equipment, and to generate annually more than US$2500 billion in gross output. This amounts to 5.5 per cent of the world's total gross national product.

These figures highlight two things: on the one hand the prominent role and contribution tourism makes to the world economy; on the other, the demand it makes on the world's resources, directly or indirectly. There is a growing realisation internationally that we need to address the relationship between tourism and the environment to ensure sustainable tourism development.

UK tourism

Tourism has always been an important element in the UK economy. Its importance has grown in recent years. The approach towards sustainable tourism in the UK is as follows

- the 1990 White Paper, *This Common Inheritance,* committed the government to preserve and enhance Britain's natural and cultural inheritance—in other words, to sustain it
- the UK tourism industry has acknowledged the sound economic sense of sustainable tourism

In May, 1991 the Tourism and Environment Task Force report *Maintaining the Balance* set out a framework for the way forward for all of us—in government, the public sector and in the private sector. As a result of the Task Force report, the government has adopted four guiding principles to shape the way tourism is supported: (1) to encourage the tourism industry itself to develop ways that contribute to rather than detract from the quality of the environment; (2) to promote respect for the quality of the environment, as well as the quality of the tourism product offered; (3) to ensure staff within the tourism industry are trained to take account of environmental considerations; and (4) to encourage and publicise those kinds of tourism that safeguard the environment.

These principles were reviewed at a conference held in mid-November 1992, hosted by the UK as President of the European Community. That conference, organised by the Department of National Heritage and the English Tourist Board, looked at tourism good practice, both in this country and around the world.

Tourism can bring benefits to everyone. But to be successful and sustainable, tourism must create a vested interest in conserving the environment and, through good management, enhance the resources it so depends on. If not, it can destroy those resources.

Ecotourism

A degree of personal unease must be expressed at the 'green' stamp of approval being given to one sector only of the global tourism industry. The key issue for the industry is to make *all* tourism sustainable. Ecotourism must not be an excuse to ignore the potential for all forms of tourism to have an impact on the environment and become unsustainable.

But what, exactly, is 'ecotourism'? There are many definitions; however, there is general agreement that ecotourism is characterised by

- attracting tourists to natural environments which are unique and accessible

- using tourism to bring about and/or improve nature conservation, through education, changing attitudes in local people and governments, community development and altered political priorities
- providing employment and entrepreneurial opportunities for local people

These characteristics suggest a number of pre-requirements before tourism can be considered to be sustainable.

Attracting tourists

The first requirement to attract tourists is political and economic stability: without this, tourists will not visit. In the words of the *World Development Report of 1992*

> (there is) . . . growing consensus that policies for economic efficiency and for environmental management are complementary. Good environmental policies are good economic policies and vice versa.

The pursuit of such policies must include good and environmentally sensitive, infrastructure-including airports, transport and communications networks, water, sanitation and electricity supplies. But above all else, sustainable tourism requires careful planning. Without this planning, tourism could do more harm than good; it could have devastating environmental and social consequences.

Improving nature conservation

There is also the need to improve nature conservation. Ecotourists are, in general, highly educated, have high income levels and have increased awareness of the importance of the environment. They ask, like Hopkins again, 'What would the world be once bereft/of wet and wildness?' Ecotourists expect high levels of ecological information. The quality of the environment and the visibility of its flora and fauna are essential features of their experience. They demand conservation.

But the lure of nature must not be at nature's expense. Nor should it be at the expense of local communities. Many governments now recognise developing tourism, as a key economic sector, and enhancing conservation as complementary aims.

In Kenya, the highly successful Naivasha Country Club is on the shores of Lake Naivasha, which is home to one of Africa's richest and most diverse bird and wildfowl populations. It attracts flocks of foreign tourists. Here is a case of profit and conservation going hand in hand.

In Belize, tourism is based almost exclusively on the diverse fauna and flora of its tropical rainforests and its unique barrier reef. These systems are under threat. So, therefore, is the very basis of the tourist industry. The Belize Government is giving greater priority to tourism, with emphasis on sustainable tourism. They have asked for help from the UK and the response of the ODA was to fund the first phase of a tourism planning consultancy to 'flesh out' the government's sustainable tourism development policy. This will include the legislative and regulatory framework within which tourism will operate.

Opportunities for local people

Another requirement for sustainable tourism is that it must involve local communities. Tourism can encourage better basic services such as water and electricity. It can create local jobs and income and support other social and environmental benefits. It must also give indigenous communities a stake in the improved management of their environment. This links sustainable tourism to sustainable development.

Preserving the natural environment means making informed choices. This means integrating tourism developments into the whole question of development within a country or a region. This involves consultation: consultation between government, the private sector, including international tourism groups, and local people.

This consultative process is vital. It is a key element of the Agenda 21 process agreed at UNCED. It is essential that direct contact is made with the local people who live close by or in the tourist destination, such as a National Park or nature reserve. It is vital to take account of their interests and knowledge and to involve them in managing and protecting the environment. It is better to discuss an issue without reaching a decision than to reach a decision without discussion.

Such consultation is already taking place; take Zambia, for example. The ODA is discussing with the National Parks and Wildlife Service support for their initiative to implement a sustainable system for managing wildlife in two areas of the Mpika district in which three National Parks are situated. These parks, and the areas surrounding them, are endowed with some of the finest wildlife resources in the world. But at present poaching is depleting the wildlife resource. It is hoped that a system of wildlife management can be introduced which will enable local people to participate in deciding and planning wildlife management. Local community groups will be able to earn greater revenues from the area through wildlife management and tourism opportunities.

Another example in Zambia shows how this can be done. This is in the Luangwa Game Reserve in the north-east of the country. The reserve is increasingly managed as a resource for local people. It is surrounded by a buffer zone, and the people from this zone are employed in the reserve, and in the provision of tourist facilities linked to the reserve. This development thus not only provides foreign exchange for Zambia, but also a source of local income, as well as revenue for conservation of the wildlife resources of the reserve.

Such work can also be done with non-governmental organisations (NGOs). The ODA is helping, through the NGO Friends of Conservation in Kenya, to promote conservation education and extension to community groups.

In Zimbabwe the ODA is supporting the Zimbabwe Trust to undertake wildlife management and other initiatives under its Communal Areas Management Programme for Indigenous Resources—the excellent CAMPFIRE Initiative (Figure 6.1). CAMPFIRE works to assist rural communities to develop their capacity to manage their wildlife and natural resources on a sustainable basis and for the benefit of the community as a whole. The initiative stems from the belief that sustainable rural development and the alleviation of poverty in many areas in Zimbabwe is best achieved through active management of wildlife resources by local communities. CAMPFIRE seeks to offer a completely different approach to development under which wildlife is regarded as the principle resource of local communities. Chiefly through providing rural communities with the proprietorial rights over local natural resources, principally wildlife, CAMPFIRE encourages community organisations to use those resources in a sustainable way and to use the benefits or revenues accruing for community needs. It therefore promotes local governance and economic self-reliance and increases employment and incomes through the wise use of local resources.

International conservation organisations such as the International Union for the Conservation of Nature and Natural Resources (IUCN) and the Worldwide Fund for Nature (WWF) are already actively promoting the CAMPFIRE approach as a practical example of environmentally sustainable development. It is a model for others to follow, not only in wildlife protection and management, but also in the promotion of ecotourism.

In 1989 the ODA began a five-year programme of financial support under its NGO Joint Funding Scheme to the Zimbabwe Trust to assist the first two districts in Zimbabwe which were interested and ready to embark on CAMP-FIRES. These two districts were Nyaminyami and Guruve, situated in the rugged and harsh Zambezi valley. In these areas people struggle to scratch a living from the barren soils, but the land is rich in biodiversity and animal life. Wild animals such as elephants, lions and buffalos trample on villagers' meagre crops and damage their property, with frequent loss of human life. The villagers therefore bore the cost of living with wildlife, but received none of the benefits such as meat, hides and income from ecotourists and safari hunting. CAMPFIRE promised to change this; to provide a means by which wildlife could contribute to villagers' livelihoods so that wildlife is no longer perceived simply as a liability, but an asset to be conserved.

The backcloth to the success of CAMPFIRE is the policy of the Zimbabwe Government to devolve the management of wildlife and natural resources

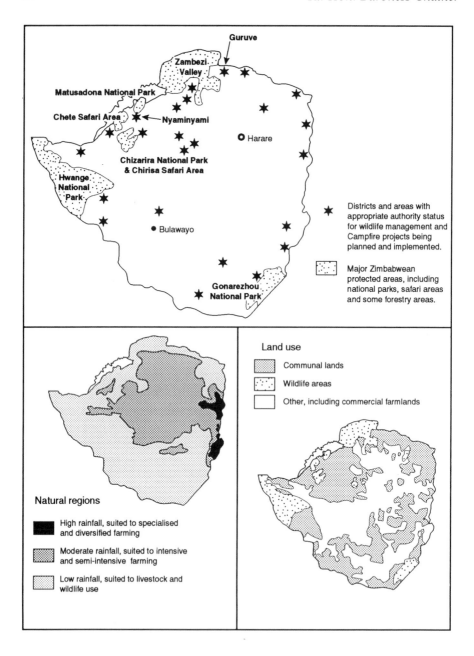

away from central government to an 'appropriate authority'. In 1989 the
people of Nyaminyami (Figure 6.2) and Guruve accepted the challenge of
CAMPFIRE and their remarkable achievement of both human welfare and
wildlife conservation soon led to the rapid spread of CAMPFIRE initiatives.

In Nyaminyami the revenues earned from sustainable wildlife activities
increased annually from 1989 to 1992 from Zimbabwe $320 000 to Zimbabwe
$1.4 million, an increase of about 450 per cent. Although some of this revenue
is retained by the Nyaminyami Wildlife Management Trust and the
Nyaminyami District Council for capital investment in wildlife management
activities and as a levy, the balance is paid direct to each of the villages or
'producer communities'. They then choose how they wish to spend their
money, including the option of cash payments of dividends to each household
in the village.

In 1992, nearly Zimbabwe $500 000 was distributed to the villagers and, as
in previous years, nearly all of this money was invested in community projects.
These projects have included the provision of a reliable water supply (Figure
6.3), the establishment of grinding mills (to reduce the distance women have
to walk to grind maize), the building of warehouses (for the storage of seeds
and grain) and, during the devastating 1992 drought, the purchase and resale
of maize meal as a community drought relief service.

In Guruve CAMPFIRE revenues have also increased from year to year
from Zimbabwe $335 000 to Zimbabwe $1 million in 1992, an increase of

FIGURE 6.2.   Village meeting, Nyaminyami (Steve Thomas, Zimbabwe Trust)

FIGURE 6.3.   A reliable water supply is ensured via the installation of water pumps
(Steve Thomas, Zimbabwe Trust)

around 300 per cent. However, the producer communities in Guruve have
received a greater proportion of total revenues than their counterparts in
Nyaminyami (Figure 6.4), and in 1992 received Zimbabwe \$603 000. More-
over, unlike Nyaminyami, communities have elected to use their income both
for household dividends and for community projects, including health and
education services (including some schools) and income-generating projects.

Apart from monetary benefits, communities of the two districts have also
benefited in kind from, for example, meat derived from the carefully selected
cropping of certain animal species whose populations are abundant enough to
allow this without affecting the species' genetic diversity and continued
growth (Figure 6.5). This benefit has been particularly significant for human
well-being as before this Nyaminyami and Guruve were characterised by
excessive protein deficiency and child malnutrition.

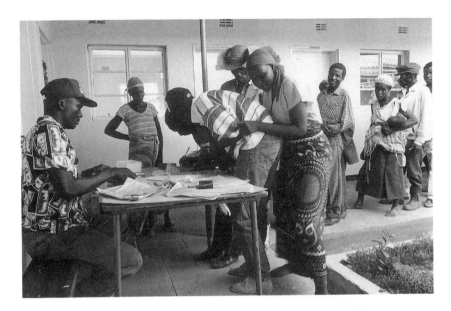

FIGURE 6.4. Dividend payout to villagers (Steve Thomas, Zimbabwe Trust)

In both districts wildlife has begun to pay its way to survival as communities seeing tangible evidence of the contribution which wildlife can make to improving their livelihoods have invested their own resources in the protection and management of their wildlife. Such protection activities and wildlife management include the deployment of community game scouts, the removal of snares, the monitoring of wildlife species and numbers and the careful control of outside access to wildlife and other natural resources in their domains.

The influence of the people of Nyaminyami and Guruve in CAMPFIRE now extends beyond their boundaries, for their initiative and example have inspired many other districts in Zimbabwe. Today there are 23 districts involved in CAMPFIRE, including every district abutting a national gamepark, and the grant pledged by the British Government in 1989 has been drawn upon to provide strategic assistance to many of these districts. Today, other donors are providing assistance to CAMPFIRE, including those from the USA, Germany and Norway. In the future the entire border of Zimbabwe will be ringed with CAMPFIRE projects.

RESEARCH NEEDS

As mentioned earlier, there are a number of areas in which the ODA sees the need for further work on this issue. The ODA is prepared to play a part by

FIGURE 6.5.   Community wildlife butchery in Nyaminyami (Steve Thomas, Zimbabwe Trust)

committing up to £150 000 over the next three years to fund research into the environmental impact of tourism in developing countries.

This sub-programme will come within the global Environmental Research Programme I, launched at the Royal Geographical Society in April 1991, which is already supporting some exciting work. It will address the relationships between local communities within National Parks, and between government and private industry in areas where tourism has become established.

What sort of tourism-related issues need to be addressed? Research might cover

- how ecotourism can be developed to ensure local populations are closely involved, and to encourage a better understanding of the value of their patrimony

- how tourism can be used as a positive stimulus to education about the environmental resources
- what should be the role of ecotourism in forests, both as an economic activity using the forests directly and in its impact upon forest resources for fuel and for local crafts?

The ODA would welcome other ideas concerning areas of necessary research and suggested methods of implementation.

CONCLUSIONS

Ecotourism is on the path to sustainability, but to continue to be sustainable, all tourism, and not just ecotourism, must take account of three interconnecting issues

- it must not damage the environment—it must be ecologically sound
- it must respect social and cultural traditions in the host country
- it must be non-exploitative of local people and ensure, as far as possible, that benefits flow to local residents.

The tourism (and ecotourism) industry must take the sustainable path. It must take an environmentally responsible view of its role in the world and must respond to the simple challenge to us all to live sustainably and enjoy life—that means on holiday as well as at home and at work.

If the development of tourism is to avoid some of the most damaging effects that have been observed on the natural and human resources of developing countries, it needs to be seen as part of the whole process of moving towards sustainable development.

REFERENCES

World Bank, 1992, *World Development Report*, Oxford University Press, Oxford.
Zimbabwe Trust, 1990, *People, Wildlife and Natural Resources—the CAMPFIRE Approach to Rural Development in Zimbabwe*, Zimbabwe Trust, Department of National Parks and Wild Life Management, The Campfire Association, Harare.

SECTION II

DESTINATION CASE STUDIES

7

Tourism and a European Strategy for the Alpine Environment

His Royal Highness Prince Sadruddin Aga Khan

PRESSURES ON THE ALPINE ENVIRONMENT

The romantic visions of the Alps, the impressions of the first tourists who discovered these mountains not so long ago, can help us to work together for their preservation.

On 17 August 1805, the first festival of Alpine herdsmen was organised on the Unspunnen meadow, near Interlaken in Switzerland. Through this festival, regional traditions increased in value and began to attract tourism—this may well have saved them from extinction.

Today, 188 years later, the total length of rail and road in the Alps is 405 000 kilometres—ten times the earth's circumference. The busiest mountain road network in the world bears 20 per cent of all passengers and 15 per cent of all goods transported in Western Europe, producing massive pollution and acid rain, major causes of the death of mountain forests.

Since the 1960s, tourism has exploded with attendant numbers of new roads, parking lots, restaurants, hotels, apartment blocks, sewage plants and other urban amenities which often function for just a few months each year. And there are, of course, the tourists! Every hour, ski-lifts can whisk one and a half million passengers to the summits. The dizzy pace of development is, in turn, putting tremendous stress on the Alps' basic resources, particularly their water system, for energy production, agriculture and human consumption.

Thus, paradoxically, though tourism has saved whole facets of Alpine culture and economy since the last century, death by tourism and over-development is one of the major threats hanging over the Alps. I remember how, when I was a boy, nature was still untouched in the Bernese Oberland. Since then, in this comparatively well preserved region, innumerable asphalt roads built for tourism and the lumber trade have cut across the mountains all the way to the summits.

Ecotourism: A Sustainable Option? Edited by E. Cater and G. Lowman
© The editors and contributors. Published in 1994 by John Wiley & Sons Ltd

The Alps are a region where conflicting trends have reached a climax. They are Europe's largest single natural system, harbouring rare species of animals and plants. However, owing to their geographical location, this vital space is shared with 12 million human beings. Also owing to their geographical location, the Alps are at the heart of Europe's north–south transit system. Transalpine traffic carries roughly 73 million tonnes of freight every year. Switzerland and Austria are the crossroads of this traffic. No reversal of this trend is expected in the future: the establishment of a single European market will double the volume of transport by the year 2010.

With their wealth of lakes and streams, the 'water towers of Europe' are the source of four major European rivers. Yet this enormous hydroelectric potential is already widely exploited. Some glaciers have been transformed into summer ski resorts. Over 5000 snow cannons busily spew artificial snow, consuming huge quantities of water. They use 2.8 million litres of water for each kilometre of piste. This artificial snow melts slowly and reduces the already short recuperation period of Alpine grasses and flowers during the summer months (Grabowski, 1992). The Alps are threatened by over-development, even desertification.

One hundred and twenty million tourists visit the Alps each year. This figure comprises 45 million tourists on vacation, together with 75 million daily and weekend tourists (Messerli, 1989). These tourists spend five hundred million nights in the Alps each year. Village populations grow five to ten-fold in the high season. The Alps' 12 000 ski lifts have a total length equivalent to three times the earth's circumference and are capable of transporting a quarter of the world's entire population each year up into the mountains. With the boom in winter tourism and the attendant development of ski resorts, the Alps have been turned into a vast playground owing to their economic success in providing skiing. According to the EEC, the Alps account for approximately one-quarter of the world's total tourism revenue and 70% of the Alpine population benefits directly or indirectly from tourism.

ALTERNATIVES TO LARGE-SCALE TOURISM

With the growth of tourism, traditional activities and mountain agriculture, increasingly less able to sustain the people, have declined. How can the traditional activities of mountain communities be preserved? What are the alternatives to large-scale tourism? How can we reconcile the economic development of a region with environmental protection?

What crucial steps would I like to see most to improve conditions in the Alps?

To harmonise tourist development with social and environmental needs, I believe that competition must be frozen in the field of regional tourism. In the entire Alps, common limits must be fixed for development and infrastructure. For that, we must achieve closer consultation and cooperation between the mountain communities, state tourism, transport and industry authorities, and competent environmental experts. Vast areas must be left intact, particularly the glaciers which have not yet been exploited. This is necessary to preserve the water resources of central Europe. It is also crucial to reduce pollution resulting from road transport and to encourage transport by rail. The use of large excavators, bulldozers, the multiplication of new roads, ski-lifts and runs should be abandoned in the high mountains to preserve the flora, fauna and natural habitats. Such environmental destruction was particularly evident in the 1992 Winter Olympics at Albertville in France (Figure 7.1), where altogether a million cubic metres of earth were carved out of the mountain sides, 30 hectares of trees were cut down and more than 320 000 square metres of land were urbanised (Keating, 1991).

In the Swiss plains, only 3.5 per cent of the land surface is uncultivated and the shrinking of natural biotopes threatens half the indigenous species of flora and fauna. Some areas have been protected through the creation of reserves and natural parks. But, between sanctuaries and concrete jungles, there are

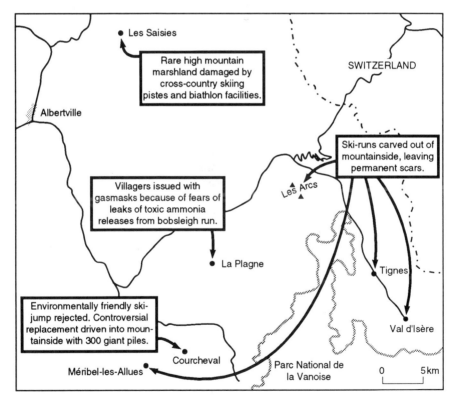

FIGURE 7.1. Environmental damage resulting from the 1992 Winter Olympics, Albertville, France

alternative ways to reconcile economic and environmental interests which favour quality over quantity. Let us not forget that many tourists visit the Alps because of their love for nature, seeking to escape from 'the greyness of their daily lives'. In an ever-shrinking world, the real question is no more whether it is possible for us to get where we wish to get, but rather whether there's any sense in getting there at all!

A new partnership: tourism and mountain agriculture

How can Alpine regions survive in the long term in harmony with tourism? This really depends on the future of mountain agriculture. In the inhabited areas of the Alps, there is no better example of harmony than the balance, diversity and beauty of nature tended over centuries by the traditional farmer. Two-thirds of the Alps consist of a landscape which has been moulded by humans and animals. Nothing can replace the heritage left behind by generations of mountain people. The Alpine farmers fulfil a crucial role as guardians of a varied landscape. In fact, it is in the direct interest of the tourist industry to ensure that the mountain farmer can continue to practise in the Alps, that the productive areas are protected and, above all, that the farmers receive their share of the economic benefits from tourism. On the other hand, mountain farmers must accept that, as tourism is their principal source of revenue, their priority can no longer be increased productivity through intensive mechanisation, but rather the maintenance of a rich, varied and attractive landscape.

Alpine tourism—that goose with the golden eggs, that magic formula—can only survive in partnership with agriculture. Alp Action is implementing this synergy in the Allgauer region of the Bavarian Alps, in the commune of Hindelang. Almost 80 per cent of the commune's 5000 inhabitants depend on tourism, directly or indirectly. The accommodation capacity of the area is 7000 beds, ranging from first class hotels to rural gîtes. It is estimated that one million visitor nights are spent in the area, as well as a considerable number of day visitors (Haug 1993). In October 1991, the farmers of Hindelang, the President of CIPRA (the International Commission for the Protection of Alpine Regions), Riso Deutschland (the German subsidiary of the Japanese Riso Corporation) and Alp Action announced the official launch of 'Hindelang Nature & Culture Land'. Here, for the first time in Germany, an entire community—its tourist operators, its shopkeepers, its public as a whole—has created a fund to help the farmers manage the environment. Partly financed by local taxes and partly by the Riso Corporation, an Alp Action Corporate Partner in Conservation, the Farmers' Fund will be allocated and invested by the farmers themselves. The farmers have signed an agreement whereby they will abide by a set of strict rules drawn up by environmental specialists and approved by the community.

Mountain farmers in Bavaria, and in the Alps in general, cannot subsist on farming activities alone. From a total of 200 farmers in Hindelang in the

1960s, 70 now remain. For generations, these farmers have depended on complementary revenue: making nails in winter, transporting salt across the mountains, working wood. Nowadays, farmers earn their complementary revenue from manning ski-lifts in winter and working in the region's industries.

Since the war, Hindelang's farmers have been selling all their milk to a large cooperative at a flat rate which barely covered their agricultural overheads. Now, with the new European Agricultural Policy which no longer subsidises productivity, the cooperative's purchasing price for milk is falling. Hindelang and other mountain farmers cannot compete with the farmers in the plains, whose overheads are significantly lower as a result of intensive, mechanised agricultural methods. For the Hindelang farmers, there was no choice but to opt out of the cooperative—they could no longer afford to produce and sell their milk at the cooperative's prices. Producing their own cheese and selling it locally, mainly to tourists, is the only means for their survival as farmers and might even provide a marginal profit. With specific Aid programmes and subsidies, such as the State of Bavaria's credits for the restoration of dairies (covering 50 per cent of costs), and the 2 DM surcharge (Kurtax) on nightly hotel rates levied in Hindelang for landscape management for tourism, all the conditions exist for the long-term success of the Hindelang Nature & Culture Land.

The role of the mountain farmer in environmental management

As long as mountain communities can preserve traditional agriculture in the mountains, they will play a part in stabilising the countryside and help to limit the thoughtless expansion of mass tourism. The farmers' very presence contributed to the struggle against erosion. Their experience in tending the fragile mountain terrain can safeguard against the construction and widening of ski-runs and help to preserve certain slopes from ski-lifts. Their economic and social needs argue against the short-term investment in tourist infrastructure which generally provides few returns for the indigenous populations and often lowers their quality of life through increased traffic and ugly buildings.

OTHER INITIATIVES

In turn, it is largely to protect the mountain communities and the tourists that Alp Action is planting hundreds of thousands of trees in six Alpine countries with the support of Jacobs Suchard International. It is to encourage and perpetuate traditional mountain crafts that the Zschokke Group, Switzerland's leading construction firm, is restoring some of the oldest Alpine chalets. And it is partly to maintain traditional agriculture that Clarins, the multinational cosmetics firm, is purchasing land on behalf of the Swiss League for the Protection of Nature to create Alpine butterfly sanctuaries.

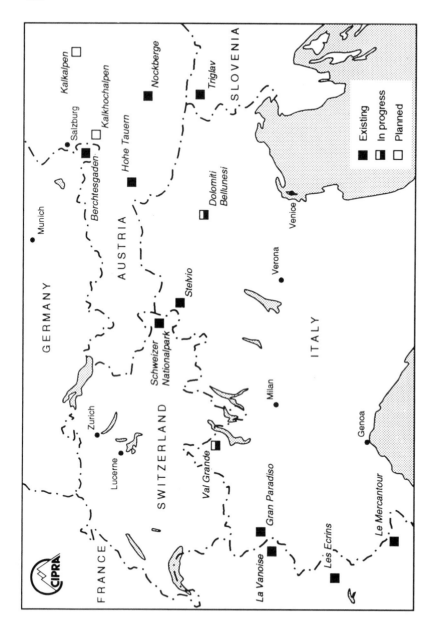

FIGURE 7.2. Location of Alpine National Parks. Reproduced by permission from CIPRA (1993)

TABLE 7.1. The Alpine National Parks. Reproduced by permission from CIPRA (1993)

National Park	Total area (ha)	Area of forest (ha)	Year established	IUCN category*
France				
1. Le Mercantour	68 500	20 637	1979	II
2. Les Ecrins	91 800	4400	1973	II
3. La Vanoise	52 839	950	1963	II
Italy				
4. Gran Paradiso	72 328	6000	1922	II
5. Stelvio	134 620	42 000	1935	V
In progress				
11. Val Grande	11 700	Unknown	1992	
12. Dolomiti Bellunesi	31 000	Unknown	1990	
Switzerland				
6. PN Suisse Engadin	16 887	5000	1914	II
Germany				
7. Berchtesgaden	20 800	8100	1978	V
Austria				
8. Hohe Tauern	178 600	17 160	1983–92	V
9. Nockberge	18 410	5966	1986	
Planned				
13. Kalkhochalpen (Salzburg)	c. 18 000	Unknown		
14. Kalkalpen (Haute Autriche)	c. 75 400	Unknown		
Slovenia				
10. Triglav	84 805	55 000	1981	II

*IUCN categories range from I to X; category I has the highest level of protection

EUROPEAN INTEGRATED ACTION

On 7 November 1991 in Salzburg, the Alpine states and the EEC agreed on a framework convention for the protection of the Alps. By signing this document Austria, France, Germany, Italy, Liechtenstein and Switzerland committed themselves to cooperate on a strategy for development based on environmental goals. Several months earlier, in June 1991, the Alps also found a champion in the European Parliament which voted a resolution reflecting the spirit of the Alpine Convention. With Europe as a whole on their side, there is hope that the Alps will evolve more harmoniously, reconciling respect for a fragile ecosystem with economic interests. There are now 14 National Parks, existing and designated, in the Alps (Figure 7.2). At the moment six are designated IUCN category II (National Park), three category V (Protected Landscape) and the remainder yet to be designated (Table 7.1).

In 1992, the first protocols for the application of the Alpine Convention were presented to environment ministers before being submitted for ratification by the various states. The alliance of all Alpine states in favour of a common desire to preserve the Alps is a great opportunity. At the Annual Meeting of the World Economic Forum in Davos, on 2 February 1993, Alp Action brought European leaders together to participate in a plenary session on a European Strategy for the Alps. This meeting was followed by the Second Awards Ceremony in honour of Alp Action's principal Partners in Conservation, in recognition of their contributions to the preservation of the Alpine heritage.

REFERENCES

CIPRA, 1993, Les parcs nationaux des Alpes, *CIPRA Info,* **29**, February.
Grabowski, P., 1992, White Gold, *In Focus,* **5**, Autumn.
Haug, R., 1993, La modèle de Hindelang, *Montagne,* **11**, 18–19.
Keating, M., 1991, Bad sports, *Geographical,* **63**, December, 26–29.
Messerli, P., 1989, *Mensch und Natur im alpinen Lebensraum Risiken, Chancen, Perspektiven*, Zentralen Erkenntnisse aus den schweizerischen MAB-Programm, Paul Haupt Bern, Stuttgart.

8

Ecotourism in Eastern Europe

DEREK HALL AND VIVIAN KINNAIRD

PREAMBLE

The short title of this chapter contains two contentious concepts. Firstly, the term 'ecotourism' itself has no consistent definition (Cohen, 1989; Boo, 1990, 1992b; Cater, 1991, 1992; Wheeller, 1992). In conformity with the rest of the book, however, this term is used in a generic sense to cover tourism development which is sympathetic to, complements and/or is employed as a vehicle for, conserving and sustaining natural and cultural environments and their resources (Ostrowski, 1991; Sofield, 1991) and which may encompass the domain of such terms as 'sustainable', 'green', 'soft' and 'alternative' tourism.

Implicit in the examination of such processes, however, is the awareness that global travel to ecotourism destinations undertaken in fuel-hungry aeroplanes is in itself incompatible with ecological sentiments. As the very support upon which all life depends is under threat as a consequence of our Western lifestyles, it is acknowledged that patterns of consumption must shift away from fossil fuel burning and the use of non-renewable resources. The extolling of ecotourism development in faraway lands (of which little may be known) may be thus viewed as paradoxical.

Secondly, 'Eastern Europe' is understood to cover the former communist ruled states of Central and Eastern Europe, excluding the erstwhile German Democratic Republic, which, within a unified Germany (Elkins, 1990), may now be conveniently regarded as part of Western Europe (but see Mellor, 1991). The lands of the former Soviet Union are also excluded, their scale and diversity being too vast for inclusion in a short review such as this (but see Shaw, 1991).

The political and economic changes which have characterised Central and Eastern Europe since 1989 have exerted a number of influences on patterns of international tourism to, within and from the region. Just as the processes of economic restructuring and social change now characterising these societies have yet to establish a settled and coherent pattern, so too do patterns of tourism development appear far from stable. For the short to medium term,

Ecotourism: A Sustainable Option? Edited by E. Cater and G. Lowman
© The editors and contributors. Published in 1994 by John Wiley & Sons Ltd

the focus of international tourism marketing in the region will be concentrated on the hard currency source countries of the West, Japan and the Middle East. While the region's economies remain crippled and their currencies inconvertible, its citizens as tourists will not play a significant economic part. However, domestic recreational demands are likely to increase considerably in the longer term with rising consumerism, and the environmental impact of this grossly underenumerated activity may be substantial. Local cross-border movement between neighbouring countries for petty trading purposes has grown to considerable proportions in recent years (Golembski, 1990), swelling international arrivals figures and complicating analyses of the scale of international tourism in the region.

The purpose of this chapter is to critically evaluate the perceptions and intended applications of ecotourism in Eastern Europe. This is placed within the context of past tourism patterns under state socialism, current issues of transition and restructuring and likely future trends in the region for tourism generally and environmentally sensitive tourism development in particular.

PAST TOURISM PATTERNS

Tourism resources

The region's tourism resources may conveniently be divided into five categories (Hall, 1990a; 1991b):

1. Sand, surf and sun—from Poland's short-season Baltic coast (Dawson, 1991) to Albania's still largely unspoilt Ionian littoral (Hall, 1991b). Marine pollution problems, arising both from the pressure of tourism itself and from other sources, are increasingly posing environmental challenges.
2. Heritage—the long and complicated history of the region is selectively represented in museums, exhibitions, statues, architecture, domestic artefacts, artisan crafts, music, song, dance and costume. Yet throughout the region, architectural splendour of notable historic centres such as Cracow in southern Poland, recognised by UNESCO as being of global importance, have long been threatened by atmospheric pollution from heavy industry and increasing levels of vehicle emissions.
3. Spas—mineral springs and curative treatments have served a wealthy, often foreign clientele, since classical times (Carter, 1991b; Turnock, 1991) and in recent years the Middle East has been a notably lucrative source of clients. Although care has been required to protect the quality of the waters of such locations, they have not been immune from atmospheric pollution.
4. Winter sports—these now attract large numbers of Western tourists and major land use conflicts have arisen, such as at Bansko in the Bulgarian

Pirin Mountains, where a winter sports resort was opened in 1981 within a National Park (Carter, 1991a).

5. Wildlife—although all countries of the region possess the equivalent of National Parks (Figure 8.1) and have designated areas devoted to the protection of fauna and flora, considerable land use conflicts exist. Hunting and fishing have been important and highly profitable tourist pursuits. The association of this activity with the now discredited former communist leaderships, however, together with increasing environmental awareness, has provoked substantial debate on the merits or otherwise of its continuation.

Tourism under state socialism

Although tourism was becoming increasingly popular in Eastern Europe in the inter-war period, particularly in upland areas, the post-war imposition of the Soviet model of political, economic and social development introduced new roles and patterns for recreational activity (Allcock and Przeclawski, 1990; Buckley and Witt, 1990).

Economic barriers, constraints on mobility, ideological hostility and the low priority given to service industries, coupled with general Cold War perceptions, rendered Europe behind the Iron Curtain an unattractive proposition for most Western vacationers. Priority was given to domestic recreational activities in the region, with administration, transport and accommodation being subsidised by state enterprises and trades unions for the benefit of (usually urban/industrial) working families. Cross-border movement normally entailed exchanges of 'friendship groups' between like-minded countries. Despite the human rights clauses of the 1975 Helsinki agreement, until the end of the 1980s the region's nationals, other than Yugoslavs (Allcock, 1991), were rarely permitted to travel westwards. Currency inconvertibility, restricted access to hard currency, relatively low living standards and stringent exit visa policies proscribed most forms of extra-bloc tourism except for the privileged *nomenklatura*, who also had access to hard currency shops and the other benefits of the 'more equal'.

Long-held fears of ideological contagion and social corruption delayed the harnessing of international tourism for such purposes as diffusing employment opportunities and promoting positive national images abroad (Hall, 1990a; 1990c; 1991b). Such structural characteristics of state socialism, as centralised and inflexible bureaucracies, and hostility towards international capitalism further inhibited tourism development.

When, therefore, the West European package holiday business was taking off in the 1960s, Eastern Europe was ill-equipped to respond to expanding market demands and was largely by-passed by Western tour operators. The one exception was Yugoslavia, which adopted a pragmatic attitude to labour and tourism mobility. There followed a rapid growth of tourist arrivals in

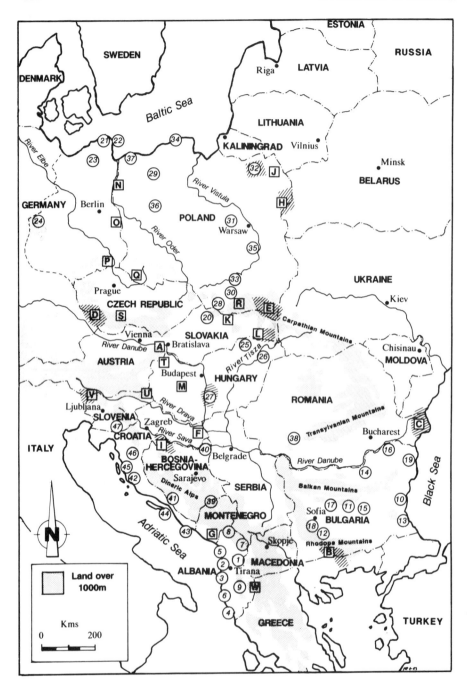

FIGURE 8.1.   National Parks and 'ecological bricks' in Eastern Europe

Key to FIGURE 8.1

'Ecological bricks'

A   Floodplains of the Danube, March and Thaya
B   Rhodope Mountains and Nestos Delta
C   Danube Delta
D   Bohemian/Bavarian Forest
E   Eastern Carpathians
F   Drau (Drava) Floodplain and Kopacki-Rit
G   Lake Shkodër
H   Bialowieza Forest
I   Sava Floodplain
J   Biebrza Marshes
K   Tatra Mountains
L   Slovakian Karst
M   Lake Balaton
N   Chorin/Schorfheide area
O   Spreewald
P   Sachsische Schweiz
Q   Karkonosze Mountains
R   Pieniny
S   Trebonsko Ponds
T   Lake of Neusiedl
U   Mur Floodplain
V   International Karst Region
W   Prespa area

Other national parks

Albania
1   Dajti Mountain
2   Divjaka
3   Karavasta
4   Ksamil
5   Kune
6   Llogora
7   Lura
8   Thethi
9   Tomori

Bulgaria
10   Atanasova Lake
11   Etura
12   Rila Mountains
13   Ropotamo
14   Rusenski Lom River
15   Sinite Kamani

16   Srebarna Lake
17   Steneto
18   Vitosha
19   Zlatni Pyassatzi

Slovakia
20   Mala Fatra Mountains

Former East Germany
21   Bottenlandschaft
22   Jasmund
23   Muritz Lake
24   Oberharz

Hungary
25   Bukk Mountains
26   Hortobagy
27   Kiskunsaq

Poland
28   Babia Gora
29   Drawski Lakes
30   Gorce Mountains
31   Kampinos
32   Mazurian Lakes
33   Ojcow
34   Slowinski
35   Swietokrzyski
36   Wielkopolski
37   Wolinski

Romania
38   Retezat

Former Yugoslavia
39   Durmitor (Montenegro)
40   Fruska Gora (Serbia–Bosnia–Croatia)
41   Hutavo Blatto (Bosnia–Croatia)
42   Krka River Reserve (Croatia)
43   Lovcen (Croatia)
44   Mijet (Croatia)
45   Paklenica (Croatia)
46   Plitvice Lakes (Croatia)
47   Risnjak (Croatia)

TABLE 8.1. Eastern Europe: international tourist arrivals 1970–90. Sources: World Tourism Organisation (1991; 1992), Hall (1993a) (with authors' additional calculations)

	No. of tourists (millions)						Percentage change			International tourism receipts (1990)	
	1970	1980	1985	1988	1989	1990	1985 –8	1988 –9	1989 –90	Receipts (US$ millions)	Receipts per tourist (US$)
Albania	nd*	nd	nd	nd	0.02	0.03	nd	nd	—	nd	nd
Bulgaria	2.5	5.5	3.4	4.0	4.3	4.5	15.8	8.8	4.3	394	87.6
Czechoslovakia	3.5	5.1	4.9	6.9	8.0	8.1	41.4	16.7	0.8	470	58.0
Hungary	4.0	9.4	9.7	10.6	14.5	20.5	8.6	37.2	41.5	1000	48.8
Poland	1.9	5.7	2.7	2.5	3.3	3.4	-9.2	32.0	3.2	266	78.2
Romania	2.3	6.7	4.8	5.5	4.9	6.5	15.5	-12.0	34.6	106	16.2
Yugoslavia	4.7	6.4	8.4	9.0	8.6	7.9	6.9	-4.1	-8.8	2774	352.0

*nd = No data.

that country from the West, a development unmatched elsewhere in the region. Although absolute numbers of international tourists to Yugoslavia were not significantly greater than those to several other countries in the region (Table 8.1), the dominance of the Western market did secure a higher level of tourist income, which, by the end of the 1980s, was greater than the total for the rest of the region and, moreover, was mostly in hard currency.

Patterns of tourist numbers

During the last years of state socialism, considerable growth in tourist (as opposed to all types of visitor) arrivals was experienced in the region (Table 8.1). Growth was particularly notable for the land-locked states of Central Europe: Czechoslovakia (41.4 per cent increase 1985–8, 16.7 per cent rise 1988–9) and Hungary (8.6 and 37.2 per cent). Poland fared less well (–9.2 per cent 1985–8), but recovered in 1989 (32.0 per cent up). The beach holiday destinations—Yugoslavia, Bulgaria and Romania—showed modest growth up to 1988, but both Yugoslavia and Romania saw downturns in 1989, a trend to be continued subsequently in the former, as the federation began to enter its death throes. By contrast, arrivals in Romania in 1990 showed a 34.6 per cent increase, albeit in large part because of a cross-border influx of low spending Soviet citizens from Moldova, emphasising the continuing need to treat all statistics in the region with great caution.

Romania aside, the most spectacular growth in tourist arrival numbers in the early transition period came about in Hungary, with increases of 37.2 per cent for 1989 and 41.5 per cent for 1990. Otherwise, somewhat surprisingly, the region witnessed a considerable reduction in the growth of tourist arrivals for 1990.

Patterns of tourist receipts

Under state socialism, with the exception of Yugoslavia, the economic impact of international tourism remained relatively small, certainly by comparison with Western Europe. In 1988, the last full year of state socialism in the region, for example, Bulgaria's tourist income was just 2.2 per cent of that of Spain and Romania's was the equivalent of just 7.3 per cent of that earned by Greece (WTO, 1990). That Turkey could raise its level of tourism receipts by more than 600 per cent between 1980 and 1988 was a salutary example for the region. By contrast, receipts declined substantially in Romania, largely as the result of the deteriorating image of the country's domestic conditions, and they fell dramatically in Poland in the early 1980s, only to later recover. In Bulgaria and Czechoslovakia, however, receipts increased at rates comparable with the major Western tourist economies, in Hungary even more rapidly, and in Yugoslavia fastest of all.

TABLE 8.2.   East-West Wetland Project Co-operation. Reproduced by permission
from Ramsar (1992)

Country/subject	Source of funding	Administered by	Amount
Hungary			
Wetland and grassland study	EU PHARE	DG I	ECU 150 000
Fertö Lake	EU PHARE	DG I	ECU 1.40 mill
Lakes Balaton and Velencei	EU PHARE	DG I	ECU 820 000
River corridors	Dutch EEP*	IUCN–EEP	SFR 124 920§
Floodplains	WWF	WWF	SFR 29 600§
Gabcikovo Dam	WWF	WWF	SFR 68 272§
Fishponds	ENHF†	ENHF†	
Poland			
Mazurian lakes	EU PHARE	DG I	ECU 1.40 mill
Warta river	EU PHARE	DG I	ECU 200 000
River corridors	Dutch EEP*	IUCN–EEP	SFR 115 900
Management of peat bogs	Dutch EEP*	IUCN–EEP	SFR 20 000
Biebrza Valley	WWF ENHF†	WWF ENHF†	SFR 144 000
Green Lungs Policy	Polish govt. and US EPA‡	Polish govt.	
Vistula river	Swedish govt.	WWF–Sweden	SWCR 3 mill‖
Romania			
Danube	Dutch EEP* WWF EBRD GEF ICBP	IUCN–EEP WWF–Auen–Institut ICBP	US$ 30 695 ECU 623 990 US$ 7 mill £25 000
Fishponds	WWF ENHF†	WWF ENHF†	SFR 101 200 DM 130 000
Croatia			
Save wetlands	EU	ENHF†	DM 1 mill
Save wetlands	ENHF†	ENHF†	
Eastern Europe			
Fishponds in Hungary, Czech Republic, Slovakia, Poland	Dutch EEP*	IUCN–EEP	SFR 101 460§

* Dutch Multilateral Programme for Eastern Europe.
† European Natural Heritage Fund, a German-based conservation NGO.
‡ United States Environmental Protection Agency.
§ Swiss Francs.
‖ Swedish Crowns.

During the early stages of transition, as intraregional mobility of low spending visitors increased in response to the easing of cross-border movements, levels of receipts rose less than proportionately, such that in 1989, all countries of the region except Romania saw a decrease in receipts per arrival, and in 1990 only Bulgaria and Yugoslavia recorded per capita increases, in the latter case reflecting declining rather than increasing tourist numbers.

The complications of post-communist transition

Despite the division of Czechoslovakia (Hall, 1992b), Central Europe, and particularly the land-locked states of the Czech Republic and Hungary, have experienced growth in international tourism development which the troubled Balkan societies have been poorly placed to pursue. Relative stability, more advanced economies, a concentration of international funding (Hamilton, 1991; Michalak and Gibb, 1993) and initial advantage have contributed to this division.

A sample of more recent figures for Hungary can exemplify that country's position as the region's leading tourist destination in terms of numbers, and, since the Yugoslav upheavals, also in terms of tourist receipts. Hungary derived a tourism income surplus of $170 million for the first seven months of 1991, a 30 per cent increase on the previous year's figure. The industry became the country's largest balance of payments contributor. For the first six months of 1992, despite a six per cent decrease in tourism income, Hungarians travelling abroad spent 21 per cent less, rendering a surplus of $202.1 million, an increase of $30 million.

The Balkan countries, despite possessing the most favourable climatic and coastal conditions for mass tourism, have experienced stagnation or even decline in tourist numbers, reflecting an initial lack of clarity of political change, continuing instability and a generally lower degree of road transport accessibility from major West European markets. Further, tourists from the northern part of the region, no longer restricted to Soviet bloc vacation destinations, started to abandon their post-war Black Sea coast holiday playgrounds for more enticing Western venues. However, in Bulgaria at least, preliminary figures for the first half of 1992 were showing an increase of 23–25 per cent in foreign visitors compared with the previous year, perhaps the result of deflection from the former Yugoslavia, where the tourism industry has been dismantled, although both Slovenia and Croatia are now vigorously promoting themselves.

In response to mass market demands, and not least the growth of 'business tourism', accommodation, transport, utilities and telecommunications are gradually being overhauled with assistance from the major international funding institutions and commercial transnational companies. For tourism to be more environmentally sensitive and sustainable, however, a greater emphasis on more modest to medium grade accommodation is required, coupled with an encouragement of small-scale rural developments which can supplement farm incomes and reduce farmers' desire to pursue ecologically harmful intensive agriculture. Previously, foreign exchange earnings flowed largely to the state, with virtually no benefits accruing to the local economy, particularly in rural areas.

Environmentally sensitive tourism must involve the local population in decision-making as well as participation in accommodation provision, conservation and education (Murphy, 1985; Wells *et al.*, 1992). Not surprisingly, however, tourism training in Eastern Europe has tended to focus on hotel management, catering, travel agenting and such areas as computing, telecommunications and languages, to cater for the new growth markets.

The region is vulnerable to tourism fashion changes, which are themselves sensitive to the instability and the short-term problems with which the region is currently beset. The impact of socio-economic change is witnessing rapidly rising crime and accident rates. Although such developments can exert a repulsion effect on tourism activity, the extent of tourism's contribution to their growth may not be insignificant. Again, one way of ameliorating such problems is to more closely involve local communities in the tourism development process.

At the same time, the uncertainty of transition and the instability of which it is a part tend to create an organisational vacuum within which the medium-term priorities for developing a tourism industry cannot be clearly established. Legislative and regulatory frameworks for privatisation and joint venture development, including provisions for insurance and guarantees, may be slow to arrive. Former members of the old communist *nomenklatura* may manage to hold onto positions of economic power while ostensibly relinquishing political power, and through their former connections can channel inward investment to their own advantage. Hidden power structures and agendas arising from such situations may not be readily apparent to outsiders. The authors are aware, for example, of one particular former active party member who is now one of the most forceful tourism entrepreneurs in his country.

The danger for the region of falling into a dependency relationship with the West, becoming dominated by Western multinational accommodation, transport, agencing and financial organisations is ever present. To become a cheap tourist playground, a number of localities could rapidly reach saturation level, with increased overcrowding, infrastructural strains, environmental deterioration and host antagonism.

CONSERVATION AND CHANGE

Past conservation policies

The history of conservation in Eastern Europe is both mixed and inconsistent. Water management, particularly for flood control and agricultural development (Turnock, 1979), extends back to at least the eighteenth century. With increasing population pressures and the growth of organised timber exploitation in the later nineteenth century, soil erosion became recognised as a serious problem and forestry protection legislation began to be introduced (Turnock, 1988). This acted as the basis for nature reserve and National Park designation, which developed from recommendations predating the First World War (Carter, 1978). The first reserves were set up in southern Bohemia as early as 1838 (Carter and Turnock, 1993: 205), although National Park legislation, inspired by North American and West European concepts of wilderness, was not elaborated until the inter-war period. Bodies set up to oversee and administer such areas included Poland's Council for Nature Protection (1919) and Romania's Commission for Natural Monuments (1933).

Although much genuine environmental concern was shown in the post-war period, in the face of policies emphasising rapid and heavy industrialisation based on outmoded technologies and inefficient fuels, environmental considerations were given a low priority (Dakov, 1976; Carter, 1985; Albrecht, 1987; Waller, 1989; Hinrichsen and Enyedi, 1990). Two forcibly promoted dogmas exacerbated this situation: (a) that socialism harnessed to science could overcome all natural obstacles; and (b) environmental problems only resulted from capitalist exploitation and thus, by definition, did not exist in socialist Eastern Europe.

The extent of resources required to ameliorate environmental damage thereby inflicted on the region has been a matter of some subsequent debate (Forster and Józán, 1990; French, 1990; Russell, 1990; Hughes, 1991; Thompson, 1991).

Change and cooperation

In 1991 the European Trust for Natural and Cultural Wealth was established in Prague with the backing of the Czech Government and a grant from the World Bank's Global Environment Facility (GEF). Inspired by the World Wide Fund for Nature (WWF) and links with environmentalists in Eastern Europe, the trust aimed to preserve the region's natural heritage by establishing an 'ecological backbone' across Europe. The first targets were the natural habitats along largely uninhabited and previously militarised border areas—'ecological bricks'—where it was hoped to foster cooperation between neighbours. Figure 8.1 shows the proposed areas together with National Parks and other areas of environmental importance (Pearce, 1992).

Although a few large sites are attracting most attention and funding, many other conservation projects have involved cooperation between Eastern and Western Europe. Bilateral and multilateral funding have been made available for an increasing number of projects appearing within assistance packages since 1989 (Table 8.2). Funding takes two forms: specific support, usually for the establishment of protected sites and their management plans, and more general funding to improve the recipient countries' administrative framework and public awareness.

At government level, the EC, particularly through the PHARE programme (European Community Environmental Assistance to Eastern European Countries, initially Poland/Hungary Assistance for Restructuring), the World Bank and the European Bank for Reconstruction and Development (EBRD) support projects and project implementation units in several countries. The Polish, US and Dutch governments are involved in the Green Lungs project, a subregional nature conservation strategy in north-eastern Poland which might be extended to neighbouring countries. At a more modest level the IUCN-East European Programme (IUCN-EEP) has, through bilateral funding, established specific nature conservation project coordination units in the Czech Republic, Poland and Romania. The WWF is involved in wetland projects in Hungary and Poland. The Ramsar Bureau has also placed a high priority on projects in Eastern Europe, having applied to the GEF for $2 million to fund small-scale wetland conservation projects (Ramsar, 1992).

Claiming the borderlands

Cross-border environmental cooperation in the region extends back to the 1920s when Czechoslovakia and Poland agreed on joint protection measures for an area which eventually became the Pieninsky/Pieniny National Park (R in Fig. 8.1) (Cerovsky and Podhaiska, 1990). In the post-war period the two countries again jointly developed cross-border National Parks in the Tatra (K) and Karkonosze (Q) mountains. Generally, however, little bilateral action was taken within the framework of the Council for Mutual Economic Assistance (CMEA or COMECON) (Carter and Turnock, 1993: 2089) and no effective supranational environmental agency was created within the region (Cerovsky, 1990: 1). Indeed, for over 40 years the borderlands between the countries of the region, and particularly between those countries and the West along the line of the 'Iron Curtain', were largely uninhabited and inaccessible. Although regularly patrolled and fortified, with large tracts forbidden to human activity and movement, these no-man's lands became unconsciously protected natural areas. With the dismantling of that 'Iron Curtain' from 1989, and the strong desire of people from both sides to travel across and explore, there arose an urgent need to protect the habitats now suddenly rendered accessible.

One of the most valuable natural areas is the Sumava Biosphere Reserve (D), 700 square kilometres of forests and wetlands on the Czech–German border. It was faced with the development of intensive agriculture and forestry, the growth of uncontrolled tourism and long-range air pollution. The Czech Government agreed to set aside 70 000 hectares as a National Park, with the remaining 92 000 hectares designated a protected landscape area, including a 3000 hectares 'strict' nature reserve. A management plan to promote sustainable resource management was sponsored by the Czech Government, the Czech Green Circle and the WWF. Completed in 1991, it envisages a core area of about 20 000 hectares, a recuperation zone of 5000 hectares, a traditional use zone of 40 000 hectares and a public use zone which it is hoped will attract ecotourism. Within the traditional use zone, forest intervention will be permitted for a 40 year period, the time required to convert artificial spruce monocultures into dynamic systems. No resource use or intervention will be allowed in the core area.

Although strong support for the plan has been forthcoming from the mayors of local communities, opposition from the forestry sector and from the Ministry of Agriculture has seen the development of an alternative plan. However, the management plan developed by the project is supported by TERPLAN, the Prague-based government agency responsible for land use planning, and by the two regional authorities. Community involvement has continued through a series of public seminars and hearings, and the WWF has provided institutional support to local non-governmental organisations (NGOs) in an effort to strengthen their involvement. Longer term problems are locally high unemployment rates and often poor cross-border cooperation.

Nonetheless, the National Park is to be used as the *Leitmotif* for the Bohemian/Bavarian forests region. Situated on the 'green roof of Europe', it is hoped that the park designation will promote, rather than hinder, the process of helping forests which are, historically, part of a single economic and cultural region, to grow back together again and to overcome political division (Kleinhenz and Hallitzky, 1991).

It is one of the Cold War's ironies that the lower Odra/Oder valley between Poland and Germany shelters the Baltic's last community of salmon, which annually swim up the river to lay their eggs in small streams on the Polish side. There are 500 types of plant, 226 species of bird, 19 species of amphibians and reptiles, 56 types of mollusc, 50 species of fish and 50 types of mammals here. Up to 100 000 migrating geese, ducks and swans rest here in spring and autumn. Osprey and sea eagles are relatively common sights, and beavers and otters live in the marshlands.

A National Park has been established which covers 32 884 hectares (22 384 in Germany, 10 500 in Poland) encompassing three zones: (1) reserve areas, with no human use (7390 hectares); (2) environmentally protected areas with some human use (9110 hectares); and (3) surrounding areas compatible with the park but with some human use (16 384 hectares).

Financed by the Government of Brandenburg, one of the new east German provinces, with support from the German Foundation for the Promotion of Culture, the park extends 60 kilometres south from Szczecin to the villages of Cedynia/Hohensaaten on either bank of the river. Aside from two outstanding land use problems—a power station and the network of border patrol roads—revived land ownership claims, attempts to exploit gravel deposits and new potential tourism pressures require strong conservation reinforcement measures (Springate, 1991). The development of ecotourism as a means of satisfying at least some of the economic pressures on the area could see the development of 'gateways' and 'honeypots' on both sides of the border, filtering tourism pressures into selected sites away from the reserve areas. Such a strategy would appear attractive to local opinion, although the two national governments have found agreement difficult.

PROBLEMS OF ECOTOURISM DEVELOPMENT IN CONTEMPORARY EASTERN EUROPE

Adoption of 'ecotourism'

The often poor environmental image of the region, coupled with the existing and potential environmental impacts of tourism activities, have seen a post-communist reappraisal of tourism and conservation strategies in the region (Jenner and Smith, 1992). Recognition is now being extended to the need for 'sustainable', 'green' and 'eco' tourism, as, for example, stated in the Romanian and Albanian national tourism programmes (RMTT, 1990: 3; Spaho, 1992; 1993) and in the objectives of a number of environmental NGOs attempting to influence policy both in the region's governments and in the major Western funding agencies (Reed, 1990).

However, there often appears to have been little conceptual discussion and analysis of the appropriateness of adopting at national (and indeed international) policy level what may be little more than fashionable buzz-words and 'marketing babble' (Wickers, 1992). This can result in contradictory and conflicting policy statements, particularly where a government's tourism and environment departments have not been coordinated. Such crucial questions as defining and recognising tourism carrying capacities and 'saturation levels' have barely begun to be addressed (Boo, 1990; 1992a) and may be neglected because of skill shortages, inadequate resources and political in-fighting (Hall, 1991a).

Further, a newly unleashed entrepreneurial sector may have neither the resources nor the inclination to take a longer term view of tourism's environmental impacts. Nor will local populations be sympathetic to environmental conservation policies if these interfere with such traditional local activities as hunting, fishing and smuggling. This emphasises the need to involve the local community in decision-making and participation in conservation and tourism provision to persuade them that environmentally sensitive tourism can be in their own economic interests.

Indeed, at a general level, as 'ecotourism' implicitly requires management, control and proscription, there will be an inevitable reaction within the region, particularly from the newly privatised sectors, against any policies echoing aspects of the old communist regimes' practices. It is no little irony that just at the time when the shackles of communist control have been thrown off and Western consultants have been flooding the region extolling the virtues of the 'free' market, so others have come along arguing that some aspects of people's newly won freedoms should be limited and that restrictions on access to certain areas should be reimposed and even extended. Superficially, for example, the old Albanian 'prescriptive' approach to tourism, whereby foreigners were herded around in a group along a few prescribed routes in prebooked state transport and full-board accommodation and were 'policed' by guides, drivers and sundry onlookers, had a great deal to commend it in minimising cultural and environmental contagion (Hall, 1984; 1990b; 1992a). The country's present tourism ministry has other ideas, however (Hall, 1993a; Spaho, 1993).

Local participation

The encouragement of active participation by the local population in the conservation and education dimensions of the tourism development process is an essential element of ecotourism. In Eastern Europe, however, attempts to involve local communities have been inhibited both by the lack of experience of bottom-up development from which citizens can draw, and the often dismissive or at best patronising attitude taken by some officials towards local populations, particularly in rural and more remote areas. Local citizen participation is often seen as a threat to the power structure of both local and central bureaucracies and to the very valuable perks which accompany the membership of such structures.

Attempts to break such ingrained structural relationships will not be easy, although local NGOs are receiving financial, organisational and moral support from their Western counterparts. Local populations in their turn may be suspicious of any 'official' approaches. For example, when researchers from the Danube Delta Institute surveyed relatively isolated local residents on their attitudes towards accommodating tourists in farm tourism and on other ways of being drawn into 'ecotourism' processes in the Delta (DDITRG, 1991), they were met with no small degree of apprehension and suspicion: an understandable response given the recent history of Romania in general and the Delta in particular.

Support requirements

Inventories of natural and human resources, entailing data collection and collation, processing, analysis and representation are still required in much of the region. Particularly in the Balkans, shortages of often basic equipment and access to literature are commonplace and constrain implementation: computers, word processors, photocopiers, fax machines and accurate measuring instruments are all urgently needed, together with access to spare parts and ease of servicing. The ability to learn from experience elsewhere is constrained by the lack of availability of appropriate literature. Documentation centres need to be established to house both comprehensive databases from which information can be easily retrieved and libraries of relevant scientific books and papers from around the world.

Linking mechanisms to ensure essential cooperation and rationalisation of effort, resources, skills and experience are often lacking. It has been the authors' experience that tensions can arise from a number of sources, such as between: (a) public and private sector representatives; (b) environment and tourism administrators; (c) ecological and economic objectives; (d) central and local government; (e) those with and those without appropriate skills and training; and (f) those differing over the perceived needs/treatment of the local population.

Staff training programme requirements reveal critical needs in such areas as ecology, social survey techniques, marketing, languages, computing, cartography, photogrammetry, geographical information systems, guiding and information centre staffing. Selective knowledge and experience, rather than holistic perspectives, have been the norm. This partly results from the activities of professionals, who, whilst specialists in their own fields, have usually received training within relatively narrow disciplinary confines and have hitherto been unable to take a broader ecological view of any particular geographical area (Hall, 1992c).

Appropriate legal and administrative frameworks may still need to be established in some countries to clarify land and property rights, control transport and accommodation and establish insurance guarantees and tax regimes. These should also include codes of tourist conduct in protected areas updated to meet new conditions.

In the case of Hungary, for example, as post-communist agricultural intensification began to threaten species and their habitats, nature conservation laws were passed in 1991 and 1992 to establish a Nature Conservation Authority (NCA). This body administers the prevention of areas of international importance from falling victim to indiscriminate privatisation and of foreigners buying protected areas. Unlike the region's traditional approach which focused mainly on species protection, the new regulations will stress habitat protection. Special attention will be paid to environmentally sensitive areas and to establishing a comprehensive network of ecological or 'green' corridors connecting major protected areas. The NCA is able to exchange land of comparable value and to lease and license land on terms favourable to farmers with the aim of compensating any losses resulting from conflicts of interest with nature conservation. A Nature Conservation Trust has been established to coordinate NGOs and government action, focusing on such issues as ecotourism development.

As a consequence of the new political and legislative framework, the WWF has been able to complete an inventory of Hungary's steppe grasslands and has prepared a legal protection and management proposal. The WWF is also promoting traditional extensive farming systems, entailing such practices as grassland management, rotation of crops and the appropriate use of marginal land such as planting native tree species rather than non-native pines. Small-scale farm tourism should be built into this process as a means of broadening the rural population's economic base and as a form of compensation and disincentive to pursue intensive agriculture. The WWF has helped to save the traditional breed of *racka* sheep, and this could act as the basis for rural heritage and ecotourism development (Anon., 1993).

Information/education requirements

Clear statements of the nature and aims of ecotourism need to be incorporated into literature and publicity material to educate and encourage active participation by interested parties (local populations, tourism organisations, local and national state bodies and individuals), as well as for potential tourists themselves.

Education and information programmes on environmental protection amongst the local population must be effective, especially through the medium of schools, and put into practice, recruiting locals as wardens and deploying them on financially beneficial training courses to strengthen tourist control mechanisms. The interest, support and participation of the local community is vital, especially where ecotourism strategies are perceived as threatening its (often black) economic interests. Bottom-up information flows may not be easy to stimulate in the short term given the nature of past decision-making practices in the region. Similarly, it will be difficult to successfully undertake social surveys, given the understandable suspicion and hostility with which previous official prying into domestic affairs was viewed.

Strategy formulation

There appear to be six types of action study required for an ecotourism strategy plan: (1) a strategy for assessing tourism demand and targeting specialist markets/niche groups; (2) an interim plan for matching different tourism activities/types of tourists, their likely environmental impacts and economic benefits; (3) the establishment of a working formula for assessing tourism carrying capacities; (4) an interim plan for a system of prescribed routeways and transport forms appropriate for different ecological conditions within and adjacent to the designated area (Hall, 1993b; 1993c); (5) an interim plan for prescribed infrastructure and services, accommodation and activity areas, their access and seasonality; and (6) a longer term plan for the nature and location of information/education centres, coordinated with local educational programmes, for 'gateways' into, and at, 'honeypots' on the periphery of protected areas. These would also act as 'tax' collection points, permit issue centres and questionnaire survey points.

Production of a final composite plan/strategy should ensure its complementarity and integration with local, regional and national environmental, tourism and other (such as education) planning strategies.

ECOTOURISM CASE STUDY: THE DANUBE DELTA

The Delta's importance

The 564 000 hectare Danube Delta is arguably the most important wildlife area in the whole of Europe (Vadineanu and Manoleli, 1990; IUCN, 1992). A major wetland area, it contains a diversity of species and habitats. At the cross-roads of several major bird migration routes and acting as a natural biofilter for Danubian waters, the importance of the Delta extends far beyond its own borders. Four-fifths of the Delta's area lies in Romania. This state, under the Ceauşescu regime, sought increasing economic exploitation of the Delta as development policies elsewhere in the country became progressively ineffective. Agriculture, fishing, tourism, reed cultivation and gravel extraction were all being considerably stepped-up during the 1980s, resulting in large-scale reclamation and destruction of important habitats.

Both the nature and extent of these activities have been a cause for grave concern. Additionally, pollution along the whole length of the Danube has been increasing, from industrial and domestic waste and effluent discharges, through the run-off of fertilisers and pesticides and from increased shipping activity, all exerting further strains on the Delta's biofiltering capabilities. The Black Sea, into which the Danube flows, is now considered to be 90 per cent biologically dead (it annually receives 4300 tonnes of nitrogen compounds, 900 tonnes of petroleum products, 600 tonnes of lead and 200 tonnes of detergents from industrial wastes, much via the Danube). Construction for hydroelectric and other developments on the river further upstream has considerably affected the river's natural regime. All of these adverse trends have acted to reduce the Delta's biodiversity.

The Danube Delta Biosphere Reserve

Following the execution of the Ceauşescus in December 1989, and the installation of the National Salvation Front government in Romania, a Ministry of the Environment was established with policies clearly at odds with past priorities and with the continuing practices of several other central ministries. The Danube Delta (Figure 8.2) was declared a biosphere reserve and given international recognition as a Ramsar site (wetland of international import-ance). The Danube Delta Biosphere Reserve Administration (DDBRA) was set up in September 1990, virtually independent of the area's local government—the Tulcea judet—and was given, in theory at least, wide-ranging powers to protect and enhance the ecological quality of the Delta. Its basic aims were the ecological restoration of the Danube Delta and the con-servation of its biodiversity and ecological structures; the formulation of a rational exploitation policy based on the area's ecological productive capacity; coordination of hydrotechnical works for improved water flow in the canals, fens and lakes, for preventing further fluvial erosion; the establishment of parameters governing the scale and access of waterway traffic, the nature and location of fishing and hunting to be pursued, and for all housing and tourism development; and, implicitly, the undertaking of research into all aspects of the Delta (Gomoiu, 1991).

Cooperation and support at international, national and local levels are imperative if this venture is to succeed. At the international level, cooperation in combating pollution is essential. In May 1990 the Danubian nations agreed in Budapest to the establishment of an environmental convention for scien-tific collaboration to extend the United Nations Economic Commission for Europe code of conduct on pollution, and to involve research and training institutions in Western Europe and North America. This was the first com-mon response by the governments of the region to an obvious collective need. Improved collaborative research, as well as technology transfer to countries such as Romania, were also required for the opening of the Rhine–Main–Danube waterway in 1992.

The IUCN brought together a group of NGOs and others to assist in the conservation of this wetland. The International Council for Bird Preservation (ICBP) has provided assistance to plan wildlife tourism, preparing awareness materials and supporting the reserve authorities with scientific and office equipment, and the EBRD and GEF are funding the management plan.

Under the governorship of a marine biologist, the Danube Delta Administra-tion was given the ministry's blessing to cut across pre-existing vested interests and to regard the Delta as almost starting from 'year zero' for purposes of ecological restitution. In practice, the legislative framework necessary to permit the authority to act to the full advantage of the Delta was only slowly put into place, and while the Administration is answerable to the Environment Ministry, strong local, regional and national interests in tourism, fishing, agriculture, hunting and navigation have exerted heavy pressures upon it. For example, a former employee of the Tourism Ministry, and, as one of the country's first tourism entrepreneurs, the owner of the Delta's first converted 'floating hotel', has taken a close interest in the DDBRA activities. At one 'ecotourism'

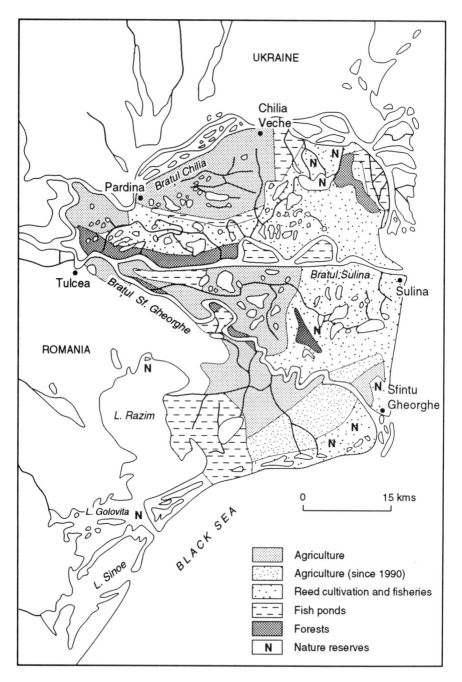

FIGURE 8.2.   Danube Delta Biosphere Reserve. Modified from IUCN (1992: 35)

workshop he presented well organised and cogently argued plans for promoting hunting trips for foreigners to the Delta. Costings were presented in such a way that much-needed hard currency income from 'organised culling' could be seen to provide a major dollar subsidy to support 'other' conservation work.

This is just one of the more obvious areas of conflict facing a country with diverse and very valuable, yet vulnerable, natural resources, strapped for cash and still only gradually emerging from a generation of brutalised repression (Turnock, 1993). Indeed, in 1990, Romania's government actually ended a 15-year ban on bear hunting, a proscription imposed by Ceauşescu to confine the 'privilege' to himself. In a desperate effort to attract hard currency, hunters were being charged a minimum of $10 000 to shoot bears in the Carpathian Mountains, where there are estimated to be fewer than 500 roaming the oak forests. Such 'tourists' are notoriously big spenders in pursuit of their game.

Ecotourism in the Danube Delta

Two clear priorities existed for the DDBRA to render 'ecotourism' an ecologically meaningful and economically profitable reality for the Delta. Firstly, detailed information on both the Delta's human and natural resources was urgently required. Although the Administration embarked on a series of questionnaire surveys of the local population to ascertain their basic demographic characteristics, patterns of economic activity, aims and aspirations, the reliability of these and of past population censuses for the area was at best questionable, given the geographical disposition of the Delta's inhabitants and the immediate political past of the country. Similarly, with a previous lack of emphasis on the intrinsic ecological merits of the Delta, only selective knowledge and experience, rather than a holistic perspective, were available. This partly resulted from the narrow disciplinary training of professionals, who had hitherto been unable to take a broader ecological view of the area, and partly from the fact that some bureaucrats appeared simply to have inappropriate disciplinary training. Past tourism administrators, for example, had often been trained as engineers.

There was, therefore, a pressing need for the Administration to undertake a comprehensive audit of the human and natural resources of the whole Delta area. To be effective, this would also require cooperation from the Ukrainian authorities in whose territory the most northerly 20 per cent of the Delta lies. Basic questions such as the definition and calculation of 'carrying capacities' for different aspects of the Delta's ecological diversity required urgent attention. Although vital in establishing a framework for the development of 'green' tourism and other activities in the Delta, such capacities in their turn could not be assessed until a fully detailed knowledge of the Delta's resources was ascertained.

Secondly, given the depressed nature of European tourism in the Balkans in general and in Romania in particular, markets for ecotourism would need to be very carefully defined and targeted. Romanian resources and expertise available for this task appeared to be minimal.

Zones of protection established in the Delta entailed the designation of 16 'core zones' (totalling over 50 000 hectares, 10.7 per cent of the total DDBRA area), surrounded by 'buffer zones' and 'transition areas', reflecting the relative ecological importance of the Delta's habitats. The ability to fully implement reinforcing controls in these areas had to follow tardy national legislation on land and property ownership. Further, a shortage of suitably trained staff and appropriate scientific equipment imposed further major handicaps on the Administration's efforts: national and international assistance in training and technology transfer was vital.

Nonetheless, with a nucleus of trained and often very experienced personnel, a corps of wardens was established, largely recruited from the local population, to serve a three-fold function: (1) most obviously, to protect the area's resources from human predators—the wardens carry firearms but have no ammunition; (2) to provide a means of skills transfer to the indigenous population; and (3) to assist the local population in understanding that protection of the Delta is in their own economic and cultural interests.

Plans to recruit local people for employment in information centres (at 'honeypots' and 'gateways') will add a further educational dimension. Encouragement and assistance in the establishment of farm tourism will additionally emphasise the economic benefits of conservation and ecotourism for local people and reduce the pressures on them to intensify their agricultural practices.

What has taken place in the Danube Delta is the establishment of a model and likely precedent for reversing environmentally detrimental processes born of political and economic bankruptcy. At the same time positive, ecologically enlightened conservation policies have been instigated which are appropriate both for an important yet vulnerable natural environment and for the human population continuing to live in, and gain its livelihood from, that environment. Properly managed, the Delta will be able to confirm that sustainable forms of tourism can have key conservation, education and economic roles in the integrated management of protected areas.

CONCLUSIONS

Sustainable forms of tourism are a relatively new concept for Eastern Europe, although past practices did see the restriction of tourists' mobility, albeit not necessarily for environmental reasons. Eastern Europe is vulnerable to tourism fashion changes, which are themselves sensitive to the instability and myriad problems besetting the region.

In spite of this, the region's cultural and environmental diversity provides the potential for substantial market segmentation. Targeting niche markets—

ideally high spending groups with minimal adverse impacts and season-extending activities—should emphasise the significance of 'green' forms of tourism (e.g. Standring, 1991). The region's substantial heritage potential and natural protected areas can be used to considerable educational as well as economic advantage to the region.

However, there are very real dangers of ecotourism being cynically taken up as a development objective simply because of: (a) the fashionability of the concept; (b) the propaganda value for governments and agencies of being seen to be 'greening' development and particularly tourism development; and (c) its role as a means of gaining access to development Aid funds from the West.

Also, it appears that too many projects are being developed based on *Western* European (or even North American) experience, despite the cultural and environmental circumstances and the nature of consequent pressures being very particular to the region itself. Indeed, there may be better lessons to be learned from the experience of the developing world than from the developed (e.g. de Kadt, 1990). In short, there is more than a slight danger of eco-ethnocentrism being superimposed on the application of ecotourism in Eastern Europe. Some projects currently being pursued have not been mentioned in this chapter precisely because they have fallen into this trap, led by people and institutions (often government departments rather than NGOs) of whom we would have expected better.

For tourism development to be successful and acceptable, sensitivity of implementation and sustainability and local participation must be more than just clichés in national or corporate plans. Most importantly, local populations must be involved and shown that conservation and tourism can complement each other to the economic advantage of the local community. Unless this is successfully achieved, longer term tourism development in Eastern Europe is likely to pose far more problems than it solves.

ACKNOWLEDGEMENTS

Grateful thanks are due to Neil Purvis for the cartography. A number of people contributed ideas and information for this paper, and the authors would like to thank particularly Gaynor Whyles, Vladimir Laska, Edmund Spaho, Zbig Karpowicz and Tony Travis.

REFERENCES

Albrecht, C., 1987, Environmental policies and politics in contemporary Czechoslovakia, *Studies in Comparative Communism,* **2**(3–4), 291–302.

Allcock, J.B., 1991, Yugoslavia, in Hall, D.R. (ed.) *Tourism and Economic Development in Eastern Europe and the Soviet Union,* Belhaven Press, London and Halstead, New York, 236–258.

Allcock, J.B. and Przeclawski, K., 1990, Introduction, *Annals of Tourism Research*, **17**, 1–6.

Anon., 1993, Hungary for change, *WWF News*, Spring, 2.

Boo, E., 1990, *Ecotourism: Potentials and Pitfalls*, 2 Vols, World Wildlife Fund, Washington.

Boo, E., 1992a, *The Concept of Visitor Carrying Capacity as it Applies to Developing Countries*, World Wildlife Fund, Washington.

Boo, E., 1992b, *The Ecotourism Boom, Planning for Development and Management*, World Wildlife Fund, Washington.

Buckley, P.J. and Witt, S.F., 1990, Tourism in the centrally-planned economies of Europe, *Annals of Tourism Research*, **17**, 7–18.

Carter, F.W., 1978, Nature reserves and national parks in Bulgaria, *L'Espace Géographique*, **1**, 69–72.

Carter, F.W., 1985, Pollution problems in post-war Czechoslovakia, *Transactions of the Institute of British Geographers (New Series)*, **10**, 17–44.

Carter, F.W., 1991a, Bulgaria, in Hall, D.R. (ed.) *Tourism and Economic Development in Eastern Europe and the Soviet Union*, Belhaven Press, London and Halstead, New York, 220–235.

Carter, F.W., 1991b, Czechoslovakia, in Hall, D.R. (ed.) *Tourism in Eastern Europe and the Soviet Union*, Belhaven Press, London and Halstead, New York, 154–172.

Carter, F.W. and Turnock, D., 1993, Problems of the pollution scenario, in *Environmental Problems in Eastern Europe*, Routledge, London, 188–213.

Cater, E., 1991, Sustainable tourism in the Third World: problems and prospects, *University of Reading Department of Geography Discussion Paper 3*.

Cater, E., 1992, Profits from paradise, *Geographical Magazine*, **64**, 16–21.

Cerovsky, J., 1990, IUCN and Eastern Europe, *IUCN Bulletin*, **21**(4), 1–4.

Cerovksy, J. and Podhaiska, Z., 1990, Czechoslovakia, in IUCN, *Environmental Status Reports 1988–1989*, Vol. 1, IUCN-EEP, Cambridge, 3–53.

Cohen, E., 1989, Alternative tourism—a critique, in Singh, B. *et al.*, *Towards Appropriate Tourism*, Lang, Frankfurt, 127–142.

Dakov, M., 1976, *Environmental Management in the People's Republic of Bulgaria*, Sofia Press, Sofia.

Dawson, A.H., 1991, Poland, in Hall, D.R. (ed.) *Tourism and Economic Development in Eastern Europe and the Soviet Union*, Belhaven Press, London and Halstead, New York, 190–202.

DDITRG (Danube Delta Institute Tourism Research Group), 1991, *Researches to Achieve a Tourism Based on the Support Capacity of Deltaic Ecosystems*, Danube Delta Institute, Tulcea.

de Kadt, E., 1990, Making the alternative sustainable: lessons from development for tourism, *Institute of Development Studies, University of Sussex, Discussion paper 272*.

Economist Intelligence Unit, 1991, *Romania: Country Profile 1991–92*, E.I.U. Publications, London.

Elkins, T., 1990, Developments in the German Democratic Republic, *Geography*, **75**, 246–249.

Forster, D.P. and Józán, P., 1990, Health in Eastern Europe, *The Lancet*, **335**, 453–460.

French, H., 1990, *Green Revolutions: Environmental Reconstruction in Eastern Europe and the Soviet Union*, Worldwatch Institute, Washington DC.

Golembski, G., 1990, Tourism in the economy of shortage, *Annals of Tourism Research*, **17**, 55–68.

Gomoiu, M.-T., 1991, *Status of the Danube Delta Biosphere Reserve Planning and Management Report 1991A*, DDBRA, Tulcea.

Hall, D.R., 1984, Foreign tourism under socialism: the Albanian 'Stalinist' model, *Annals of Tourism Research,* **11**, 539–555.

Hall, D.R., 1990a, Eastern Europe opens its doors, *Geographical Magazine,* **62**, 10–15.

Hall, D.R., 1990b, Stalinism and tourism: a study of Albania and North Korea, *Annals of Tourism Research,* **17**, 36–54.

Hall, D.R., 1990c, The changing face of tourism in Eastern Europe, *Town and Country Planning,* **59,** 348–351.

Hall, D.R., 1991a, New hope for the Danube Delta, *Town and Country Planning,* **60**, 251–252.

Hall, D.R. (ed.), 1991b, *Tourism and Economic Development in Eastern Europe,* Belhaven Press, London and Halstead, New York.

Hall, D.R., 1992a, Albania's changing tourism environment, *Journal of Cultural Geography,* **12**, 35–44.

Hall, D.R., 1992b, Czech mates no more? *Town and Country Planning,* **61**, 250–251.

Hall, D.R., 1992c, Skills transfer for appropriate development, *Town and Country Planning,* **61**, 87–89.

Hall, D.R., 1993a, *Albania into the Twenty-first Century,* Pinter, London.

Hall, D.R., 1993b, Impacts of economic and political transition on the transport geography of Central and Eastern Europe, *Journal of Transport Geography,* **1**, 20–35.

Hall, D.R., 1993c, Transport implications of tourism development, in Hall, D.R. (ed.) *Transport and Economic Development in the New Central and Eastern Europe,* Belhaven Press, London, 206–225.

Hamilton, G., 1991, Amex sets initiative for EE tourism development, *Business Eastern Europe,* **20**, 412.

Hinrichsen, D. and Enyedi, G. (eds), 1990, *State of the Hungarian Environment,* Statistical Publishing House, Budapest.

Hughes, G., 1991, Are the costs of cleaning up Eastern Europe exaggerated? Economic reform and the environment, *Oxford Review of Economic Policy,* **7**(4), 12–24.

International Union for the Conservation of Nature (IUCN), 1992, *Conservation Status of the Danube Delta, IUCN-EEP Environmental Status Reports* Vol. 4, IUCN-EEP Cambridge.

Jenner, P. and Smith, C., 1992, *The Tourism Industry and the Environment,* E.I.U. Publications, London.

Kleinhenz, C. and Hallitzky, E. 1991, *Costs and Benefits of the Sumava National Park, Management Plan for the WWF,* University of Passau, Passau.

Mellor, R.E.H., 1991, Eastern Germany, in Hall, D.R. (ed.) *Tourism and Economic Development in Eastern Europe and the Soviet Union,* Belhaven Press, London and Halstead, New York, 142–153.

Michalak, W. and Gibb, R., 1993, Development of the transport system: prospects for East/West integration, in Hall, D.R. (ed.), *Transport and Communication Development in the New Central and Eastern Europe,* Belhaven Press, London.

Murphy, P.E., 1985, *Tourism: a community approach,* Methuen, London.

Ostrowski, S., 1991, Ethnic tourism—focus on Poland, *Tourism Management,* **12**, 125–131.

Pearce, F., 1992, The wild East, *BBC Wildlife,* April, 40–42.

Ramsar, 1992, New opportunities for cooperation in Europe, *Ramsar Newsletter,* **13**, 2–7.

Reed, D., 1990, *The European Bank for Reconstruction and Development: an Environmental Opportunity,* World Wide Fund for Nature, Washington.

RMTT (Romania Ministry of Trade and Tourism), 1990, *The Programme of Modernisation and Development of the Romanian tourism 1990–1992,* Ministry of Trade and Tourism, Bucharest.

Russell, J., 1990, *Environmental Issues in Eastern Europe: Setting an Agenda,* RIIA and IUCN, London.

Shaw, D.J.B., 1991, The Soviet Union, in Hall, D.R. (ed.) *Tourism and economic development in Eastern Europe and the Soviet Union,* Belhaven Press, London and Halstead, New York, 119–141.

Sofield, T., 1991, Sustainable ethnic tourism in the South Pacific: some principles, *Journal of Tourism Studies,* **2**, 56–72.

Spaho, E., 1992, Tourism: promising contracts, *Albanian Economic Tribune,* **6**(10), 17–19.

Spaho, E., 1993, Personal interview, Deputy Minister of Tourism, Tirana, 27 March.

Springate, C., 1991, Where eagles dare, *Green Magazine,* **3**(3), 26–29.

Standring, K., 1991, Eastern bloc-buster, *Birds Illustrated,* **1**(1), 76–81.

Thompson, J., 1991, East Europe's dark dawn, *National Geographic,* **179**(5), 37–69.

Turnock, D., 1979, Water management resources in Romania, *GeoJournal,* **3**, 609–622.

Turnock, D., 1988, Woodland conservation: the emergence of rational land use policies in Romania, *GeoJournal,* **17**, 59–70.

Turnock, D., 1991, Romania, in Hall, D.R. (ed.) *Tourism and Economic Development in Eastern Europe and the Soviet Union,* Belhaven Press, London and Halstead, New York, 203–219.

Turnock, D., 1993, Romania, in Carter, F.W. and Turnock, D. (eds) *Environmental Problems in Eastern Europe,* Routledge, London, 135–163.

Vadineanu, A. and Manoleli, D., 1990, Romania, in IUCN, *Environmental Status Reports,* Vol. 2, IUCN-EEP, Cambridge, 83–131.

Waller, M., 1989, The ecology issue in Eastern Europe: protest and movements, *Journal of Communist Studies,* **5**, 303–328.

Wells, M., Brandon, K. and Hannah, L., 1992, *People and parks: Linking Protected Area Management with Local Communities,* The World Bank/World Wildlife Fund/ US Agency for International Development, Washington.

Wheeller, B., 1992, Alternative tourism—a deceptive ploy, *Progress in Tourism, Recreation and Hospitality Management,* **4**, 140–145.

Wickers, D., 1992, Whither green?, *The Sunday Times,* 5 January.

World Tourism Organisation (WTO), 1990, *Annual Yearbook of Tourism Statistics,* WTO, Madrid.

World Tourism Organisation (WTO), 1991, *Annual Yearbook of Tourism Statistics,* Vol. 1, WTO, Madrid, 104.

World Tourism Organisation (WTO), 1992, *Annual Yearbook of Tourism Statistics,* Vol. 1, WTO, Madrid, 103.

9

Ecotourism in Australia, New Zealand and the South Pacific: Appropriate Tourism or a New Form of Ecological Imperialism?

C. MICHAEL HALL

INTRODUCTION

In few regions around the world has interest in ecotourism been as pronounced as it has been in Australia, New Zealand and the countries of the South Pacific (Figure 9.1). Ecotourism has become one of the 'buzz-words' of the tourism industry in the south-west Pacific to the point where it has become a cliché (e.g. Hay, 1992). Nevertheless, the discovery of the environment by tourism marketers is no accident. Tourism is subject to broader shifts in societal values; however, the emergence of a conservation ethic in Western society has been commodified for the needs of the tourist industry. Conservation and the development of 'environmentally friendly' products has now become a major selling point of tourism destinations and specific tourist packages (Huie, 1992). As Helu-Thaman (1992: 26) argued

> Ecotourism is fast becoming the modern marketing manager's source of inspiration for the new sale. It's got a lot going for it: it gives great pictures; it offers pretty much what people want when they wish to escape from pressured polluted urban living, and it offers a sort of moral expiation of guilt for our contribution to the degradation of our own planet.

Relationship between tourism and the environment

The natural environment of the south-west Pacific is a major tourist drawcard. New Zealand promotes itself as 'clean and green' in its search for the tourist dollar, whereas Australia uses images of natural attractions such as the Great Barrier Reef, Kakadu National Park and Uluru (Ayers Rock) in its overseas promotion. Similarly, in their search for foreign exchange and economic

Ecotourism: A Sustainable Option? Edited by E. Cater and G. Lowman
© The editors and contributors. Published in 1994 by John Wiley & Sons Ltd

138

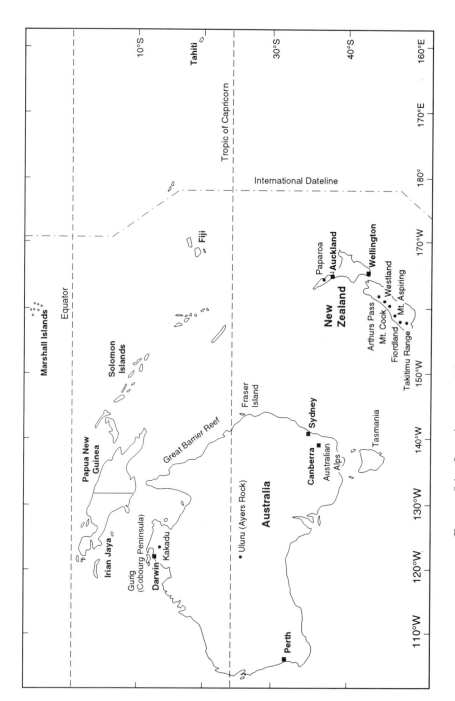

FIGURE 9.1.   Location map of the south-west Pacific

TABLE 9.1.   Recent trends in tourism to selected nations of the south-west Pacific.
Source: World Tourism Organisation (1990; 1992)

	Tourist arrivals (thousands)		Tourism receipts (US$ millions)	
	1985	1990	1985	1990
Australia	1143	3191	1062	3797
New Zealand	670	976	413	1072
Fiji	228	251	147	230
Papua New Guinea	30	41	10	28
Solomon Islands	12	9	3	4
Marshall Islands	2	7	NA	NA
French Polynesia	122	132	98	142

development many South Pacific nations are seeking to attract nature-based tourism development. Nevertheless, although the environment is one of the major attractions of the region, the dramatic increase in the number of visitors is affecting its integrity and quality. In 1980 Australia received 904 600 visitors; by 1990 the figure had more than doubled to 3.1 million (Table 9.1). For the year 2000 Australia is targeting around seven million tourists (Commonwealth Department of Tourism, 1992). Similarly, New Zealand has also witnessed rapid tourism growth. In 1980 New Zealand received 445 000 visitors and 976 000 in 1990. For the year 2000 the New Zealand Tourism Board (1991) has set a target of three million visitors.

At one time developed nations such as Australia and New Zealand regarded negative socio-cultural and physical impacts of tourism as something which happened elsewhere. However, the rapid increase in inbound tourism, greater environmental awareness, fear of foreign control and the realisation by many tourist destinations that tourism, while smokeless, is not harmless, has meant that there is now a general acknowledgement in Australia and New Zealand that tourism can have substantial negative impacts on host communities (Craik, 1991; Hall, 1991; 1992b).

Awareness of the relationship between tourism and the environment occurs in both the demand and supply components of the tourist product. The term 'ecotourism', as it is commonly used in the south-west Pacific, refers to two different dimensions of tourism which, although interrelated, pose distinct management, policy, planning and development problems (Hall, 1992b).

- ecotourism as 'green' or 'nature-based' tourism, which is essentially a form of *special interest* tourism and refers to a specific market segment and the products generated for that segment.
- ecotourism as *any* form of tourism development which is regarded as environmentally friendly

In both of its common usages, ecotourism is regarded as a positive dimension of tourism. Who can argue with the concept of a form of economic development or income generator which helps preserve the environment? The concept of ecotourism has been used as a kind of propaganda and has become 'good' or 'desirable'. Nevertheless, some words of caution have been heard (e.g. Johnston, 1990). As Berle (1990: 6) commented:

> Ecotourism is big business. It can provide foreign exchange and economic reward for the preservation of natural systems and wildlife. But ecotourism also threatens to destroy the resources on which it depends. Tour boats dump garbage in the water off Antarctica, shutterbugs harass wildlife in National Parks, hordes of us trample fragile areas. This frenzied activity threatens the viability of natural systems. At times we seem to be loving nature to death.

Concern over the impacts of inappropriate forms of ecotourism have concentrated on the effects of ecotourists on the physical environment. After all, the impacts of the footprint of an ecotourist are the same as that of a 'mass' tourist. Indeed, several workers have argued that it is essential that conservation is put back into our understanding of ecotourism (e.g. Bragg, 1990; Valentine, 1992a), particularly as ecotourism has come to represent the potentially symbiotic relationship between tourism and environmental conservation suggested in the oft-quoted paper of Budowski (1976). More often than not ecotourism has come to be regarded as tourist visitation to National Parks and Reserves. However, such a notion of ecotourism not only provides an extremely limited approach to ideas of environment, ecology and the maintenance of biodiversity, but it also indicates the inherent bias of much ecotourism toward Cartesian ideas of environmental conservation which separate humankind from nature.

In most Western societies in which land is set aside solely for conservation purposes, ecotourism occurs in designated areas in which natural heritage values predominate and in which evidence of modern human settlement is often removed or not interpreted to visitors. Nevertheless, the split of heritage into natural and cultural components is somewhat artificial, as the values which are associated with areas such as National Parks, wilderness and scientific reserves are cultural in nature. To retain an area as a National Park is as much a cultural decision, and hence a cultural landscape, as it is to use the land for grazing, intensive farming or slash/burn cultivation. Indeed, the legitimacy of the cultural practices of indigenous peoples in areas now set aside as National Parks and Reserves is slowly being recognised by some governments and conservation agencies.

For much of humanity, and particularly for the indigenous peoples of the south-west Pacific, humankind is not regarded as separate from the landscape but is part of an indivisible whole, i.e. the physical environment is an everyday lived-in experience (Hall and McArthur, 1993). However, many ecotourism businesses, consultancies, researchers and advocates, particularly some environmental conservation groups, tend to either ignore or fail to understand the quite different relationship of indigenous people and of certain local communities to their land and environment compared with Western society.

The following discussion reviews the current state of ecotourism in the south-west Pacific. Australia, New Zealand and several South Pacific nations (Figure 9.1) are examined in terms of environmental aspects of policy formulation, legislation, development and marketing. Specific attention is paid to the application of sustainable development principles to tourism and the appropriateness of ecotourism, particularly in the light of indigenous perceptions of tourism development. The chapter concludes by arguing that ecotourism has been promoted within a particularly narrow band of conservation and business thought which has failed to appreciate the role of social values within sustainable tourism development and the maintenance of biodiversity.

AUSTRALIA

Tourism is a major contributor to economic development and employment generation in Australia. Tourism is Australia's biggest export earner and accounts for approximately 5.6 per cent of the GDP. Domestic tourism accounts for almost three-quarters of tourist expenditure. Tourism accounted for an estimated 10 per cent of all new positions, both part-time and full-time, created annually in Australia from 1982 to 1989 (Economist Intelligence Unit, 1990). In the early 1990s tourism employed approximately six per cent of the workforce, with nearly all of the employment growth being generated by inbound tourism. The Australian Tourist Commission has predicted that tourism will generate 200 000 new jobs in the next decade and generate between A\$20 billion and \$30 billion in income from overseas (Edwards and Murphy, 1992: 33). The national government emphasises inbound tourism because of the potential foreign exchange earnings and their contribution to the balance of payments (Hall, 1991). However, although tourism is improving Australia's balance of payments by virtue of the substantial contribution international visitors make to export income, this contribution is offset by the social and environmental impacts of tourism.

Managing tourism's impact on the environment

One of the primary costs of the substantial growth of inbound tourism in Australia is the impact of increased visitation on the physical environment. Major destination regions such as the Great Barrier Reef, the Australian Alps, Fraser Island, the Tasmanian Wilderness Parks, Kakadu National Park and Uluru National Park (Ayers Rock) are all starting to show the effects of both direct visitor impacts, such as trampling, and associated impacts through the construction of tourist facilities, particularly in coastal regions (Craik, 1991; Hall, 1991).

Tourism operators are increasingly becoming aware of the pressures that are being placed upon them by environmentalists and are responding with the development of guidelines for operators. For example, the Australian Tourism Industry Association (1989) has put considerable effort into the production of a self-regulatory code of environmental practice that members should adhere to; the West Australian Government has been developing a set of guidelines for sustainable tourism development (O'Brien 1989), whereas the Commonwealth (federal) Government has also produced a report in its own search for sustainable forms of tourism development (Ecologically Sustainable Development Working Groups, 1991). However, despite the value of such codes and guidelines in raising industry awareness of environmental issues, considerable doubts may be expressed at the efficacy of a self-regulatory code without accompanying consideration of the strategic planning and policy implications of tourism development (Dutton and Hall, 1990; Hall, 1992b). Indeed, such developments may have only occurred to reduce the likelihood of greater government intervention in the environmental dimensions of the tourism industry.

One of the major difficulties in managing the impact of tourism on the environment in Australia is the nature of the country's political system. Australia is a federation in which primary constitutional responsibility for environmental management and land use lie with the individual states. The Commonwealth Government has only a limited range of powers relating to foreign affairs, trade, commerce and foreign investment, which can be used in relation to environmental matters. Similarly, in the case of tourism promotion, marketing and planning, control is divided between the Commonwealth and the States (Hall, 1991). Nevertheless, under the Labour Government which has been in power since 1983, the Commonwealth has attempted to provide leadership on environmental issues, particularly in terms of promoting the notion of sustainable development.

In 1990 the Commonwealth Government established a series of Ecologically Sustainable Development Working Groups to develop a series of sustainable development strategies for Australia's major industry groups, including tourism. Although the recognition of the need for ecologically sustainable tourism is laudable, and clearly necessary in a country such as Australia which suffers from substantial environmental degradation as a result of tourist activities (Craik, 1991; Hall, 1991; 1992a), two problems arise in the activities of the Working Groups. Firstly, given the limited legal powers open to the Commonwealth in tourism and land use matters, the recommendations of the Working Groups are extremely difficult to implement at all levels of government in Australia. Secondly, the focus of the Working Groups on *ecologically sustainable* development fails to pay adequate attention to the integration of economic, ecological and social factors within the idea of sustainable development (e.g. Redclift, 1987; Turner, 1988; Pearce *et al.*, 1990).

The concept of the environment in the search for sustainable forms of tourism development, such as ecotourism, must include social factors as well as physical features. As Brookfield (1991: 42) has argued, environmental sustainability not only refers to environmental regeneration and the maintenance of biodiversity, but must also 'be measured by progress along a vector made up of attributes that include improvements in income and its distribution, in health, in education, freedoms, and access to resources'.

The Ecologically Sustainable Development Working Groups (1991: 41) have suggested that tourism will move towards ecological sustainability if it

- develops in accordance with the wisest use of environmental resources and services at the national, regional and local levels
- operates within the biophysical limits of natural resource use
- maintains a full range of recreational, educational and cultural opportunities across generations
- maintains biodiversity and ecological systems and processes
- develops in a manner which does not compromise the capacity of other sectors of the economy to achieve ecological sustainability

Inclusion of the social dimension

Undoubtedly, the findings of the Working Groups are part way along the path to sustainability, but the missing element in the programme is the social dimension of the relationship between tourism and the environment. Ecotourism in Australia, as elsewhere in the region, tends to be seen in terms of visits to National Parks and other 'natural landscapes'. However, many conservationists and visitors fail to realise that they are seeing a cultural landscape that has developed in response to 50 000 years of Aboriginal land management practices and 200 years of European introductions.

In many of Australia's National Parks and public lands the traditional landowners are seeking a degree of control over the lands they lost with the coming of the European colonists. Some National Parks, such as Gurig, Kakadu and Uluru in the Northern Territory are Aboriginal-owned and leased back to the management agency. They are living, dynamic examples of the interrelationship between society and nature. Ecotourism is strongly promoted in the Northern Territory. However, there is a fear from many Aboriginal groups that contact with tourists may devalue Aboriginal culture and lead to further social breakdown in some communities. For example, Mr S. Brennan from the Bureau of the Northern Land Council commented that Gagudju people in the Kakadu region of the Northern Territory 'do not like the idea of being a bit like a zoo, feeling that they are on display for tourists to come and see what an Aboriginal person looks like in his environment, to see whether he still walks around with a spear. They certainly do not like that concept of tourism' (in Senate Standing Committee on Environment, Recreation and the Arts 1988: 28–9).

In the case of Gurig National Park, the Cobourg Peninsula Sanctuary Board established a small-scale tourism development, Seven Spirit Bay, to provide additional income for the traditional owners. The lodge and associated infrastructure were subject to stringent environmental planning and design standards. The traditional owners also provide a range of activities for visitors which highlight Aboriginal use of the environment. At all times, however, ultimate control over this extremely successful ecotourism development, which has won numerous tourism awards, has rested with the traditional owners (Metcalfe, 1992).

Both the Australian Tourism Commission, the authority chartered with the responsibility of promoting Australia overseas, and the various state tourism commissions have embraced ecotourism as a promotional mechanism and for the development of the new tourist product. For example, the Victorian Department of Conservation and the Environment (1992a) has produced an ecotourism brochure which lists 38 different products available in the state ranging from visits to National Parks to trips to the zoo. In addition, the Department has produced a detailed strategic policy and marketing document on the value of the ecotourism market to Victoria (Department of Conservation and the Environment, 1992b). However, although employment benefits of nature conservation and positive economic returns are highlighted, the broader social impacts of ecotourism are ignored.

Australia is placing substantial emphasis on tourism as a source of employment and economic development. Ecotourism is regarded as a major market segment to be targeted for the development and promotion of the nature-based tourist product. At the national level ecotourism has been tied in with attempts to develop policies for ecologically sustainable tourism, whereas at the state level ecotourism has been embraced as a mechanism to provide financial assistance for the National Park system and to create employment where other alternative land uses such as mining, grazing or timber cutting can be prohibited. At all levels of government the focus on ecotourism has been marked by a lack of understanding of the social dimensions of ecotourism and the effects of visitors on host communities and their relationship with the environment. With the exception of a few product developments, such as Seven Spirit Bay, tourism has been linked with the economy and the environment, but the third element of sustainability, that of society, has been sadly missing.

NEW ZEALAND

Nature-based and heritage orientated tourism is given considerable prominence in New Zealand's domestic and international tourism marketing strategies. New Zealand is marketed as 'clean and green' to the overseas visitor (Burt, 1992). Somewhat paradoxically, the New Zealand Tourism Board (1991: 11) in its strategic plan has described this image as 'boring', even though they also note that 'interest in the environment is a major theme' in global tourism trends 'which New Zealand's marketing must address'. Nevertheless, ecotourism-type activities have been a major feature of New Zealand's tourism product development in recent years, with the New Zealand Tourism Board's Natural Heritage Guide (1993) listing 49 operators active in the field. In addition, several regions, such as Coromandel and the West Coast of South Island, are concentrating on attracting the ecotourism market segment (Pacific Asia Travel Association, 1991).

Natural heritage attractions such as regional parks, urban parks and public gardens attract large numbers of domestic and international tourists. According to the 1991 Deloitte Ross Tohmatsu annual survey of attractions, natural attractions accounted for 28.9 per cent of all visits in New Zealand, a total of approximately 4.95 million visits. This figure did not include visits to New Zealand's National Parks. Indeed, although figures on National Parks visitation are not well maintained by the Department of Conservation, Molloy (1993) has noted that approximately 55 per cent of all overseas tourists visit a National Park during their stay in New Zealand. According to Dingwall (1992: 118), 'A 1989 survey revealed that 21 sites are experiencing severe impacts on existing facilities'. Therefore, it would appear that the three-fold increase in inbound tourism sought by the New Zealand Tourism Board, noted above, would potentially have a major impact on New Zealand's conservation estate.

Domestic interest in ecotourism-related activities is also high. The New Zealand Tourism and Publicity Department's 1989 domestic travel segmentation study categorised 21 per cent of the New Zealand population (12 per cent of the annual holiday volume) as 'heritage minded' tourists. Preferred holiday activities included visits to historic sites, museums, art galleries and exploring National and Forest Parks. In terms of general attitudes the sample of tourists questioned expressed concerns about the environment and a desire for the keeping of Maori culture.

Conflicting views on environmental conservation and the role of ecotourism

The role of Maori people in tourism is emerging as a major issue in New Zealand. Since the early 1970s there has been a renaissance of Maori culture, which has been reinforced by formal legal measures to give weight to Maori rights under the Treaty of Waitangi, signed between the British Crown and Maori chiefs in 1840. Maori people, who make up approximately 13 per cent of New Zealand's population, traditionally have extremely close ties to the land. In promoting ecotourism in New Zealand it is therefore becoming apparent that failing to address Maori concerns over the relationship between tourism and environment may not only restrict a richer understanding of the environment for visitors, but is also culturally insensitive (Hall *et al.*, 1992).

The increase in European (*Pakeha*) concern for the natural heritage of New Zealand is seen by some Maoris as prejudicially affecting them. For example, Maori groups at present own more than 50 per cent of native bushland in private hands, the reservation of which has been a central point of *Pakeha* conservation group concerns over the past 20 years. As one Maori put it '*Pakehas* are all conservationists when it comes to Maori land—the *Pakeha* attitude seems to be what's yours is ours, but what's mine is my own' (*The Dominion*, 18 October 1989).

The divergence in Western and Maori perceptions of environmental conservation can be illustrated in the Ngai Tahu claim to the Waitangi Tribunal, which examines and makes recommendations on Maori grievances concerning the implementation of the Treaty. The claim amounted to more than 70 per cent of South Island and included substantial portions of National Parks, high country areas and lakes and waterways. Aspirations of the Ngai Tahu in respect to some of the Crown Lands which they claim and which relate directly to ecotourism include (Barr, 1992)

- joint title to all or some National Parks in the claim area; these parks are Fiordland, Mt Aspiring, Mt Cook, Westland, Arthur's Pass and Paparoa
- some responsibility for management of some or all of the parks, called co-management
- sole responsibility to control tourism and possibly other concessions in parks—the Ngai Tahu have said they will give preference to Maoris and to concessions 'with the right culture'
- outright legal title to natural features of special cultural value including Mt Cook and the Takitimu Range in Southland

Many *Pakeha* are concerned that Maori land claims will prohibit tourist access to natural areas. The Federated Mountain Clubs (FMC), in their submission to the Waitangi Tribunal on the Ngai Tahu claim, expressed concern about transferring areas of Crown Land, which have recreation and conservation value, into Maori title (Hall *et al.*, 1993). They argued that privatisation of any Crown Land will reduce freedom of access for the general public to enjoy such lands (by banning access or charging entrance fees). The FMC do not question the validity of the Maori claims, but their attitude indicates the difficulties of reconciling Western and indigenous notions of appropriate environmental conservation measures. For example, with reference to the possibility of National Park land being transferred to Maori control, the FMC argue (Barr, 1992:9):

But even if the Ngai Tahu were the greenest group in the nation, they shouldn't be granted control, because whoever manages these lands must be answerable to the people, and private owners are not . . .

Maori claims cover almost all of our country. If private land is excluded, then most of the land left is conservation land. If the Ngai Tahu claims are successful they will have set an unstoppable precedent that other tribes will want to follow.

Barr's comments indicate the potential implications for ecotourism from Maori claims. Many Maori people do want greater control and input into product promotion, visitor interpretation and tourism development. Tourism is seen by the Maori as an employment generator, but many also have substantial reservations as to its cultural impacts and they fear a loss of control over their heritage. Several Maori ecotourism operations, the most famous being the whalewatching operation at Kaikoura in South Island, have illustrated the potential benefits of ecotourism for Maori people, but the *tangata whenua* (people of the land) have generally not, as yet, become substantially involved in the management of New Zealand's National Parks and Reserves (James, 1991). The Resource Management Act 1991, which incorporates sustainability into legislation and which compels local government to consult with the Maori on any aspect of policy which affects Maori cultural rights, will also have major impacts on ecotourism developments, although given the recency of the legislation the full effects are as yet unknown (Ministry of Tourism, 1992a; 1992b).

Ecotourism is destined to be a major feature of the promotion of New Zealand overseas. Nevertheless, the target of three million visitors by the year 2000 is bound to have significant environmental consequences. The government is using a combination of factors to manage environmental impacts, including legislation, economic instruments and industry self-management, but the value of these measures remains unknown given the recent radical restructuring of government involvement in tourism in New Zealand (Hall, 1993). However, the greatest challenge facing ecotourism development will be the ability of the tourism industry and government to understand and meet the wishes of the Maori people to control their relationship with the environment.

SOUTH PACIFIC

What we have seen so far in terms of tourism development in the Pacific Islands has made some of us rather pessimistic about the potential of Ecotourism and to ask whether it is really in our best long-term interests (Helu-Thaman, 1992: 26)

The small island nations of the South Pacific lie at the margins of the world economy and face massive problems of economic and social development. Given the slow rates of economic development and increasing population pressures, great importance has been attached by Pacific Island governments to service sector activities such as tourism. 'For island states that have very few resources, virtually the only resources where there may be some comparative advantage in favour of (island microstates) are clean beaches, unpolluted seas and warm weather and water, and at least vestiges of distinctive cultures' (Connell, 1988: 62). Although many Pacific islands appear to have competitive advantages in natural tourism resources, they lack the capital to develop tourism infrastructures and products. Therefore, the South Pacific is highly dependent on foreign Aid and investment programmes from Australia, France and New Zealand, with Japan becoming a major Aid provider in recent years (Hall, 1993).

In global terms the South Pacific island region accounts for only approximately 0.15 per cent of the world's international tourism arrivals, with an estimated 621 000 arrivals in 1991, of which two-thirds are taken up by Fiji (42 per cent) and Tahiti (26 per cent) (Yacoumis, 1990; Kudu, 1992). In spite of its small size in global terms, tourism is one of the mainstays of the region's economy and is a major employment provider for many of the countries in the region (Milne, 1992). The projected growth in intra-Pacific travel and special interest tourism activities is seen as holding good prospects for further tourism growth and lessening dependence on external aid, despite long-held concerns over foreign ownership, uneven patterns of economic development and negative socio-cultural and environmental impacts (Farrell, 1977; Finney and Watson, 1977; Rajotte and Crocombe 1980; Rajotte 1982; Milne, 1992).

The environment, long part of the attractiveness of the South Pacific to pleasure tourists, has become a major component of tourism development in the region. The European Union (EU) funded Tourism Council of the South Pacific (TCSP) has undertaken a series of visitor surveys in member countries which indicated that between 50 and 80 per cent of all tourists to the region felt that the natural environment was one of the principal attractions of the host country (Kudu, 1992).

Promotion of ecotourism in the South Pacific

Under the EU-funded Pacific Regional Tourism Development Programme (PRTDP), the TCSP has been actively promoting ecotourism projects. As part of the PRTDP the TCSP has released a series of reports on nature legislation, nature conservation and development guidelines and their relationship with ecotourism. In addition, the PRTDP has helped fund a series of pilot ecotourism projects and regional tourism product development schemes. However, despite the funding and production of numerous reports and consultancies advocating the establishment of protected areas such as National Parks, wildlife reserves and forest parks in the South Pacific (e.g. TCSP, 1988), 'It has been found that not many protected areas have actually been established and very few areas have been established as protected areas with the prime aim of attracting tourism' (Kudu, 1992: 158). According to Kudu, the most common reason for this situation, 'is that there does not seem to be a need by the residents of the area, and when this perception is coupled by the problem of land tenure—you are not going very far' (Kudu, 1992: 158).

Ecotourism is being promoted by the TCSP to ensure the establishment of protected areas on communal land through the 'potential of considerable economic benefits to the landowners'. Nevertheless, 'the TCSP is cognizant of the problems of convincing communal landowners that their land often serves them better unexploited than exploited, particularly as exploitation often provides the landowners with immediate and visible economic benefits (Kudu, 1992: 158). The TCSP primarily perceives the difficulties in establishing nature reserves, supported by ecotourism development, as being the result of the failure of the indigenous people to see the economic returns that would accrue to them from ecotourism. It is suggested that the problem lies with the local communities and not the TCSP, the consultants, conservation groups, or the tourism industry. However, is this in fact the case?

Much of the driving force for the promotion of ecotourism comes from foreign donors, investors, academic institutions, consultants and conservation groups, such as the World Wide Fund for Nature, Greenpeace and the Maruia Society, who perceive ecotourism as an opportunity to conserve a particular aspect of the environment through the reservation process, and from the local élites who can gain financially (Lees, 1991; 1992; Alebua, 1992; Hamilton and Nena, 1992; Rapaport, 1992; Sofield, 1992; Young, 1992). Undoubtedly, the environment is of critical economic and social importance to the indigenous peoples of the Pacific. The biodiversity of the land and water resources is the element which sustains human society and economy. In this context, the environment has been conserved for millennia, but perhaps more importantly Westerners need to recognise that for the indigenous peoples of the South Pacific the environment is above all a cultural resource (Helu-Thaman, 1992). However, in the promotion of the vast majority of ecotourism projects in the region, such as those proposed by the TCSP, the environment is primarily seen as an economic and ecological resource only.

Ecotourism is promoted as an opportunity to halt or restrict the local use of natural resources which some Western conservationists perceive as ecologically harmful and replace them with an economic alternative in the form of tourism. For example, in the case of Wotho Atoll in the Marshall Islands, a project undertaken by the East–West Centre, the Pacific Island Network and the Government of the Republic of the Marshall Islands includes a proposal that three islets be given protection with no harvesting of birds, crabs, turtles and other marine species from adjacent reefs. In return the island community would receive 'capital and technical support to establish a small scale ecotourism venture; two or three thatched cottages with associated facilities, including nature interpretation. The weekly air service would provide adequate access and allow a small flow of nature tourists to visit this exquisite jewel in the Pacific' (Valentine, 1992a: 7).

Conflicting views and interests

Land tenure systems vary throughout the South Pacific, but are generally based on patterns of communal land ownership. Often negotiations on land use, such as the harvest of timber or the conservation of forests through reservation and ecotourism, are not undertaken by national or provincial governments, but directly between developers and the custom landowners (Fuavao, 1992). Despite the attentions of the TCSP to the establishment of conservation legislation for tourism, 'existing legislation is usually unenforceable, particularly where it conflicts with the national culture' (Fuavao, 1992: 153). Indeed, he also notes that the weight of environmental policy and the degree of on-site control that government agencies have is quite restricted and, in some cases, may expose landowners to exploitation.

Despite its claim for a high moral ground over mass forms of tourism (Hall, 1992b), ecotourism can have substantial social impacts on host communities. In the case of Society Expedition's ship *World Discoverer*'s visit to northern Australia and Papua New Guinea, Goodfellow (1992) argued that even though the company promoted tourism that was relatively ecologically and culturally sensitive (Society Expedition's motto is 'leave only footprints'), substantial cultural impacts still occurred. For example, many passengers, who were largely wealthy, elderly Americans and Europeans, felt it hard to accept local practices in terms of the killing of animals such as crocodiles and turtles, whereas in the case of several Asmat villages in Irian Jaya, traditional customs and trading patterns were clearly being distorted by the tourist presence as they were gradually being brought into a cash economy. As Goodfellow (1992: 29) observed in the case of the reactions of the tourists who had visited the villages

> Some were completely sobered by the thoughts of what we might have left behind and said they would never return. They had come to find common ground with another culture and perhaps to discover warmth and acceptance lacking in their own. In doing so they threaten to destroy the very values they held in high esteem.

Inappropriate ecotourism can also have marked effects on community social structures. The TCSP has placed a substantial proportion of EU funds into the development of ecotourism in the Solomon Islands in recent years. Ecotourism has been seen as a potential alternative to the logging of lowland rainforest by providing for the reservation of rainforest species. As the Solomon Islands tourism development plan states (TCSP, 1990a: 42)

In those areas where environmental protection is needed, tourism can provide the custom owner with the needed cash, the area is left undisturbed, and the cash return is ongoing.

Tourism, therefore, allows for cash to be received for the privilege of visiting the land, but with no resource depletion. Economic benefits are thus gained with future land use options being retained.

In traditional indigenous Solomon Islands' society 'custodianship of the land was so central to the culture that any new idea which impinged on land rights would be greeted with caution' (Sofield, 1992: 90). However, Melanesian society has been drastically affected by Westernisation, although significant attention is still given to 'big men' and consensus decision-making in non-urban areas. Nevertheless, Kudu (in Sofield, 1992: 90), a Solomon Islander who is Director of Development and Planning for the TCSP, has suggested that traditional values have been eroded to the point that 'when it comes to placing priority in terms of environment versus commercial venture, the determining factor is always the question of benefits, not so much collectively but individually'. According to Sofield the increasing individualisation of the Solomon Islands' society has led to the exploitation of lowland rainforest (Sofield, 1992: 91)

> The slow move towards a cash economy has contributed to a breakdown of the previously strong moral sanctions supporting conservation practices at a clan level.
>
> Often individual rights will be pursued over clan rights as exploitative practices accelerated access to consumer goods, creating intra-clan conflict. It should be noted that the ability to exploit timber resources for virtually instant wealth is reinforced by that fundamental element of Melanesian society . . . the constant striving for 'big man' status and consequent competition among 'big men'. The very structure of Melanesian society impels landowners to sell their trees to the highest bidder . . .

So is ecotourism an alternative?

Alebua (1992: 38) has observed that conservation organisations, such as the Australian Conservation Foundation, have tried to introduce environmental education programmes, but they 'offered idealism without cash, and the resource owners decided to stick with the logging companies'. In contrast, since the late 1980s a series of government and consultants' reports, mainly funded by the EU, Australia and New Zealand, has recommended the establishment of a representative protected reserves system for the Solomon Islands which is funded through ecotourism projects (TCSP, 1990a; Lees, 1991). However, substantial problems have emerged in the implementation of the protected forests system because of community doubts as to the benefits of ecotourism developments (Rudkin, 1994). As Fuavao (1992: 152) commented, Pacific islanders 'do not want the pursuit of material benefits to undermine their cultural systems and values, nor to cause any permanent harm to the land and marine resources which allowed them to sustain island life for many centuries'.

In her study of ecotourism in the Solomon Islands, Rudkin (1994) noted that the development proposals put forward by the TCSP, Western conservation organisations and Aid donors served only to reinforce the power and wealth of 'big men' at the expense of the wider indigenous community. The attraction of ecotourism for big men is therefore no different than that of timber cutting. For example, Sofield (1992: 97) noted that the Guadalcanal rainforest wilderness trail, proposed by him in 1988, only became possible because of the intervention of a former Prime Minister, Ezekiel Alebua, 'a prominent Solomon Islands "big man" who is a customary landowner from the area'.

The input of Western funds to achieve the twin goals of economic and social development and the conservation of biodiversity is laudable. Unfortunately, such funds often seem to benefit the local élite, developers and consultants rather than being distributed at the village level. The combined interests of Western conservation and tourism interests and local 'big men' has meant that many communities are unaware of tourism development proposals, but even when objections and concerns are voiced their wishes may be ignored. Kudu (1992: 158) observed that ecotourism projects need 'to be managed by local landowners' so that they are 'not seen as an alien imposition'. However, Rudkin (1994) has gone further and has argued that a more representative decision-making process is required which integrates social, economic and environmental considerations and gives the final say on ecotourism developments to the residents of villages, rather than the developers or 'big men', often residing in urban centres. She observed that in sharp contradiction to the tourism development plan for the Solomon Islands quoted above, ecotourism does deplete local resources. The hosting of tourists can strain the food and water resources of a semi-subsistence economy, take time away from food production and places pressure on what little infrastructure exists. In addition, she noted that the difficulty in providing tourist access to sites, the threat of tropical diseases such as malaria, the erosion of walking tracks and the impact of cyclones, all combine to make ecotourism an unsustainable form of development.

The countries of the South Pacific face major problems of economic and social development. Tourism is one of the primary measures which governments of the region see as able to achieve development objectives. Given current interest in the environment in tourism-generating regions and the area's unique flora and fauna, ecotourism has been seized upon as a means to generate both income and conserve the environment. However, Western notions of conservation and the promise of ecotourism have not been widely supported at the 'grass roots' level because of different cultural perceptions of the relationship between society and the environment. Some ecotourism proposals have served to reinforce the local élite rather than distribute income throughout the destination region. Without further critical appraisal and a greater awareness of the social dimensions of development and its interrelationship with environment and economy, ecotourism may therefore extend the dependency of the region on foreign capital rather than become a force for self-sufficiency and cultural and economic independence.

ECOTOURISM: APPROPRIATE TOURISM OR A NEW FORM OF ECOLOGICAL IMPERIALISM?

Tourism is an environmentally dependent industry. Ecotourism is only the latest expression of this relationship. Different concepts of 'ecotourism' meaning different things have led to a substantial loss in the explanatory power of the term and its potential to be a rallying point for those wanting to ensure that tourism can contribute to sustainable development. This has been particularly apparent in the south-west Pacific where many, often urban, supporters of ecotourism have focused on species preservation at the expense of indigenous peoples and local communities. If ecotourism is everything, then maybe it is nothing! We should go beyond ecotourism and start talking of 'sustainable' or 'appropriate' tourism which emphasises the connectivity of ecology, society and economy in sustainable tourism development and the role of local people in making decisions which affect their land and senses of place. For example, Helu-Thaman (1992) refers to the need for 'ecocultural' tourism in the South Pacific rather than ecotourism *per se* because she seeks to emphasise the cultural context within which ecotourism occurs.

Ecotourism development needs to be based not on the culture of the tourist or developers, Aid-givers or conservation groups, but on the values and culture of the host community. Throughout the south-west Pacific, many nature-based tour operators have neglected the concerns of local people, particularly indigenous peoples. The natural environment is a cultural resource, a factor of particular significance when the rights and heritage values of indigenous peoples have often been ignored.

In his book *Ecological Imperialism: the Biological Expansion of Europe, 900–1900*, Crosby (1986) describes the, sometimes forced, Europeanisation of the global environment through the spread of the plant and animal species most desired by European peoples. In the current age of supposed environmental awareness, many European peoples are seeking ways to restrain gene, species and ecosystem loss and preserve biodiversity through National Park and associated reserve systems. Ecotourism is being promoted throughout the world, and in the south-west Pacific in particular, as a means to achieve both environmental conservation and economic return in conjunction with these systems. Undoubtedly, the maintenance of biodiversity is a critical component of sustainable development. However, sustainable development also teaches us that the environment and economy are integrated with society. Many promoters of ecotourism in the south-west Pacific have either forgotten or ignored this lesson. Therefore, we are perhaps facing a form of ecological imperialism in the region in which a new set of European cultural values is being impressed on indigenous cultures through ecotourism development.

Ecotourism does have a part to play in economic development and environmental conservation. However, to neglect the social dimension of development and people's relationshp to their environment is in opposition to the principles of sustainable development which ecotourism is supposedly supporting and implementing.

ACKNOWLEDGEMENTS

The author gratefully acknowledges the assistance of Brenda Rudkin, Brian Springett and Jody Cowper in the preparation of this chapter.

REFERENCES

Alebua, E., 1992, Eco-forestry in Solomon Islands, *The Courier*, **132**, 38–39.

Australian Tourism Industry Association (ATIA), 1989, *An Environmental Code of Practice for the Tourism Industry, Second Draft*, ATIA, Canberra.

Barr, H., 1992, Worries over Maori bid to control parks, *The Dominion*, 21 July, 6.

Berle, P.A., 1990, Two faces of ecotourism, *Audobon*, **92** (2), 6.

Bragg, L., 1990, Ecotourism: a working definition, *Institute for Tropical Rainforest Studies Newsletter*, **2**(2), 7.

Brookfield, H., 1991, Environmental sustainability with development: what prospects for a research agenda? in Stokke, O. (ed.) *Sustainable Development*, Frank Cass, London, 42–46.

Budowski, G., 1976, Tourism and conservation: conflict, coexistence or symbiosis, *Environmental Conservation*, **3**(1), 27–31.

Burt, D., 1992, Marketing New Zealand's natural heritage to the international visitor, in Hay, J.E. (ed.) *Ecotourism Business in the Pacific: Promoting a Sustainable Experience, Conference Proceedings*, Environmental Science, University of Auckland, Auckland, 214–218.

Commonwealth Department of Tourism, 1992, *Tourism Australia's Passport to Growth: a National Tourism Strategy*, Department of Tourism, Canberra.

Connell, J., 1988, Sovereignty and survival: island microstates in the third world, *Research Monograph No. 3*, Department of Geography, University of Sydney, Sydney.

Craik, J., 1991, *Resorting to Tourism: Cultural Policies for Tourist Development*, Allen and Unwin, Sydney.

Crosby, A.W., 1986, *Ecological Imperialism: the Biological Expansion of Europe, 900–1900*, Cambridge University Press, Cambridge.

Deloitte Ross Tohmatsu, 1991, *New Zealand Tourist Attraction Survey 1991*, Deloitte Ross Tohmatsu Tourism and Leisure Consulting Group, Wellington.

Department of Conservation and the Environment, 1992a, *Ecotourism Victoria Australia*, Department of Conservation and the Environment, Melbourne.

Department of Conservation and the Environment, 1992b, *Ecotourism a Natural Strength for Victoria—Australia*, Department of Conservation and the Environment, Melbourne.

Dingwall, P.R., 1992, Tourism in protected areas: conflict or saviour? in *Heritage Management: Parks, Heritage and Tourism*, Royal Australian Institute of Parks and Recreation, Hobart, 117–122.

Dutton, I. and Hall, C.M., 1990, Making tourism sustainable: the policy/practice conundrum, in *Environment, Tourism and Development: an Agenda for Action? A Workshop to Consider Strategies for Sustainable Tourism Development*, Centre for Environmental Management and Planning, Old Aberdeen.

Ecologically Sustainable Development Working Groups, 1991, *Final Report—Tourism*, Australian Government Publishing Service, Canberra.

Economist Intelligence Unit, 1990, Australia, *EIU International Tourism Reports*, No. 4, 64–83.

Edwards, K. and Murphy, D., 1992, Mixed blessings, *Time Australia*, **7**(6), 32–41.

Farrell, B.H. (ed.), 1977, *The Social and Economic Impact of Tourism on Pacific Communities*, Center for South Pacific Studies, University of California, Santa Cruz.

Finney, B.R. and Watson, K.A. (eds), 1977, *A New Kind of Sugar: Tourism in the Pacific*, Center for South Pacific Studies, University of California Santa Cruz, Santa Cruz.

Fuavao, V.A., 1992, Operating within natural policy and legal environments, in Hay, J.E. (ed.) *Ecotourism Business in the Pacific: Promoting a Sustainable Experience, Conference Proceedings*, Environmental Science, University of Auckland, Auckland, 151–153.

Goodfellow, D., 1992, Hosts versus guests—the desires and concerns of the passengers on Society Expedition's ship *World Discoverer*, in Weiler, B. (ed.) *Ecotourism Incorporating The Global Classroom, 1991, International Conference Papers*, Bureau of Tourism Research, Canberra, 26–29.

Hall, C.M., 1991, *Introduction of Tourism in Australia: Impacts, Planning and Development*, Longman Cheshire, South Melbourne.

Hall, C.M., 1992a, *Wasteland to World Heritage: Preserving Australia's Wilderness*, Melbourne University Press, Carlton.

Hall, C.M., 1992b, Issues in ecotourism: from susceptible to sustainable development, in *Heritage Management: Parks, Heritage and Tourism*, Royal Australian Institute of Parks and Recreation, Hobart.

Hall, C.M., 1993, *Introduction to tourism in the Pacific: development, impacts and markets*, Longman Cheshire, South Melbourne.

Hall, C.M. and McArthur, S., 1993, Heritage management: an introductory framework, in Hall, C.M. and McArthur, S. (eds) *Heritage management in New Zealand and Australia: Visitor Management, Interpretation and Marketing*, Oxford University Press, Auckland, 1–17.

Hall, C.M., Mitchell, I. and Keelan, N., 1992, Maori culture and heritage tourism in New Zealand, *Journal of Cultural Geography*, **12**(3), 115–128.

Hall, C.M., Keelan, N. and Mitchell, I., The implications of Maori perspectives on the interpretation, management and promotion of tourism in New Zealand, *Geojournal*, in press.

Hamilton, L.S. and Nena, M., 1992, Assessment of coastal resources for nature conservation and nature tourism, Kosrae Island State F.S.M., in Hay, J.E. (ed.) *Ecotourism Business in the Pacific: Promoting a Sustainable Experience, Conference Proceedings*, Environmental Science, University of Auckland, Auckland, 79–85.

Hay, J.E. (ed.), 1992, *Ecotourism Business in the Pacific: Promoting a Sustainable Experience, Conference Proceedings*, Environmental Science, University of Auckland, Auckland.

Helu-Thaman, K., 1992, Ecocultural tourism: a personal view for maintaining cultural integrity in ecotourism development, in Hay, J.E. (ed.) *Ecotourism Business in the Pacific: Promoting a Sustainable Experience, Conference Proceedings*, Environmental Science, University of Auckland, Auckland, 24–29.

Huie, J., 1992, Trends in tourism today and their relevance to parks and heritage, in *Heritage Management: Parks, Heritage and Tourism*, Royal Australian Institute of Parks and Recreation, Hobart, 8–14.

James, B., 1991, Public participation in Department of Conservation management planning, *New Zealand Geographer*, **47**(2), 51–59.

Johnston, B.R., 1990, Introduction: breaking out of the tourist trap, *Cultural Survival Quarterly*, **14**(1), 2–5.

Kudu, D., 1992, The role and activities of the Tourism Council of the South Pacific, particularly in relation to ecotourism development, in Hay, J.E. (ed.) *Ecotourism Business in the Pacific: Promoting a Sustainable Experience, Conference Proceedings*, Environmental Science, University of Auckland, Auckland, 154–160.

Lees, A., 1991, A representative protected forests system for the Solomon Islands, *Report to the Australian National Parks and Wildlife Service*, Maruia Society, Nelson.

Lees, A., 1992, Ecotourism—restraining the big promise, in Hay, J.E. (ed.) *Ecotourism Business in the Pacific: Promoting a Sustainable Experience, Conference Proceedings*, Environmental Science, University of Auckland, Auckland, 61–64.

Metcalfe, D., 1992, Seven Spirit Bay: an ecotourism development in Western Arnhem Land, Northern Territory in Weiler, B. (ed.) *Ecotourism Incorporating The Global Classroom, 1991 international conference papers*, Bureau of Tourism Research, Canberra, 199–207.

Milne, S., 1992, Tourism and development in South Pacific microstates, *Annals of Tourism Research*, **19**(3), 191–212.

Ministry of Tourism, 1992a, *Tourism Sustainability: a Discussion Paper*, Ministry of Tourism, Wellington.

Ministry of Tourism, 1992b, *Resource Management Act: a Guide for the Tourism Industry*, Ministry of Tourism, Wellington.

Malloy, L., 1993, The interpretation of New Zealand's natural heritage, in Hall, C.M. and McArthur, S. (eds) *Heritage Management in New Zealand and Australia: Visitor management, Interpretation, and Marketing*, Oxford University Press, Auckland, 59–60.

New Zealand Tourism and Publicity Department, 1991, *Domestic Travel Segmentation Study*, New Zealand Tourism and Publicity Department, Wellington.

New Zealand Tourism Board, 1991, *Tourism in New Zealand: a Strategy for Growth*, New Zealand Tourism Board, Wellington.

New Zealand Tourism Board, 1993, *New Zealand: Natural Heritage Guide*, New Zealand Tourism Board, Wellington.

O'Brien, B., 1989, *The Eco Ethics of Tourism Development*, Western Australian Tourism Commission and Environmental Protection Authority, Perth.

Pacific Asia Travel Association, 1991, *The Coromandel Experience: a PATA Task Force Study*, Pacific Asia Travel Association, Sydney.

Pearce, D.W., Barbier, E.B. and Markandya, A., 1990, *Sustainable Development: Economics and Environment in the Third World*, Edward Elgar, Aldershot.

Rajotte, F., (ed.), 1982, *The Impact of Tourism Development in the Pacific*, Environmental and Resource Studies Programme, Trent University, Peterborough.

Rajotte, F. and Crocombe, R. (eds), 1980, *Pacific Tourism as Islanders See It*, Institute of Pacific Studies, Suva.

Rapaport, D., 1992, Encouraging environmentally sound tourism development in the Pacific, in Hay, J.E. (ed.) *Ecotourism Business in the Pacific: Promoting a Sustainable Experience, Conference Proceedings*, Environmental Science, University of Auckland, Auckland, 111–117.

Redclift, M., 1987, *Sustainable Development: Exploring the Contradictions*, Methuen, London and New York.

Rudkin, B., 1994, Ecotourism: passage to sustainable development? *Unpublished Masters Thesis*, Massey University, Palmerston North, forthcoming.

Senate Standing Committee on Environment, Recreation and the Arts, 1988, *The Potential of the Kakadu National Park Region*, Australian Government Publishing Service, Canberra.

Sofield, T., 1992, The Guadalcanal, track ecotourism project in the Solomon Islands, in Hay, J.E. (ed.) *Ecotourism Business in the Pacific: Promoting a Sustainable Experience, Conference Proceedings*, Environmental Science, University of Auckland, Auckland, 89–100.

The Dominion, 18 October 1989.

Tourism Council of the South Pacific (TCSP), 1988, *Nature Legislation and Nature Conservation as Part of Tourism Development in the Island Pacific*, TCSP, Suva.

Tourism Council of the South Pacific (TCSP), 1990a, *Solomon Islands Tourism Development Plan 1991–2000, Vol. 1—Summary*, TCSP for the Ministry of Tourism and Aviation, Government of Solomon Islands, Suva.

Turner, R.K. (ed.), 1988, *Sustainable Environmental Management: Principles and Practice*, Belhaven Press, London.

Valentine, P.S., 1992a, Ecotourism and nature conservation: a definition with some recent developments in Micronesia, in Weiler, B. (ed.) *Ecotourism Incorporating the Global Classroom, 1991 International Conference Papers*, Bureau of Tourism Research, Canberra, 4–9.

Valentine, P.S., 1992b, 'Nature-based tourism, in Weiler, B. and Hall, C.M. (eds) *Special Interest Tourism*, Belhaven Press, London, 105–127.

World Tourism Organisation, 1990, *Yearbook of Tourism Statistics*, WTO, Madrid.

World Tourism Organisation, 1992, *Yearbook of Tourism Statistics*, WTO, Madrid.

Yacoumis, J., 1990, Tourism in the South Pacific: a significant development potential, *The Courier,* **122**, 81–83.

Young, M., 1992, Ecotourism—profitable conservation, in Hay, J.E. (ed.) *Ecotourism Business in the Pacific: Promoting a Sustainable Experience, Conference Proceedings*, Environmental Science, University of Auckland, Auckland, 55–60.

10

Ecotourism in the Caribbean Basin

DAVID WEAVER

INTRODUCTION

In its examination of ecotourism within the Caribbean Basin, this chapter distinguishes between the insular Caribbean (defined as the islands of the Caribbean Sea, along with the Bahamas and Turks and Caicos groups) and the mainland Caribbean (nine Central and South American countries possessing a Caribbean coastline and El Salvador) (Figure 10.1). For each group, the outline of present trends and future prospects in ecotourism is preceded by an overview of the traditional tourism product. Dominica and Costa Rica are featured as high profile ecotourism case studies representing the insular and mainland Caribbean, respectively.

THE INSULAR CARIBBEAN

The traditional Caribbean tourism product

The insular Caribbean has emerged as one of the world's most tourism-intensive destination regions by merit of its tropical climate, extensive coastline, pro-tourism government policies and proximity to the North American market. This status is reflected in the regional host to guest ratio of 2:1 (based upon 17 million international tourist arrivals in 1989 and 33 million permanent residents), which contrasts with the global ratio of 13:1 (World Tourism Organisation, 1990). However, visitation levels vary widely within the region (see Table 10.1). While St Maarten, the Virgin Islands and many other entities accommodate tourist numbers far in excess of the local population, the opposite holds true for Cuba and Haiti. Low host to guest ratios tend to characterise the smaller, less populated islands, many of which have become dependent upon tourism revenues. The relative economic contribution of international tourism among these smaller island destinations ranges from 10 per cent of the GNP in Guadeloupe and Martinique to 50 per cent or more in the Bahamas, the British Virgin Islands, Anguilla and Antigua (World Tourism Organisation, 1990).

Ecotourism: A Sustainable Option? Edited by E. Cater and G. Lowman
© The editors and contributors. Published in 1994 by John Wiley & Sons Ltd

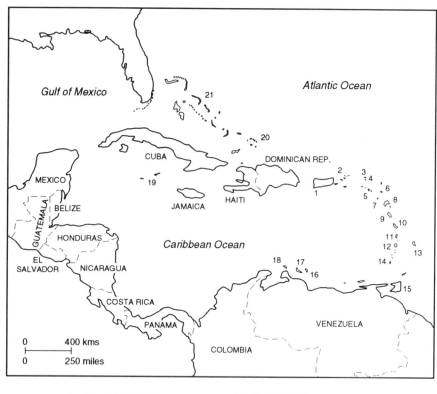

1. Puerto Rica (USA)
2. Virgin Islands (US/UK)
3. Anguilla (UK)
4. St. Maarten (Neth. Fr.)
5. St. KITTS-NEVIS
6. ANTIGUA & BARBUDA
7. Montserrat (UK)
8. Guadeloupe (Fr.)
9. DOMINICA
10. Martinique (Fr.)
11. St. LUCIA

12. St. VINCENT
13. BARBADOS
14. GRENADA
15. TRINIDAD & TOBAGO
16. Bonaire (Neth.)
17. Curacao (Neth.)
18. Aruba (Neth.)
19. Cayman Islands (UK)
20. Turks & Caicos Islands (UK)
21. BAHAMAS

FIGURE 10.1.   Location map (1993) of the Caribbean basin

The Caribbean is known primarily as a 3S (sea, sand, sun) destination of beach resorts and cruise ship ports, supplemented by historical and cultural attractions. Although allusions to an unspoiled natural environment have always been prominent in the promotion of Caribbean tourist destinations, the sea, sand and sun have usually functioned as the setting for play- and rest-focused activities which bear little resemblance to ecotourism. This disassociation between 3S tourism and ecotourism is reinforced by evidence of negative environmental and social impacts resulting from the former, particularly

TABLE 10.1. Caribbean basin destinations ranked by host to guest ratio. Sources: World Tourism Organisation (1990) and Hoffman (1991)

Destination	1990 population	Tourists (thousands) (1989) Stayovers	Cruise	Host to guest ratio
Insular Caribbean				
St Maarten	15	504	472	0.02:1
Cayman Islands	24	210	404	0.04:1
British Virgin Islands	12	176	72	0.05:1
US Virgin Islands	102	492	1063	0.07:1
Bahamas	251	1575	1645	0.08:1
Aruba	63	345	70	0.15:1
Turks and Caicos Islands	9	47	—	0.19:1
Antigua and Barbuda	75	189	208	0.19:1
Bonaire	9	37	8	0.20:1
Anguilla	7	29	—	0.25:1
Barbados	260	461	337	0.33:1
St Kitts-Nevis	40	72	37	0.37:1
Montserrat	12	17	10	0.44:1
Curaçao	155	193	125	0.49:1
Martinique	340	312	368	0.50:1
Grenada	114	69	120	0.60:1
St Lucia	153	135	104	0.64:1
Puerto Rico	3336	2450	777	1.00:1
St Vincent	106	50	50	1.00:1
Guadeloupe	340	123	86	1.63:1
Dominica	85	35	6	2.00:1
Jamaica	2513	715	444	2.20:1
Dominican Republic	7253	1300	100	5.00:1
Trinidad and Tobago	1270	194	21	5.90:1
Cuba	10 582	314	5	33.00:1
Haiti	5862	122	—	48.00:1
Total	32 988	10 166	6532	2.00:1
Mainland destinations				
Belize	180	220	—	0.80:1
Costa Rica	3032	376	—	8.00:1
Mexico	88 335	6257	1039	12.00:1
Panama	2423	190	—	13.00:1
Guatemala	9340	437	—	21.00:1
Honduras	5261	250	—	21.00:1
El Salvador	5221	131	—	40.00:1
Colombia	32 598	733	—	44.00:1
Venezuela	19 753	412	—	48.00:1
Nicaragua	3606	69	—	52.00:1
Total	169 749	9075	1039	17.00:1

within the underdeveloped world (Cohen, 1978; Britton and Clarke, 1987; Edwards, 1988; Lea, 1988). In contrast with the high demand, high priority 3S product, ecotourism has never attained a significant profile within the region. On the supply side, terrestrial ecotourism opportunities are constrained by a limited land base which has been densely settled and extensively degraded during the past 500 years. Also, the insular Caribbean, with the exception of Trinidad, is not as biologically diverse or as rich in unusual or endemic species as the mainland rainforests or isolated insular destinations such as the Galapagos Islands and Madagascar.

Recent ecotourism trends

The pursuit of ecotourism by most Caribbean destinations during the past few years represents a logical strategy for these islands to follow, despite the appearance of a bandwagon effect. Three distinct forms of ecotourism can be identified. First, many destinations are reassessing the way in which their current 3S product is being delivered, and are introducing the principles of sustainable development to reduce the negative environmental and social impacts without changing the basic nature of the product. This strategy recognises and accepts that 3S tourism is likely to remain as the product core for many destinations, but that improvements can be made, and market shares retained or increased, through the application of certain ecotourism principles. Issues of sustainability and resort tourism have been discussed at recent regional meetings, including the workshop on Environmentally Sound Tourism Development, held in 1987 in Barbados (Edwards, 1988) and the conference on the Public Policy Implications of Sustainable Development in the Caribbean Region, held in Kingston, Jamaica in 1990 (Jackson, 1990). Second, in an attempt to diversify the 3S product, soft ecotourism opportunities are being made available to visitors whose primary motives remain more conventional. A guided tour of a road-accessible wildlife reserve, or a scuba dive experience, thus function as diversions from a beach-centred agenda. The provision of non-3S opportunities also recognises a growing concern over the link between skin cancer and ozone depletion, and the increasing influence of an environmentalist ethos, both of which call into question the long-term prospects of strictly specialised 3S destinations. Third, destinations are recognising that certain areas unsuited to conventional beach tourism may be able to accommodate a hard ecotourism component catering to nature-specific tourists. Four types of locations are appropriate for this form of ecotourism.

Mountainous interiors of main islands

Most Caribbean islands (excluding the Bahamas, Turks and Caicos Islands, Cayman Islands, Barbados and several others) possess hilly or mountainous interiors where population densities and levels of exploitation are relatively low, and where some vestige of the natural vegetation cover persists. Examples of forested interiors where ecotourism initiatives are being undertaken include the Cordillera Central of the Dominican Republic, Jamaica's Cockpit Country and Blue Mountain Range, El Yunque in Puerto Rico, the interior of Guadeloupe's Basse-Terre island, the Northern Range of Trinidad and the Soufrière district of St Vincent. The semi-desert uplands within Curaçao's Christoffel Park and Aruba's Arikok National Park have also been targeted for their ecotourism possibilities.

Peripheral islands

A number of Caribbean states and dependencies include outlying islands where the low level of tourism development and overall economic activity are amenable to alternative forms of tourism. Peripheral islands where ecotourism is being consciously promoted include Barbuda (Antigua and Barbuda), the Family Islands of the Bahamas, St John (US Virgin Islands), Tobago (Trinidad and Tobago) and Saba and Bonaire (Netherlands Antilles). Also included in this category are the numerous uninhabited islets, such as Buck Island Reef (US Virgin Islands) and Bird of Paradise Island (Trinidad and Tobago), which harbour bird colonies, deserted beaches or other natural attractions.

Undeveloped coastal areas

Many beaches, wetlands, dunes, mangroves and cliffs remain undeveloped owing to an absence of development pressure, or because of their remoteness or unsuitability for 3S tourism. Ecotourism initiatives are being pursued on the north coasts of Curaçao and Aruba, the south-west coast of Jamaica and along the northern coast of Trinidad.

Offshore reefs

If the insular Caribbean can be described as land-poor, then it can also be characterised as sea-rich, given the high quality diving environment and the extensive territorial waters and Exclusive Economic Zones which surround each island. Although all Caribbean destinations offer diving opportunities, higher profile venues include the Bahamas, Bonaire and the Cayman Islands, where this sector generated US$80–90 million, US$30 million and US$52.3 million, respectively, during 1985 (Dixon and Sherman, 1990: 180–181). Although the island is smaller in absolute terms, diving is even more relatively important to Saba, Netherlands Antilles, where 2100 divers generated between US$1 million and US$1.5 million in 1988. It is anticipated that diver use will increase to 5000 visitors by 1994 (Dixon and Sherman, 1990: 182). Of course, not all scuba divers are ecotourists, particularly if they are engaged in such destructive activities as spearfishing and shell or coral collecting.

Discussion

In all the four environments discussed above, protected areas constitute the primary venue for ecotourism. Although some Caribbean protected areas are long-established [e.g. J. Armando Bermudez National Park (1956) and J. del Carmen Ramirez N.P. (1958) in the Dominican Republic, Culebra National Wildlife Refuge (1909) in Puerto Rico and Virgin Islands N.P. (1956) in the US Virgin Islands], most are of more recent origin (IUCN, 1990). This is particularly true for the more than 100 legally established marine and coastal protected areas in the greater Caribbean basin noted by the Organisation of American States (OAS/NPS, 1988).

Ecotourism in Dominica

Through a combination of circumstances and strategy, Dominica has been transformed from the poor sister of insular Caribbean destinations to the island most closely associated with ecotourism (Boo, 1990; Weaver, 1991). It is clear that although Dominican governments wanted to develop the island as a 3S destination during the post-war period, efforts to do so were hindered by political uncertainties, lack of infrastructure and most notably, a physical geography unsuited to 3S tourism (i.e. mountainous terrain, heavy forest cover, lack of white sand beaches). The rejection by the Dominican Government of a major consultant's report in 1971 may be seen as the turning point in the Dominican tourism industry. This report by Shankland-Cox and Associates, although acknowledging that the island's scenery should constitute the basis for its tourism strategy, used wildly optimistic visitation predictions (200 000 to 300 000 by 1990, compared with 13 000 in 1970) to advocate an accommodation target of 5200 beds by 1990 (versus about 200 in 1970). The Kasterlak Report of 1975, in sharp contrast, acknowledged the limitations of Dominica, and recommended the gradual, selective development of a small-scale, nature-based tourism product capitalising upon the emergent environmental movement. The acceptance of the major philosophical thrust of the Kasterlak Report indicated a fundamental shift of perception, whereby a physical setting hitherto maligned as a tourist liability (e.g. Dominica's possession of the largest intact rainforest in the small-island Caribbean) would be deliberately marketed as a tourism asset. Subsequent National Structure Plans and consultants' reports have reinforced this ecotourism-centred philosophy, although Boo (1990) points out that the major overall reason given by tourists for visiting Dominica was visiting friends or family, presumably cited by visitors with local origins. North Americans and Europeans were more likely to cite nature visitation as their primary motive. The domestic ecotourist market is small, as a result mainly of the small population of the island.

The release of the Kasterlak Report coincided with the establishment of Dominica's first National Park, Morne Trois Pitons, in the southern interior (Figure 10.2). Although set up primarily for purposes of watershed and species protection, the park has become a major feature of Dominica's ecotourism product, containing two freshwater lakes, a boiling lake, numerous fumaroles and hot springs and relatively undisturbed tracts of rain and montane forest. Other areas with anticipated ecotourism potential, such as the Northern and Central Forest Reserves, are complemented by historical and cultural attractions such as Cabrits National Historic Park and the Carib Reserve on the eastern coast.

Structurally, the accommodation sector is dominated by small hotels and guest houses divided into three geographical categories: a cluster of accommodation in the capital city of Roseau; several beach-based facilities along the

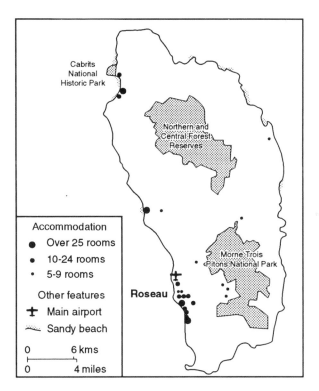

FIGURE 10.2.   Protected areas and accommodation, Dominica 1990

west coast; and a number of dispersed lodge-type facilities in the interior, particularly near Morne Trois Pitons. The small size and dispersed location of facilities, along with the encouragement of local participation (70 per cent of all accommodation units were owned wholly by Dominicans in 1988), year-round patronage and the emphasis upon local foods and architectural traditions, all conform to the principles of ecotourism.

In addition, ecotourism is being pursued as one supplementary component of a diversified economy dominated by agriculture. The Division of Tourism hopes to increase tourism's share of the GNP from 1.5 per cent to about 5 per cent by the mid-1990s—a modest target when contrasted with the percentages for Antigua and many other islands.

However, several recent developments in the tourism sector have raised questions about Dominica's long-term commitment to an ecotourism-centred strategy. These include the construction of a cruise ship pier off Cabrits National Historic Park (cruise ship excursionists are not generally nature-oriented), a 100-unit hotel/condo project near Portsmouth and a proposal to expand Melville Hall Airport to accommodate jet aircraft. Although these developments do not necessarily indicate a transition to a more intensive conventional product, they do illustrate the perennial ecotourism dilemma, which is the attainment of an appropriate balance between development and environmental and social carrying capacities.

Although no thorough studies on the negative impacts of tourism have yet been carried out in Dominica, anecdotal evidence already points to litter problems caused by cruise ship passengers and trekkers, the use of soap in rivers and springs and the illegal collection of wild plants in protected areas (Boo, 1990). Of course, many of the problems attributed to tourists may result from the activities or cooperation of local residents. Other concerns which need to be addressed include inadequately trained guides, a lack of basic tourist infrastructure in the interior, poorly maintained trails vulnerable to erosion and over-concentrations of visitors within a small number of readily accessible natural sites, such as the Emerald Pool (a few minutes walk from a main road). The 1994 target of 60 000 stayover tourists suggested in the 1991 Tourism Sector Plan (compared with 30 000 in 1991) may also be excessive, although such a visitation level need not generate environmental stress if it is staggered both temporally and spatially.

Ecotourism prospects of the insular Caribbean

Although Dominica is the clear front runner in ecotourism among insular Caribbean desitnations, several other islands at a relatively early stage of tourism development also appear to be emphasising an unspoiled environment and lack of resort development as the primary attraction for visitors. The recent promotional slogans of St Vincent and the Grenadines ('The

Natural Place to Be'), Montserrat ('The Way the Caribbean Used to Be') and Grenada ('The Original Caribbean') are similar in appeal to Dominica's 'Nature Island of the Caribbean'. Montserrat is hoping to feature ecotourism as the centrepiece of its long-term tourism strategy; already 80 per cent of its international visitors indicate an interest in nature-based tourism (Gill, 1992). The government of the Turks and Caicos Islands (slogan: 'Beautiful by Nature') has also apparently embarked on an ecotourism-centred tourism strategy, albeit based mainly on marine rather than terrestrial natural attractions. Ecotourists in the Turks and Caicos Islands currently account for about 20 per cent of international visitors (Gill, 1992). It remains to be seen whether ecotourism will attain the same status in these four destinations as it has in Dominica, or whether the more conventional 3S variety will eventually prevail as access improves and developmental pressures increase. Of all the insular Caribbean destinations, the brightest long-term ecotourism prospects probably belong to Cuba, with its extensive undeveloped coastline, numerous uninhabited offshore islands and tracts of inland forest. Although the current regime is attempting to diversify the Cuban economy through 3S tourism, the ecotourism potential of the many undeveloped areas has also been recognised. The island's proximity to the USA will result in an influx of American tourists, including ecotourists, once travel restrictions are eased.

To summarise, the developments in the insular Caribbean region suggest that it is highly unlikely that ecotourism will ever come to dominate that large majority of destinations in which natural resources, marketing image and infrastructure are already geared toward 3S tourism. For these places, ecotourism will probably find its niche as an inspiration for an improved 3S product, a diversion for 3S tourists and an important activity in natural or semi-natural areas removed from the beach.

THE MAINLAND CARIBBEAN

The traditional mainland tourism product

The mainland is much less tourism-intensive and dependent than the insular Caribbean, as measured by a regional host to guest ratio of 17:1 (see Table 10.1) and a two per cent contribution of international tourism to the cumulative regional GNP (World Tourism Organisation, 1990). However, as with the islands, significant internal variations are disguised by the regional statistic. Although the resident population and host to guest ratio of Belize resemble the smaller Caribbean islands, other mainland destinations are superficially similar to Haiti, Cuba and the Dominican Republic. Tourism contributions to individual GNPs range from 26 per cent in Belize to one per cent or less in Colombia, El Salvador, Honduras, Nicaragua and Venezuela. Mexico's status as the largest recipient of international tourists in the entire study area is masked by an unimpressive host to guest ratio of 12:1 and a tourism contribution of two per cent to GNP.

A case could be made for differentiating the Caribbean basin study area by host to guest ratio rather than by the island to mainland distinction. The decision to use geography in this chapter reflects the fact that whereas the insular Caribbean is dominated by 3S tourism, the mainland product is more variable as a result of the broader array of available cultural, historical and environmental attractions (World Tourism Organisation, 1986). In addition to important social and business tourism sectors, five major elements of the traditional product can be distinguished.

Urban tourism

Mainland capital cities (except for Belmopan, Belize) are large, dominantly metropolitan areas containing a wealth of historical and cultural attractions, services and shopping opportunities. For this reason, and because of their pleasant inland climates (Panama City excepted) and their proximity to major international airports, capital cities have emerged as major, if not primary, nodes of tourist activity.

Sites related to indigenous culture and history

Unlike the insular Caribbean, the mainland retains a strong native American presence, both contemporary and historical. Meso-American archaeological sites (e.g. Mexico alone has catalogued 11 000 such sites) and contemporary native settlements (Chichicastenango in Guatemala, Tipitapa in Nicaragua, San Blas Islands of Panama) constitute an important element of the regional tourism sector.

Sites related to colonial history (outside the capital)

The rich Spanish colonial heritage of the mainland, conspicuous in the capitals, is also well represented in other cities. Colonial centres which have become tourist attractions include Antigua (Guatemala), Granada and León (Nicaragua), Cartago (Costa Rica), Cartagena (Colombia), Portobelo (Panama) and Cumaná (Venezuela).

Beach resorts

Major beach resorts have developed in Mexico (e.g. Acapulco, Cozumel, Cancún, Mazatlán, Puerto Vallerto), Colombia (Cartagena, Santa Marta) and Venezuela (La Guara, Barcelona, Isla de Margarita). Beach resort tourism is much less evident in the smaller Central American countries, especially along the relatively isolated Caribbean coast. Domestic tourists account for a much higher proportion of beach visitors than in the smaller Caribbean islands.

Natural areas

Although the natural endowment of the mainland is extensive and diverse, nature-based tourism has mainly been of the soft variety oriented to sites accessible to main roads and/or near metropolitan areas, and catering to domestic tourists. Prominent examples include Lake Atitlán (Guatemala) and Poás National Park (Costa Rica). The hard ecotourism component has traditionally maintained a very low profile on the mainland.

Recent ecotourism trends on the Caribbean mainland

Like the insular Caribbean, mainland destinations are beginning to exploit their ecotourism potential for both the specialised market and as an add-on to other forms of tourism. Most of the attention is being focused upon protected area systems, which were originally established to protect watersheds and wildlife, but which were often subsequently neglected owing to lack of funds and civil unrest. By 1989 the mainland (excluding Belize) had established 205 public protected areas encompassing 22 481 270 hectares (World Resources Institute, 1990). Increasingly, it is the prospect of lucrative ecotourism revenue which helps to justify the retention, enhancement and enlargement of these areas in the face of competition from cattle ranchers, peasants and loggers. The recent Guatemalan initiative to protect a substantial portion of its land base, including most of the remaining lowland forests of northern Petén province, is an example of a major national environmental programme with an explicit ecotourism component. Mexico's incipient ecotourism sector is also focused upon the national protected areas system, which functions 'to promote and conserve the natural richness of the country, introducing visitors to the knowledge of the vital values found in nature and the need for its protection to benefit present and future generations' (Boo, 1990: 116). The Monarch Butterfly Reserve, one of the best known natural attractions, has experienced an increase in visits from 9000 in 1984–5 to 70 000 in 1987–8 (Boo, 1990).

Bilateral and multilateral projects related to ecotourism include the Paseo Pantera, which is an attempt to integrate the park systems and protection efforts of all Central American states, especially through the creation of transnational mega-parks such as La Amistad International Park (Costa Rica/Panama), Bosawas/Río Plátano reserve (Nicaragua/Honduras) and the International Biosphere Reserve La Fraternidad (Guatemala/Honduras/El Salvador). National governments and conservation groups, both local and foreign, are also promoting the Ruta Maya, a cultural and ecotourism circuit of Mayan sites and natural areas in Mexico, Guatemala, Belize, El Salvador and Honduras. Management plans for certain native-controlled areas, such as the Darien Biosphere Reserve and the Kuna lands in Panama, are advocating ecotourism as one element of a sustainable economy (Houseal *et al.*, 1985). Despite all of these initiatives and good intentions, ecotourism in most mainland destinations is still in its infancy, accounting for no more than a tiny fraction of regional tourist revenues and traffic. The exceptions are Belize, which hosted the first Caribbean Ecotourism Conference in 1991, and Costa Rica, profiled in the following section.

Ecotourism in Costa Rica

Costa Rica's status as the most advanced ecotourism destination of any Latin American country is attributable to several factors. Firstly, having been spared the chronic political instability which has plagued most areas of Central America, Costa Rica has acquired a reputation as a stable, relatively prosperous and safe country for visitors. Secondly, the country possesses unusually high biodiversity despite its small size, as a result of its pivotal location between North and South America and its extreme range of elevation. Within 12 distinct life zones, Costa Rica is estimated to harbour between 1260 and 1500 species of trees (Hall, 1985; Rovinski, 1991), 205 mammals, 849 birds, 160 amphibians, 218 reptiles and at least 9000 vascular plants, representing four per cent of the global total (Boza, 1988). Thirdly, Costa Rica has established a comprehensive system of public and private protected areas representing most of its biodiversity. This system has received extensive exposure through media, government promotional efforts and the activities of conservation groups such as the Organization for Tropical Studies, a consortium of universities and research institutes which operates three research sites in Costa Rica (Rovinski, 1991).

The public protected areas system was initiated in 1970 with the formation of the National Parks Service, under the auspices of the Ministry of Agriculture (Rovinski, 1991). The initiative came from an influential group of conservationists who were concerned about the rate at which cattle ranchers, peasants and loggers were deforesting the country (Fennell and Eagles, 1990). As in the case of Dominica, there is little evidence to suggest that ecotourism played any significant part in the early development of the park network. By the late 1980s the public system had expanded to include at least 35 widely distributed entities covering 573 000 hectares or 11.23 per cent of Costa Rica (Figure 10.3). The public system has been augmented by a growing number of privately protected spaces, including the well-known 13 000 hectare Monteverde reserve, and other protected spaces such as Indian-controlled lands. Taken together, approximately one-fifth of Costa Rica's land base, in theory, receives protection from deforestation.

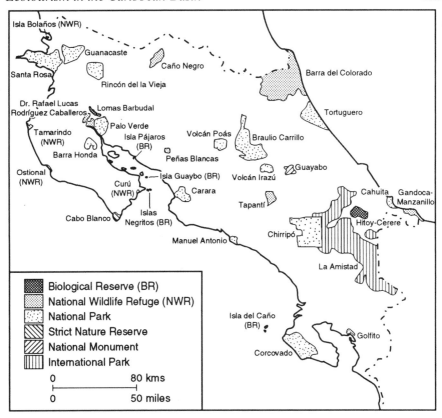

FIGURE 10.3. Public protected areas, Costa Rica 1992. Sources: Boza (1988), Rovinski (1991) and Carey and Jones (1993)

Ecotourism remained virtually non-existent as an organised sector in Costa Rica until the late 1970s. Most of the 300 000 international tourists arriving in 1976 originated from within Central America and had San José, the capital, as their primary destination (Boo, 1990). The first major ecotourism initiatives were undertaken by private sector entrepreneurs, capitalising on the emerging reputation of the expanding park system (Fennell and Eagles, 1990). Pioneering companies included the American-founded Costa Rica Expeditions Travel Agency (1979) and the Costa Rican-owned Tikal (1983) and Horizontes (1984) groups (Boo, 1990). Although the number of ecotourist arrivals did increase through the early 1980s, local entrepreneurs attributed the boom of the late 1980s to two specific high profile events: the awarding of the Nobel Peace Prize to President Oscar Arias in 1987 and the holding of the Seventeenth General Assembly of the World Conservation Union in San José during 1988 (Rovinski, 1991). These events followed the transfer of the National Parks Service from Agriculture to the newly created Ministry of

Natural Resources in 1986, which was accompanied by a change in management philosophy from preservation to sustainable development. According to Rovinski (1991: 45), 'the use of protected areas for lucrative and nondestructive activities, such as ecotourism, became a priority'. This change in strategy reinforced the Tourism Development Strategy of 1984–90, which targeted nature and adventure tourism as one of four market niches to be pursued, along with 3S, cruise ship and business/convention tourism (Boo, 1990). Not only did the number of international arrivals subsequently grow to over 500 000 by 1992 (when tourism emerged as the single largest earner of foreign exchange), but fully 50 per cent of these tourists paid at least one visit to a National Park, compared with about 20 per cent in 1986 (Wood, 1993). As anticipated, many of these visits were undertaken as add-on ecotourism excursions by visitors whose primary motives were not nature-oriented. However, the significance of ecotourism among international tourists is apparent from a Board of Tourism Survey conducted in 1987, in which 36.1 per cent of arrivals cited ecotourism as a major motivation for their visit, whereas 72.3 per cent cited the natural beauty of Costa Rica (Boo, 1990).

Other indicators corroborate the growth of ecotourism in Costa Rica while also providing evidence of its impacts. For example, one-third of the country's 30 travel agencies cater mainly to the ecotourism market, generating significant amounts of foreign exchange (Boo, 1990). The Costa Rica Expeditions Travel Agency now attracts 20 000 clients annually, three-quarters of whom arrive for ecotourism purposes, with each visitor spending an average of US$148 each day (Rovinski, 1991). In 1989, the 13 000 ecotourists who visited the privately owned La Selva Biological Field Station spent US$291 000, whereas the nearby Rara Avis private reserve generates an annual income of US$80 000 in the adjacent settlement of Horquetas (Rovinski, 1991).

Such revenues may not appear very large by national standards, but their economic impact on local communities is extremely important. Other evidence points to a more ambiguous impact. In an analysis of Tortuguero National Park's socio-economic impact on the adjacent community of the same name, Place (1988) found that the local population's traditional self-reliance, based on the exploitation of the area's biological resources (e.g. bush meat, fish, etc.), has been replaced by a dependence on mainly part-time jobs generated by park visitors and other tourists. This transition from a largely subsistence to a market economy had, however, already begun before the park was created, and Place (1988) suggests that small-scale nature-based tourism has so far proved more benign than other modern economic alternatives which could have dominated instead. The key appears to be the retention of this type of tourism within the context of a village-based delivery system ensuring participation by the largest possible number of locals, some of whom still resent the confiscation of their traditional hunting and gathering areas to create the park.

The environmental impacts of ecotourism in Costa Rica are also ambiguous. Although the large number and size of protected areas could allow for the wide dispersal of park visitors, certain popular and/or readily accessible areas are experiencing visitation levels in excess of their environmental carrying capacities. Serious problems of overcrowding, water pollution, trail erosion and changes in wildlife behaviour have been noted in Manuel Antonio National Park (Rovinski, 1991), though much of the disruption can be attributed to beach-oriented excursionists. Unfortunately, most parks still lack sustainable management plans, trained personnel and research into the carrying capacities of individual areas, while facing unregulated commercial development near and sometimes within the parks (Rovinski, 1991). Some attempts have been made to harmonise visitation levels with carrying capacity. For example, no more than 25 visitors are allowed to view the sea turtle nesting sites each night at Nancite Beach, Santa Rosa National Park (Clark, 1991).

Noting the increase in international visits to the park system from 50 000 in 1986 to 250 000 in 1991, Wood (1993) warns that the parks are becoming the victims of their own success through overvisitation, and that the commitment of government funds to park maintenance has been highly irregular despite the revenue potential of protected areas. Wood therefore advocates a differential structure whereby foreigners would pay a higher park entrance fee than Costa Rican nationals, with the extra revenues being allocated toward the enhancement of the park system. Currently, entrance fee revenues are not necessarily used for this purpose. A differential fee structure could also serve to regulate visitation by allowing for the increase in entrance costs to a level where visitor numbers are in concordance with carrying capacity (Lindberg, 1991). Certain private reserves have already raised their entrance fees as a means of controlling visitation and increasing their revenues. Monteverde, where visitation has risen from 500 in 1974 to 15 322 in 1988 (Fennell and Eagles, 1990), charged an entrance fee of US$2.75 in 1989, compared with US$0.65 in the National Parks (Boo, 1990).

A broader issue facing the park system is the continuing deforestation of the countryside, which threatens to eliminate virtually all natural habitat outside the protected areas within the next two decades. Not only does this belie the country's progressive environmental image, it suggests that high quality ecotourism opportunities will soon be available only within the increasingly stressed parks and reserves.

Ecotourism prospects of the mainland Caribbean

Although the ecotourism potential of the mainland is considerable, several factors currently militate against the long-term success of this sector in most parts of the region. Firstly, the reputation of regional instability persists, fuelled by continuing guerrilla activity in Guatemala, an uneasy truce in El Salvador, the recent American invasion of Panama, coup attempts in Venezuela and the drug war in Colombia. Remote areas ideal for ecotourism can also accommodate insurrectionists and drug runners, as demonstrated by Contra activity in the Nicaragua/Honduras border region during the Nicaraguan civil war. Secondly, all mainland countries continue to suffer from rampant deforestation (World Resource Institute, 1990), which not only reduces the potential venues for ecotourism, but sustains the impression that the region is environmentally irresponsible. A third problem is that the so-called ecotourism promoted by some operators does not meet the criteria expected of the genuine product, thereby placing the whole concept into disrepute. Evidence from Belize suggests that many ecotourism facilities and activities are actually bringing about the negative impacts usually associated with conventional mass tourism (Cater, 1992). Costa Rica itself is not immune to this problem, as described earlier.

Of any mainland destination, the most promising ecotourism prospects probably belong to Mexico, given its political stability, increasing prosperity, diversity, size, proximity to the USA and the emergence of an environmentally aware middle class. Colombia and Venezuela, though also diverse and relatively prosperous, are less politically stable and the number of visitors from the critical North American market is also liable to be negatively affected by intervening ecotourism opportunities available in Mexico, Costa Rica and Belize. However, this could be compensated for by increases in the number of domestic ecotourists.

CONCLUSIONS

Ecotourism has never occupied a significant place in the traditional tourism industry of the Caribbean basin. Although the insular Caribbean has become closely identified as a 3S destination region, the mainland tourism sector has been more diverse as a result of a greater range of cultural and physical resources and the dominance of large capital cities. However, virtually all destinations within the study area are now trying to introduce an ecotourism component into their tourism product. Recognising the entrenched status of 3S tourism, most island governments perceive ecotourism as a supplementary activity aimed at both the resort tourist and the growing ecotourist market, best suited to hilly interiors, peripheral islands, remote coasts, offshore reefs and other quasi-natural areas. Concurrently, efforts are being made to enhance conventional tourism through the application of ecotourism principles. Although the potential for terrestrial ecotourism in particular is greater on the mainland, its prospects are threatened by rampant environmental degradation and a reputation for political instability. Larger mainland populations, however, also suggest a greater potential for the development of a domestic ecotourist market. Throughout the Caribbean basin, ecotourism is closely linked to public protected areas originally established for environmental reasons, but also recently upgraded and enlarged because of the potential revenues to be derived from ecotourism.

Dominica and Costa Rica have emerged as the best known ecotourism destinations within the region. For Dominica, the adoption of a deliberate ecotourism strategy in the 1970s represented a departure from previous attempts to develop a 3S product and resulted from a decision to promote former tourist liabilities as assets. Costa Rica's success has been based upon its stability, exceptional biodiversity, extensive publicity and the interaction between a comprehensive protected areas network and a private sector actively promoting ecotourism. Even in these two destinations, however, this sector is in its infancy and it is too early to tell whether they will emerge in the long-term as models of sustainable ecotourism. Legitimate concerns are raised by rapid increases in international tourist visitation levels and by anecdotal evidence of environmental damage from various sites. However, as the number of destinations offering ecotourism opportunities increases, the wider dispersal of ecotourists should ease demand in the two or three current hot-spots, especially if the size of the ecotourist market stabilises. In the long term, Mexico and Cuba could emerge as two of the most important ecotourist destinations in the study area because of their great number of potential attractions and proximity to the North American market. However, 3S tourism will probably continue to dominate the tourism industries of both.

REFERENCES

Boo, E., 1990, *Ecotourism: the Potentials and Pitfalls*, Vol. 2—Country Case Studies, World Wildlife Fund, Washington.

Boza, M., 1988, *Costa Rica National Parks*, Editorial Heliconia, Fundación Neotropica, San José.

Britton, S. and Clarke, W. (eds), 1987, *Ambiguous alternative: Tourism in Small Developing Countries*, University of the South Pacific, Suva.

Carey, A. and Jones, L. (eds), 1993, *The Buzzworm Magazine Guide to Ecotravel*, Buzzworm Books, Boulder.

Cater, E., 1992, Profits from paradise, *Geographical Magazine,* **64** (3), 16–21.

Clark, J.R., 1991, Carrying capacity and tourism in coastal and marine areas, *Parks,* **2**(3), 13–17.

Cohen, E., 1978, The impact of tourism on the physical environment, *Annals of Tourism Research,* **5**(2), 215–237.

Dixon, J.A. and Sherman, P.B., 1990, *Economics of Protected Areas: a New Look at Benefits and Costs*, Island Press, Washington.

Edwards, F. (ed), 1988, *Environmentally Sound Tourism in the Caribbean*, The University of Calgary Press, Calgary.

Fennell, D.A. and Eagles, P.F., 1990, Ecotourism in Costa Rica: a conceptual framework, *Journal of Park and Recreation Administration,* **8**(1), 23–34.

Gill, C., 1992, Balancing tourism and the environment, *Tourism Today,* September/ October, 34–41.

Hall, C., 1985, *Costa Rica: a Geographical Interpretation in Historical Perspective, Dellplain Latin American Studies, No. 17,* Westview Press, Boulder, Colorado.

Hoffman, M.S. (ed.), 1991, *The World Almanac and Book of Facts 1992*, Pharos Books, New York.

Houseal, B., MacFarland, C., Archibold, G. and Chiari, A., 1985, Indigenous cultures and protected areas in Central America, *Cultural Survival Quarterly,* **9**(1), 10–20.

International Union for the Conservation of Nature (IUCN), 1990, *1990 United Nations List of National Parks and Protected Areas*, IUCN, Gland.

Jackson, I., 1990, Tourism and sustainable development in the Caribbean, in Cox, J. and Embree, C. (eds) *Sustainable Development in the Caribbean,* Institute for Research on Public Policy, Halifax, 127–138.

Lea, J., 1988, *Tourism and Development in the Third World,* Routledge, Chapman and Hall, New York.

Lindberg, K., 1991, *Policies for Maximizing Nature Tourism's Ecological and Economic Benefits,* World Resources Institute, Washington.

Organization of American States/National Park Service (OAS/NPS), 1988, *Inventory of Caribbean Marine and Coastal Protected Areas*, Washington.

Place, S., 1988, The impact of National Park development on Tortuguero, Costa Rica, *Journal of Cultural Geography,* **9**(1), 37–52.

Rovinski, Y., 1991, Private reserves, parks and ecotourism in Costa Rica, in Whelan, T. (ed.) *Nature Tourism: Managing for the Environment,* Island Press, Washington, 39–57.

Weaver, D.B., 1991, Alternative to mass tourism in Dominica, *Annals of Tourism Research,* **18**(3), 414–432.

Wood, M.E., 1993, Costa Rican parks threatened by tourism boom: society launches letter-writing campaign, *The Ecotourism Society Newsletter,* **3**(1), 1–2.

World Resources Institute, 1990, *World Resources, 1990–91,* World Resources Institute, Oxford University Press, New York.

World Tourism Organisation (WTO), 1986, *Country Tourism Profiles*, WTO, Madrid.

World Tourism Organisation (WTO), 1990, *Compendium of Tourism Statistics 1985–89,* 11th edn, WTO, Madrid.

11

The Annapurna Conservation Area Project: a Pioneering Example of Sustainable Tourism?

CHANDRA P. GURUNG AND MAUREEN DE COURSEY

THE ANNAPURNA REGION: MOUNTAIN AGRICULTURE AND TREKKING TOURISM

The area surrounding the Annapurna mountain range in western Nepal has long been recognised, both nationally and internationally, as one of the world's most spectacular landscapes. Over 7000 square kilometres in size, this region harbours an outstanding array of both biological and cultural diversity. Nine distinct ethnic groups—approximately 100 000 people (living inside and outside the region)—have for centuries carved an existence out of its subtropical, temperate and high alpine settings. The world's deepest river valley, the Kali Gandaki, cuts a thin, 1824 metre chasm between the lofty summits of Annapurna 1 (8091 m) and Dhaulagiri (8151 m), two of the world's highest mountains. Extremes of climate and topography create excellent habitats for a wide variety of flora and fauna, including the endangered snow leopard (*Panthera uncia*), blue sheep (*Pseudois nayaur*), musk deer (*Moschus chrysogaster*), over 100 varieties of orchids and expansive stands of rhododendron, bamboo and pine forests.

The majority of Annapurna's residents live at subsistence level or below, primarily as farmers, labourers, herders or traders. Although some inhabitants are able to meet their daily requirements fairly comfortably, many in the more remote regions still suffer from food deficits. However, they are all dependent on the natural resources as over 90 per cent of local energy needs are met by forests. Forests also provide a host of other essential products such as fodder, building materials, medicines, game, wild foodstuffs and raw materials for domestic purposes.

Unlike the tropical lowlands to the south, the Annapurna region never experienced the acute population pressures that contributed to massive deforestation and environmental degradation in those areas. The harsh and

Ecotourism: A Sustainable Option? Edited by E. Cater and G. Lowman
© The editors and contributors. Published in 1994 by John Wiley & Sons Ltd

unforgiving terrain kept most outsiders away, allowing residents to use and manage their nearby resources as they saw fit. Although local populations have grown significantly over the years (2.6 per cent annually), basic needs remained at a level readily accommodated by the existing resource base. To sustain local livelihoods, numerous indigenous systems evolved to manage natural resources. Although not perfect, these systems have helped to maintain the quality of Annapurna's environment.

Over the last two decades, the explosion in trekking tourism has upset this delicate ecological balance and contributed significantly to a loss of cultural integrity in the Annapurna region. Its unparalleled attributes and the relative ease by which one could reach the heart of the Himalaya have made the Annapurna region the number one trekking destination in all of Nepal. In 1991, a total of 270 000 tourists visited Nepal. Seventy thousand of these visitors were trekkers, out of which 38 500 (55 per cent) headed for some part of the Annapurna region (Table 11.1). It is estimated that for every trekker there is at least one outside support staff, pushing the annual number of visitors to well over 77 000, almost twice the local population. A standard commercial trek around the Annapurna Circuit (22–25 days) for 12 clients sets off with a support staff of approximately 50 members. The situation is further exacerbated by the fact that the majority of trekkers tend to bottle-neck in three areas: the Annapurna Sanctuary, the base of the 6000 metre Thorong Pass (Thorong Phedi) and Ghorepani village, a major trail intersection. The trekkers are also seasonally concentrated: owing to the prevailing weather pattern, over 60 per cent of the trekkers come in four months of the

TABLE 11.1. Growth in number of trekkers, 1980–92. Reproduced by permission from Fleming (1991)

Year	Everest	Langtang	Annapurna	Other	Total	Percentage increase/ decrease
1980	5836	4113	14 332	3197	27 478	—
1981	5804	4488	17 053	2155	29 500	+7.4
1982	6240	4535	19 702	1855	32 332	+9.6
1983	6732	4030	21 119	417	32 298	−0.1
1984	7724	4792	25 422	3268	41 206	+27.6
1985	8347	4610	18 960	813	32 730	−20.6
1986	9900	5250	33 620	805	49 575	+51.5
1987	8998	6107	30 914	1256	47 275	−4.6
1988	11 366	8423	37 902	3582	61 273	+29.6
1989						
1990	11 314	7826	36 361	7497	62 998	+2.8
1991*			38 447			
1992*			44 417			

*Based on ACAP's records.

FIGURE 11.1.   Stock of fuelwood outside tourist lodge, Chandrakot, Annapurna District, Nepal (Erlet Cater)

year—October, November, March and April. These high impact areas, and to a lesser extent along the rest of the main trekking routes, have suffered tremendously from *laissez-faire* tourist development. Over 700 tea shops and lodges have been built that cater to a tourist population whose needs are much greater than local standards (Figure 11.1).

Localised deforestation from spiralling fuelwood and construction demands has led to a decrease in forest habitats—including Nepal's showcase rhododendron forests—and further destabilisation of the surrounding hillsides. Virtually all food and housekeeping items have to be imported from Kathmandu and Pokhara, inflating local economies and introducing non-nutritious diets. Inadequate sanitation facilities and indiscriminate practices by tourists and trekking groups have left virtual 'minefields' of human excreta and toilet paper. Toilets, if they exist at all, are often dangerously close to water sources. Non-biodegradable litter such as plastics, tins and bottles, used primarily by tourists, are disposed of in nearby streams or strewn in piles at the edge of the settlements (Figure 11.2). Tourism, as a messenger of outside values and behaviours, has also affected local cultures. Village youths are easy prey to the seductiveness of Western consumer culture as tourists are laden with expensive trappings such as hi-tech hiking gear, flashy clothes, cameras and a variety of electronic gadgetry.

FIGURE 11.2.   Litter on the outskirts of Landruk, Annapurna District, Nepal (Erlet Cater)

THE NEED FOR A NEW CONCEPT IN PROTECTED AREA MANAGEMENT: THE CREATION OF THE ANNAPURNA CONSERVATION AREA PROJECT

Popular participation in conservation is not new in Nepal. People have developed various resource management systems which have been practised for centuries to fulfil their daily needs. However, as the population grew and their demands and needs were multiplied by modernisation, environmental problems became severe. The loss of habitats for rhinoceros and tiger in the Chitwan valley, as a result of resettlement and malaria eradication projects (the first foreign-aided projects), culminated in the loss of these endangered species. However, without adequate understanding, such areas were declared National Parks with the sole intention of protecting the wildlife and forest while forgetting the needs of the people. Certainly this approach achieved one set of goals, the protection of flora and fauna, but it also created unforeseen socio-economic problems. The park/people conflict is still an unresolved issue (Mishra and Sherpa, 1987; Sharma, 1991).

In the Annapurna region, environmental problems are multifaceted. Hence, instead of prescribing one single mitigative measure, the problems have been addressed holistically. Integrated strategies have been devised that will incorporate all the relevant issues. To avoid resistance from the people by designating the area as the National Park for the Annapurna region, a new designation was needed which addressed the needs of the local people, of *human development*, as well as the need for *nature conservation* and the need for *tourism management.*

As a result of the Annapurna region's unique socio-economic, cultural and environmental factors, a new designation was called for which encompassed the three main components discussed above. Thus, Conservation Area designation means slightly less restrictive management policies than those of Nepal's National Parks, but is broader in scope and coverage. With the assignment of a large degree of management responsibility to local populations, Conservation Area status is designed to avoid excessive bureaucracy (Sherpa *et al.*, 1986).

With the approval of His Majesty's Government of Nepal, the operational plan was implemented by the King Mahendra Trust for Nature Conservation (KMTNC) in 1986, establishing the Annapurna Conservation Area Project (ACAP) (Figure 11.3).

The study had found that virtually 40 000 people were living within the Annapurna region, dependent upon local natural resources for their livelihood. Owing to its large size, the region encompasses a variety of cultures and microclimates, which have given rise to many indigenous management schemes. These traditional practices were much more effective than those of projects initiated and implemented by government agencies with much larger foreign assistance. Consequently, the study team felt strongly that, unless the local people were brought into the mainstream of conservation, measures taken to conserve the natural and cultural heritage of the region may not be successful. Hence a new approach was necessary to allow the local residents to remain within and around the conservation area and permit them to use the resources in a sustainable manner. In essence, the local people would be the custodians of the resources.

AN APPLIED EXPERIMENT IN INTEGRATED CONSERVATION AND DEVELOPMENT: ESSENTIAL ELEMENTS OF THE ANNAPURNA CONSERVATION AREA PROJECT

Guiding principles

The main guiding principles of ACAP are

- sustainability
- people's participation
- catalyst (or Lami/a match-maker)
- conservation for development

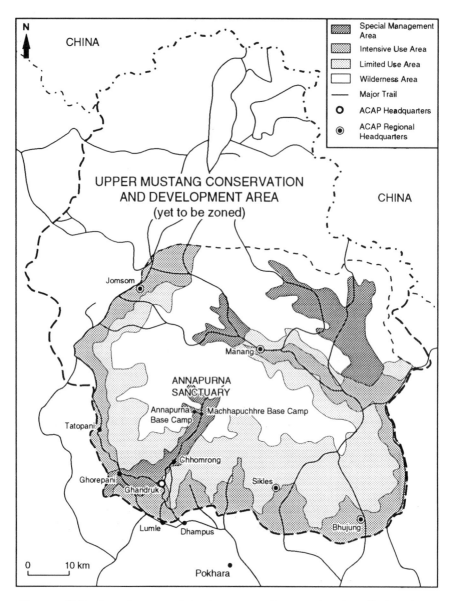

FIGURE 11.3.   Location map of the Annapurna Conservation Area Project Area

- grass-roots methods
- multiple use
- implementation of programmes by stages

Sustainability

The ACAP team realised from the beginning that conservation efforts require substantial capital. The financial structure was designed so that, initially, programme costs were borne primarily by support from outside donors, such as the World Wild Fund for Nature (WWF) (USA), the King Mahendra UK Trust and the Netherlands Development Organization (SNV/Nepal). However, the ACAP would eventually become financially self-supporting through user fees, a mechanism to generate its own income, thereby diminishing the dependency on foreign investment. The ACAP recognised from the very beginning that it should develop its own scheme to become financially self-reliant once the funding from donors was exhausted. As a result, with the approval of His Majesty's Government of Nepal, an entry user's fee (like the National Park fee) was charged to all international visitors. Although the grants from donors were still being received, all the fees collected were deposited in an endowment trust fund. Since 1992, the fund has been partially used for conservation and development programmes in the conservation area.

Sustainability in this context does not only mean financial sustenance. It also refers to the availability of trained personnel in and from the region, utilising both formal and informal expertise. Both of these aspects are incorporated in any community development and conservation projects implemented by ACAP through the local people.

People's participation

The sustainability of conservation and development projects depends on the participation and motivation of the local people. Fundamentally, motivation comes from a realisation that it is their own project, that they are the main beneficiaries and that they truly have ownership in their future. As people are involved in the planning, decision-making and implementation of the projects, locals must contribute at least 50 per cent towards any development programme. This is matched by funds from the ACAP or other sources, as many of ACAP's programmes are experimental. Thus the sharing of both successes and failures is part of the development process. The involvement of local people is also necessary in tourism management. Hence training is given to trekking lodge owners and lodge management committees (LMC) are formed, delegating responsibilities for proper management of the lodges.

Catalyst or Lami approach

Various development and conservation projects have been implemented by both national and international agencies in the region. It is not the aim of the ACAP to take over or duplicate the work of the government; rather it is to work closely with it. As most of the population is deprived of basic facilities such as drinking water, health care and education, the ACAP plays the part of facilitator by bringing in outside resources to fulfil the needs of the local residents.

Conservation for development

The ACAP contends that conservation and development are complementary rather than opposing forces. Development programmes, if incorporated within the conservation aspects, will be more sustainable. For either to be sustainable, they must both be carried out in a coordinated manner with the same main objective: the long-term welfare of the people and the environment that sustains them. Adopting proper conservation methods in tourism planning should generate more revenue, which could contribute towards the development of the country.

Grass-roots methods

History shows that it is no longer feasible to effect environmental conservation, especially in developing countries, to the exclusion of human needs. Flora and fauna may be temporarily protected, but the needs of growing populations will soon supersede even the best protection efforts. With a long-term view in mind, the ACAP adopts a more decentralised, bottom-up approach to revive conservation. Local people are actively encouraged to take a leading role in conservation and development activities, expressing their needs and concerns in open forums. The ACAP supplies the technical expertise and know-how so that they undertake many of the projects themselves. It is hoped that, by these grass-roots methods, the socio-economic problems and alienation often associated with National Parks will be avoided.

The multiple-use concept

Tourism, farming, forestry and biodiversity conservation are carried out jointly in the Annapurna Conservation Area. To avoid possible conflicts, as an initial step the ACAP was zoned according to various levels of use, both by tourists and villagers (Figure 11.3). Studies are currently being conducted to extend the conservation area on the basis of biological diversity and intact ecosystems. Not only will this promote informed decision-making, but it will give great assurance that the best management practices will be implemented in the most suitable areas.

Implementation of programmes by stages

Owing to its large size, existing administrative structure [five Districts, 70 Village Development Committees (VDCs)] and the varying levels of impact, ACAP is designed to be implemented in stages. The areas hardest hit by

FIGURE 11.4.   Demonstration back boiler at ACAP headquarters, Ghandruk (Erlet Cater)

trekking were addressed first, not only because of their acute problems but also because suitable trails were needed to test new methods and technologies before promoting them in other regions. Initially, the project was implemented in only one VDC area of approximately 900 households, covering approximately 200 square kilometres. Three years later, in 1989, 12 additional VDCs were incorporated, encompassing nearly 1200 square kilometres. In 1993, the project reached all areas within the protected zone. Additionally, it has assumed responsibility for managing the newly designated Upper Mustang Conservation and Development Project (see Figure 11.3), bringing the total land area under the ACAP jurisdiction to 7000 square kilometres.

Major programmes

Alternative energy   Deforestation is a major issue in the Annapurna region. Certain localised areas have been devastated by the sudden influx of trekking tourism. Forests are depleted to fulfil energy and construction requirements to meet the needs of tourists and the fodder requirement of the local residents. Thus the problem of deforestation is tackled from many different angles, including alternative energy sources, energy-saving technologies, reforestation and community forest management schemes. The ACAP has been promoting several alternative sources of energy and fuelwood-saving devices in the conservation area to reduce the pressure on forests. Some of these are discussed in detail here.

Back-boiler water heaters   The residents of the Annapurna region still use the open-hearth system for cooking. The stove is neither smoke-free nor fuel-efficient. At the same time, on the main trekking routes, people are using a separate fireplace for hot water. The ACAP has introduced a fuelwood-saving device known as the back-boiler water heater (Figure 11.4). A number of circulatory pipes are attached to the drum. The pipes are fitted onto the existing stoves. These stoves are also improved. Thus, during cooking, the water in the back boiler is automatically heated up. The introduction of this simple technology has already saved 40 per cent of fuelwood consumption. Over 200 of these back-boiler water heaters have been introduced in the Annapurna region. (Figure 11.5).

Solar water heaters   The ACAP also introduced solar water heaters which the local lodge owners were initially reluctant to use. However, over the last two years more than a dozen solar water heaters have been installed in various lodges.

FIGURE 11.5.   Back-boiler system installed at a lodge at Tolka, Annapurna District, Nepal (Erlet Cater)

Kerosene   In part of the area of most acute fuelwood shortage the ACAP has implemented a kerosene-only policy. However, as kerosene has to be imported from outside Nepal, sudden geopolitical problems create shortages of this resource, leading to a disruption of the programme.

Micro-hydroelectricity projects   Based on the above experiences, the ACAP has realised that its alternative energy technologies cannot depend on imported fossil fuels or on the forest resources. Thus, based on the available technology in Nepal, as well as depending on a renewable resource, micro-hydroelectricity projects have been found to be the most appropriate solution. This involves tapping small local streams to produce hydroelectricity, which is used for lighting and cooking.

The introduction of these fuelwood saving devices, as well as other alternative energy sources, may have a positive impact on the tourism industry, making it more profitable.

A micro-hydroelectricity project has recently been implemented in the village of Ghandruk, which is on one of the most popular trekking routes, towards the Annapurna Sanctuary. To cater for the demands of a growing number of tourists (10 000 each year), there are now 20 lodges and six campsites in the village. The village has a total of 250 households. The amount of fuelwood that is being consumed by the lodges is more than the total consumption by local residents.

To reduce the pressure on forest resources the ACAP, in conjunction with the local population, installed a small micro-hydroelectricity project with a total capacity of 50 kW in May 1992. The total cost of the project was 3.6 million rupees (£50 000 sterling). Financial assistance for the project came from the Canadian Cooperation Office, King Mahendra UK Trust, the WWF and the Agricultural Development Bank, Nepal. Technical assistance came from the Intermediate Technology Development Group (ITDG), UK and the Development Consulting Services (DCS), Nepal. The local people bore 30 per cent of the total costs, partly in cash and also in the form of voluntary labour.

Two new technologies have been introduced in Ghandruk which store energy produced from micro-hydroelectricity. Both these technological developments are produced in Nepal and can be easily repaired and maintained by the Nepali technicians.

Bijuli Deckchi (low wattage cooker)   It was found that, with the Nepali style of cooking, 80 per cent of the energy used is usually spent in boiling water. It was realised that if the hot water was readily available, only 20 per cent of the original energy requirements would be needed for cooking the food. Furthermore, electricity would only be used for seven to eight hours a day for cooking and lighting. The rest of the time, if not stored, the energy would be wasted as energy from water would be produced 24 hours a day. In addition to cooking and boiling water for food, the Bijuli Deckchi also stores energy in the form of hot water, which is used for cooking. This cooker is now very popular in Ghandruk. Virtually all the lodge owners are using the Bijuli Deckchi for cooking.

Heat-storage cooker   As the Nepali style of cooking also requires a lot of frying, a new device is now being introduced as a prototype. This new technology is a heat-storage cooker where the energy is stored in rocks and boulders. With the help of a small fan, cold air is blown into the rocks, displacing the hot air. Food is fried using this hot air. The temperature of the air reaches up to 500°C.

Conclusions   With the introduction of these two new technologies, it is expected that dependency on fuelwood will be drastically reduced. Ultimately, it will have a significant impact on curtailing deforestation.

Tree nurseries and reforestation

In addition to the introduction of alternative cooking technologies, more than ten tree nurseries have been established in various places. The ACAP staff are trained to collect the seeds from the forest and produce seedlings in these nurseries. The seedlings produced in the nurseries are mostly of fodder, firewood and timber species. The ACAP has a policy of not introducing any exotic species. Seedlings are distributed free of charge to the local people. In the last six years, over 300 000 seedlings have been distributed for both individual and community plantations.

Community forest management

To protect the existing forest, local level Conservation and Development Committees (CDCs) and Forest Management Committees (FMCs) are formed. The local 15 member CDC is selected by the people themselves. This committee is empowered to protect the forest, to allow the members of the community to collect firewood and fodder in a sustainable manner and to keep the fines collected from those people who have broken the rules.

Community development programmes

Through the project the ACAP has been helping various community development projects to fulfil their basic needs. Thus health posts have been established; maternal and child health clinics have been set up; and mothers' groups have been formed to carry out the various community development and conservation projects. The mothers' groups concentrate their efforts mainly on trail repairs, school repairs, tree planting and sometimes getting rid of undesirable social activities such as gambling and public drinking. Drinking water programmes and the construction of schools, trails and bridges are some of the community development undertakings of the ACAP.

Conservation education and extension

Lack of conservation awareness at both the government and local level has contributed to the plight of the natural system. Conservation efforts in Nepal often failed because they focused mainly on an arbitrary enforcement of regulations (Sherpa, 1987). Thus the ACAP strongly believes that the heart of its programme - is education and public awareness. Unless awareness is raised among the users of the resources, both locals and outsiders, sustainable development cannot be achieved. As a result, the ACAP has identified three target groups, the children in the village, the adult population and the international visitors. Environmental education is taught as part of regular classwork at schools for the children between the sixth and eighth grade. Similarly, adult education, slides and video programmes, study tours, group discussions, appropriate training and awareness raising campaigns (such as cleaning campaigns) are carried out, targeting the local adult population. To motivate the international tourist, information centres have been set up and the ACAP has developed a *minimum impact code* which is incorporated in a brochure distributed to all trekkers going into the Annapurna region.

Research and training

One of the main aims of the project is to develop locally trained labour, ensuring that the project should become sustainable in terms of employment. About 80 per cent of the project staff are local residents. Furthermore, the inclusion of female staff is also promoted as far as possible. About 30 per cent of the staff are women. Appropriate training is provided for the staff both in Nepal and abroad to motivate them as well as to upgrade their efficiency.

The project is also providing appropriate training in income-generating activities as well as training the trekking lodge operators. A week-long integrated lodge owners' training course has been provided for all the lodge operators of the Annapurna region. The curriculum includes food preparation, sanitation and hygiene, garbage disposal systems, menu-costing, fuelwood-saving devices, cultural differences and, finally, the safety and security of the trekkers. Local LMCs are formed which are authorised to control prices and be responsible for the safety and security of trekkers. This training has already promoted changes among the local lodge operators.

At present, there are several research programmes underway, e.g. a floristic survey of the Annapurna region and the Biodiversity Conservation Data Project. These programmes are compiling an inventory of the flora, fauna and non-timber forest products. The information collected will be very useful in updating the management plans of the conservation area.

Financial sustainability

Once the basic infrastructure is established with financial assistance from donors, the ACAP will have its own financial base to cover the operating costs of the project, relieving the government of an additional burden.

ECOTOURISM AS A SUSTAINING FORCE: ECOTOURISM AS IF PEOPLE MATTERED

'Uncover a world of savage beauty on this trek to the Annapurna . . .' (Mountain Travel-Sobek Catalogue, 1992).

Environmentally and culturally friendly tourism becomes a tool which can

- generate income for local communities
- promote understanding between different cultures
- provide a range of options for an enjoyable educational and challenging experience for both nationals and foreign tourists
- educate local populations on matters of health, education, energy use, business and environmental conservation
- provide a financial incentive to protect and conserve a globally significant natural/cultural resource

The ACAP believes that tourism, properly managed, can bring great benefits to the land and the people of the Annapurna region. Rather than a necessary evil, tourists are regarded as partners in fulfilling the goals of biodiversity conservation, cultural revitalisation and sustainable economic development. In the Annapurna region nature and culture share the tourist spotlight. Trekking is a unique form of recreation that allows tourists to enjoy these features in an interactive, challenging and educational manner. In return, they can supply the region with much-needed capital to carry out conservation and local development programmes. The challenge remains to develop pro-active policies and practical methods to mitigate the negative effects of tourism and highlight the positive effects.

The ACAP has recognised that ecotourism needs to be based on both nature and culture so that all participants—villagers, visitors, guides, travel agents and the natural environment—can benefit. The ACAP strives to sensitise all users through brochures, displays, information booths, periodic meetings and the like, as well as providing viable alternatives to potentially destructive practices. The project's thoughts on ecotourism go beyond the standard definitions of Ceballos-Lascurain (1988) and Boo (1992). The ACAP seeks not only to generate financial support for conservation and grass-roots development, but also to integrate the local residents and their economy into the mainstream of national tourism planning, giving them a meaningful role. This will hopefully avoid patronising them by giving money so that they can remain where they are. Financial patronisation is not a long-term solution.

With such objectivity, the ACAP's working definition of ecotourism becomes that of applying environmental and cultural sensitivity whereby all the users, both locals and visitors, minimize their impacts.

'Nepal is here to change you not for you to change Nepal'

Sustainable tourism, benefiting the country in the long term, can still be achieved if all concerned—the government and private sector—can work together. The responsibility of conservation and the protection of natural and cultural heritage should not be left wholly in the hands of the locals, but responsibility should be borne by all concerned and the users—the locals, the private agencies, the government and the visitors (tourists).

For a developing country such as Nepal, revenue generated from tourism should be ploughed back into the local economic development programmes. National level programmes ought to be devised in such a way that the tourism industry is not based on imported materials, but on the resources that are available within the country. In this way, a larger proportion of the foreign currency earned from tourism could be retained within the country. According to a World Bank report, almost 50–60 per cent of the revenue earned from tourism in Nepal flows out of the country in the form of import leakages. In the mountain region, less than 10 per cent of the revenue generated is retained in the local areas. Thus proper management is necessary for sustainability. Otherwise, 'the goose that lays golden eggs not only fouls its own nest but will ruin the economy with unforeseen socio-economic, cultural and natural environmental problems, at a cost that a developing country may not be able to afford'. A vivid example of this is the litter accumulated on the slopes of Mount Sagarmatha (Mount Everest), which is estimated to amount to 50 tonnes and will cost US$500 000 to clean up (NMA, 1991). Nepal cannot afford such an operation.

THE FUTURE: CONTINUING ISSUES AND NEW CHALLENGES

The ACAP has begun two projects: the Upper Mustang Conservation and Development Project and the Ghalegaun-Sikles Ecotourism Project (GSEP). The aim of these two projects is to develop environmentally sensitive tourism which will have an effect on the natural and cultural environment, at the same time fulfilling the basic needs of the local people by using the revenue generated by tourism.

The Upper Mustang Conservation and Development Project

The Upper Mustang area is situated in the north-central part of Nepal adjoining the Tibetan border (Figure 11.3). Most of the region is located in the rainshadow area above 3000 metres. Although rich in culture, Mustang is very dry and has very little vegetation cover. Owing to the lack of fuelwood, the local population use yak dung and goat dung pellets for heating and cooking. The population is sparse. As a result of harsh climatic conditions, with severe winter cold and snow, almost 50 per cent of the local population migrates to the south for seasonal employment. The government offices, schools and health care facilities are virtually closed for six months every year. Only one crop is grown each year. Livestock rearing provides the main source of income. His Majesty's Government of Nepal has opened the area to trekking tourism since March 1992. The royalty for trekking in the region is US$700 for a ten-day trek. Each year, 1000 tourists are allowed to trek. The government has decided to plough back 60 per cent of the revenue generated from tourism into the conservation and development programmes of the area. The responsibility for management of the project has been given to the ACAP. The project places emphasis on energy issues, improving the living conditions of the people by providing health care facilities and irrigation, and preservation of the cultural heritage of the region.

Ghalegaun-Sikles Ecotourism Project

The Ghalegaun-Sikles area is a trekking route of one week's duration, starting from about 900 metres and reaching up to 2700 metres above sea level. It is located on the southern slopes of the Annapurna region, in the middle hills of Nepal. The route traverses rhododendron forests as well as culturally rich villages.

The GSEP is the second project, started in 1992, that ACAP is undertaking with financial assistance from the Nepalese Government and the Asian Development Bank. The ACAP plans to develop a model trek route with proper environmental considerations. The route will have a garbage disposal system, sanitation and hygiene and the use of passive energy or alternative sources of energy rather than depending on fuelwood for cooking and heating. Various community development programmes are planned along the route which will provide basic facilities such as drinking water, health care and schools. Tourism will be of direct economic benefit to the local people and stimulate the revival of a cultural heritage which is gradually being lost.

CONCLUSIONS

In Nepal, which lacks large-scale industries, tourism can play an important part in the country's economic development. However, a continued lack of environmental sensitivity on the part of the government and private sector will prejudice the future of the tourism industry. In the Annapurna region, it has been suggested that the carrying capacity of the region may have been exceeded. The authors believe that the carrying capacity of a given area depends on the development of services and the sensitivity of the people who are using the resources. Given the existing facilities in the region with regard to energy, lodging and other relevant services, the present 45 000 tourists may be more than is sustainable. However, the authors are of the opinion that neither the closing of an area nor the opening up of a new area to diversify tourism will help, unless tourism is managed at both macro and micro levels.

Tourism is still one of the most promising 'industries' in Nepal, with a great potential for increasing the country's scarce resources. Sustainable tourism is still possible if proper environmental conservation consideration is given by both the government and the private sector. The recent initiatives (Mustang and Ghalegaun-Sikles projects) by the Ministry of Tourism show that the government is keen on developing environmentally sensitive tourism, but responsibility must be taken by all the users, both the private sector and tourists alike.

The past seven years' experience in the ACAP has led the authors to believe that an area's depleted natural and cultural environments can be restored from the revenue generated from tourism, if tourism is properly managed. Blaming tourism for deforestation, litter and inflation will serve no purpose.

REFERENCES

Boo, E., 1992, The ecotourism boom: planning for development and management. Wildlands and human needs: a program of the World Wildlife Fund, *WHN Technical Paper Series, Paper # 2.*

Ceballos-Lascurain, H., 1988, The future of ecotourism, *Mexico Journal,* January 27.

Fleming, W.B., 1991, *Tourism: Environmental Management and Sustainable Development in the Arun Basin,* Vol. 12, King Mahendra Trust for Nature Conservation, Kathmandu.

Mishra, H.R. and Sherpa, M.N., 1987, Nature conservation and human needs: conflicts or coexistence: Nepal's experiment with the Annapurna Conservation Area Project, paper presented at the *4th World Wilderness Congress, 11–18 September 1987, Denver, CO, USA.*

Nepal Mountaineering Association (NMA), 1991, *A Proposal for Cleaning Mount Sagarmatha 1993–1994 as a Part of Clean Himalaya Campaign,* NMA, Nepal.

Sharma, U.R., 1991, Park–people interactions in Royal Chitwan National Park, Nepal, *Dissertation* submitted to the Faculty of the Committee on Wildlife and Fisheries Science in partial fulfilment of the requirements for the Degree of Doctor of Philosophy, in the Graduate College, the University of Arizona.

Sherpa, M.N., 1987, People, park problems and challenges in the Annapurna Conservation Area in Nepal, paper presented at the *International Symposium on Protected Landscapes, Grange-over-Sands, 5–10 October 1987, Cumbria, UK.*

Sherpa, M.N., Coburn, Broughton, Gurung, Chandra Prasad, 1986, *Annapurna Conservation Area, Nepal: Operational Plan,* King Mahendra Trust for Nature Conservation, Nepal.

FURTHER READING

Bjonness, I.M., 1980, Ecological conflicts and economic dependency on tourist trekking in Sagarmatha (Mt Everest) National Park, Nepal: an alternative approach to park planning, *Norsk Geografiske Tidsskrift,* **3,** 119–138.

Boo, E., 1990, *Ecotourism: the Potentials and Pitfalls,* World Wildlife Fund, Washington, DC.

Eber, S. (ed.), 1992, *Beyond the Green Horizon: a Discussion Paper on Principles for Sustainable Tourism,* World Wildlife Fund, Godalming.

Griffith, L., 1993, Roads less travelled, *WWF News,* 13–16.

Gurung, H., 1990, Environmental management of mountain tourism in Nepal, paper presented at *ESCAP Symposium on Tourism Promotion in the Asian Region, 12–15 November 1990, Hangzhou, China.*

Gurung, Lal P., 1989, Socio-cultural, economic and physical impacts of tourism in the southern part of Annapurna Region, Nepal, *Diploma Dissertation* submitted in partial fulfilment of the requirements for the Diploma in Parks and Recreation Management in Lincoln College, New Zealand.

Mason, P., 1990, *Tourism: Environment and Development Perspectives,* World Wildlife Fund, Godalming.

Thompson, S., 1992, Trekking to save the tree line, *Geographical Magazine,* August, 30–33.

West, P.C. and Brechin, S.R. (eds), 1991, *Resident Peoples and National Parks: Social Dilemmas and Strategies in International Conservation,* The University of Arizona Press, Tucson.

Whelan, T. (ed.), 1991, *Nature Tourism: Managing for the Environment,* Island Press, Washington.

Yap, S.K. and Lee, S.W. (eds), 1992, *In Harmony with Nature, Proceedings of the International Conference on Conservation of Tropical Biodiversity,* Malayan Nature Kuala Lumpur Society, Kuala Lumpur.

12

Ecotourism in Antarctica

BERNARD STONEHOUSE

INTRODUCTION

Antarctica lies far to the south of all other continents, ringed by the ice-ridden Southern Ocean. Known to humankind for less than a century, with no human population of its own, it was for long protected from exploitation by pack ice and a harsh climate. For conventional tour operators it held little appeal: distant, dangerous and totally lacking in the standard amenities that conventional tourists demand. Adventure travel during the 1950s brought Antarctica into the tourist world. From 1966 onwards the more accessible points of the continent have become tourist venues, visited annually during brief summers by tour ships and aircraft. Antarctic tourism has grown most rapidly within the last decade, doubling and redoubling to an annual total of about 7000. This chapter traces the history of Antarctic tourism, examines the kinds of tourism currently practised, discusses ecological implications and outlines current research towards the management of tourism under the Antarctic Treaty regime.

Last of the continents to fall to humanity, Antarctica was believed to exist long before its actual discovery. Captain James Cook RN sought it assiduously in the 1770s, circumnavigating the Southern Ocean and penetrating the pack ice far beyond the Antarctic Circle. Foiled by the continent's maritime defences—icebergs, sea ice, poor visibility and foul wealther—Cook sailed away convinced that Antarctica existed, but equally certain that land in so high a latitude would prove neither habitable nor useful to humans.

For long he was right. Although sealers throughout the nineteenth century exploited peripheral islands in the Southern Oceans, taking a rich harvest of sealskins and oil, only a very few found time and curiosity to penetrate southward, into and beyond the pack ice. No human saw Antarctica before about 1820. French, American and British explorers criss-crossed the Southern Ocean and drew in the outlines of a vast new continent, but it is doubtful whether anyone landed on Antarctica before 1894, or wintered ashore before 1899.

In the first decade of the twentieth century explorers from several nations tackled the more readily accessible parts of the coast. Scott and Shackleton

Ecotourism: A Sustainable Option? Edited by E. Cater and G. Lowman
© The editors and contributors. Published in 1994 by John Wiley & Sons Ltd

penetrated the ice-covered interior: Amundsen reached the South Pole on 17 December 1911. During the 1920s and 1930s Norwegian whalers explored more of the coastline and aircraft first flew over the continent itself, photographing and recording some of its vast interior ice sheets, glaciers and mountain ranges.

Only in the final years of the Second World War were the first permanent settlements established—small research stations manned year-round by transient populations of scientists, explorers and technical support staff. Up to the mid-1950s Antarctica's meagre population was lodged in a scattering of such stations, present more to establish sovereignty than to explore. The total population of Antarctica seldom exceeded a few hundred in summer, a few dozen in winter.

After 1957–8, the International Geophysical Year (IGY), human effort intensified: Antarctica became a continent for science—a continent still with no permanent human population, but one where scientists of many nations pursued research under a unique international political regime, the Antarctic Treaty. Sovereignty claims were shelved in the interests of the Treaty; nations that elsewhere squabbled to the point of warfare found cause for cooperation south of the 60th parallel of latitude.

Throughout the 1960s, increasing amounts of public money were spent on Antarctic research and exploration: Antarctic affairs were well publicised, but it was scientists and their support staff, including ships' companies and aviation teams, that remained the most numerous users of Antarctica. Few visited Antarctica for fun or recreation: nearly all to be found there were government-employed, or sponsored by nationally funded expeditions.

THE START OF ANTARCTIC TOURISM

The first-ever tourist aircraft flew to Antarctica in December 1956; the first tourist ship arrived in January 1958. Since then tourism has increased slowly and erratically, catering mainly to a small up-market sector of adventure travellers and natural history buffs, and limited by the formidable expenses arising from Antarctica's remoteness. In winter a few hundred scientists still have Antarctica to themselves. In summer their numbers rise to seven to eight thousand, but tourists start to outnumber them, to the consternation of many who work there and the concern of legislators charged with the task of protecting the Antarctic environment.

The *Shorter Oxford English Dictionary* (1983) defines a tourist as '. . . one who travels for pleasure or culture, visiting a number of places for their objects of interest, scenery or the like'. Tourists discovered the north polar region during the mid-nineteenth century, attracted by sailing, hunting and huge-scale wilderness. Arctic exploring expeditions of the nineteenth and early twentieth centuries sometimes defrayed expenses by carrying a few paying passengers, who thereby gained an adventurous summer vacation. Antarctica waited longer for its tourists. None sailed there casually and expedition ships, outward bound usually for a year or more, were traditionally overloaded with men and equipment, with no room for supernumeraries.

In 1980 Reich recorded an early attempt to promote Antarctic tourism, reported in the Christchurch (New Zealand) *Press* of 4 November 1910. Messrs Thomas Cook and Sons at that time proposed a 50-day tourist voyage to McMurdo Sound, in the sector of Antarctica immediately south of New Zealand, widely known throughout the Dominion as the starting-off point of both Scott's and Shackleton's polar expeditions. The tour did not materialise and there is no further evidence of recreational voyages to Antarctica for almost half a century.

Summer visitors to the US McMurdo Station during the early 1960s usually included journalists, cameramen, politicians and dignitaries—official visitors brought in to publicise or provide Congressional support for US activities in the area. Given VIP treatment, often including a flight to Amundsen Scott (South Pole) Station, such visitors were unofficially dubbed tourists and regarded with mistrust and mild derision by the working scientists and support staff (Stonehouse, 1965). By this time more authentic forms of Antarctic tourism had already begun. Sadly, the mistrust and derision, delicately tinged with macho, were transferred to the real tourists: the industry began in an aura of hostility that even now tends to persist among other users of Antarctica.

AIR-BORNE TOURISM

The first genuine Antarctic tourists were a planeload of passengers who, on 23 December 1956, flew in a DC6B aircraft from Punta Arenas, Chile to Antarctic Peninsula. They enjoyed a scenic flight that penetrated over 150 kilometres south of the Antarctic Circle (Reich, 1980; *Explorers Journal*, 1957). In the following season a chartered Pan American Stratocruiser carried US military personnel from Christchurch, New Zealand to McMurdo Station. Thereafter for over a decade, passenger flights on either side of the continent were rare.

The first commercial transpolar flight, in November 1968, carried 75 passengers from New Zealand to South America, refuelling at McMurdo Station. During the early 1970s plans were considered to carry passengers by air from New Zealand to a cruise ship in McMurdo Sound; this scheme was never developed. From February 1976 Boeing 747s of Qantas, and later DC 10s of Air New Zealand, carried passengers on long scenic tours of Victoria Land, overflying without landing. These became popular flights, carrying a total of several thousands of passengers. They ended in disaster on 28 November 1979, when a New Zealand aircraft crashed into the side of Mount Erebus with the loss of 257 lives (Chippindale, 1980; Auburn, 1983).

In 1979–80 the Chilean Government installed a 1300 metre long hard run-
way and a hostel for passengers at Teniente Rodolfo Marsh Station, King
George Island, South Shetland Islands (Figure 12.1). This made possible tourist flights from Punta Arenas, using both Chilean Air Force and private aircraft. For the period 1982–4 Boswall (1986) records a menu of flights, giving
passengers the choice of returning the same day, staying briefly on King
George Island for walks or helicopter flights, or joining tour ships for seven-
day cruises of Antarctic Peninsula.

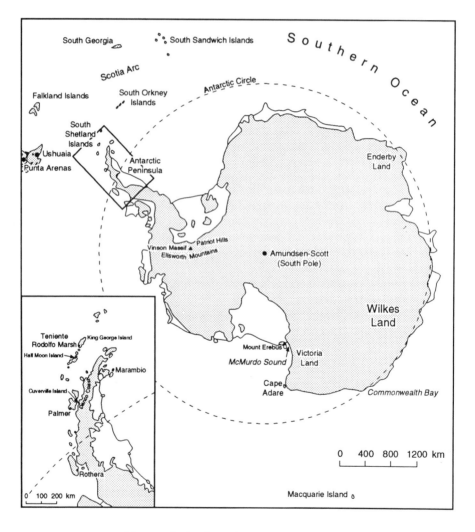

FIGURE 12.1.   Location map of Antarctica

Teniente Marsh Station is still often used for commercial flights; other hard runways are only available for emergency use at Argentine Marambio Station, Seymour Island and British Rothera Station, further south along Antarctic Peninsula. However, bare ice patches in the interior of Antarctica are now being used as runways for wheeled aircraft, making possible a much wider range of tourist flights. The North American company Adventure Network International, for example, flies exploring parties, camera crews and climbers, trekkers, ornithologists and other kinds of tourists from southern Chile to the Patriot Hills, Vincent Massif (Antarctica's highest peak), the South Pole and other remote corners of Antarctica (Swithinbank, 1992a; 1992b). In 1989–90 this company operated a nine month season from July to March, supporting expeditions and carrying its own passengers from an advanced base in Ellsworth Mountains.

Such enterprise has opened virtually the whole of Antarctica to air-borne tourism; for a review of possibilities see Swithinbank (1993). The main factor limiting expansion is the high cost of safe and ecologically sound operations, currently restricting uptake to a few hundred passengers each year, or less than five per cent of the total number visiting Antarctica.

SHIP-BORNE TOURISM

The first ship to carry tourists to continental Antarctica appears to have been *Les Eclaireurs*, an Argentine naval transport ship used in servicing government operation stations. This made two voyages to the Antarctic Peninsula in January and February 1958, carrying about 100 paying passengers on each voyage. In the following year both Chilean and Argentine government ships made similar short voyages, between them carrying over 300 passengers (Reich, 1980).

No further voyages are recorded until January 1966, when the first US-inspired cruise took place. Using the Argentine naval vessel *Lapataia* and carrying 58 passengers, Lars-Eric Lindblad of Lindblad Travel Inc. made a single voyage to the Antarctic Peninsula. In the following season Lindblad promoted two similar voyages, again to the Antarctic Peninsula. In 1968 Lindblad Travel Inc. promoted two voyages to the Peninsula in the Chilean transport *Navarino* and two to the Ross Sea region, including McMurdo Sound, in the Danish ice-strengthened ship *Magga Dan*. So began Lindblad's long association with Antarctic tourism and his establishment of a benign pattern of tourist handling and behaviour that has since permeated the whole of the Antarctic tourist industry.

Over the following quarter of a century Antarctic ship-borne tourism grew erratically but surely (Reich, 1980; Codling, 1982; Enzenbacher, 1992). Statistics covering the late 1960s to the mid-1980s, though not entirely reliable, indicate passenger numbers fluctuating between 500 and 2000, with an unusual peak of over 3500 in 1974–5, owing to repeated voyages by one large Argentine-operated ship, *Regina Prima*. From 1986 to 1990 numbers fluctuated between 2000 and 3500. More reliable data gathered during the past three years by the US National Science Foundation indicate continuing increases in the number of ships employed, journeys made and passengers carried. In 1990–1 more than 4600 ship-borne tourists visited Antarctica; during 1991–2 over 6000 and during 1992–3 about 7000.

Ship-borne tourists, currently accounting for more than 95 per cent of all tourists visiting Antarctica, are necessarily restricted to readily accessible parts of the coast. More visit the South American sector than any other area of the continent. Most Antarctic cruise ships sail from southern South America (Montevideo, Buenos Aires, or the Tierra del Fuego ports of Punta Arenas or Ushuaia) to the Falkland Islands, Antarctic Peninsula and islands of the Scotia Arc (the South Shetland and South Orkney islands and sub-Antarctic South Georgia). Those on the other side of Antarctica leave southern ports in New Zealand and Tasmania for McMurdo Sound, Cape Adare and Commonwealth Bay, occasionally also Wilkes Land and Enderby Land. Macquarie Island and the southern islands of New Zealand are often included in their itineraries.

Ship-borne visits extend from mid-November to late March, when weather and ice conditions are best and wildlife is most spectacular. The ships range in passenger capacity from fewer than 50 to over 1000, though seldom in the past have more than 450 been carried on each voyage, even in ships with capacity to carry more. Some, but not all, are ice-strengthened (Figure 12.2); most are cruise liners that alternate visits to Antarctica with voyages in warmer waters and the Arctic. Recently ships with true ice-breaking capacity have appeared, chartered from Russian fleets and adapted for tourist use. Privately owned and chartered yachts, some with paying passengers, add slightly to the traffic. Most are summer visitors; a few overwinter each year. A few round the world cruise liners pay brief visits to the South Shetland Islands on the Antarctic fringe.

Paying passengers continue to be carried on naval transports and other expedition ships, usually in less luxury, though more cheaply. One such ship, the Argentine naval transport *Bahia Paraiso*, on 28 January 1989 struck a reef and was wrecked off southern Anvers Island, Antarctic Peninsula. No lives were lost, but oil and other contaminants spread over a large area of inshore waters. The wreck occurred just off US Palmer Station, where long-term programmes of marine ecological work were in progress.

Though *Bahia Paraiso* was not a dedicated tourist ship, some who condemn tourism unhesitatingly cite this misfortune as evidence of the environmental hazards that tourists impose on Antarctica. By grace and good management no true tourist ship has as yet had such an accident, though more than one has come close. However, it is worth recording that the tourist ship *World Discoverer* was first on the scene of the *Bahia Paraiso* disaster, equipped with excellent facilities to ensure the safety of the shipwrecked passengers and

FIGURE 12.2. M.V. *Society Explorer*, veteran ice-strengthened passenger ship, in pack ice off the Antarctic Peninsula (Bernard Stonehouse)

crew. Many who work in the relative isolation of Antarctica find comfort in the presence, thoughout summer, of a fleet of efficient, well-equipped tourist ships, whose captains, crews and passengers are almost invariably hospitable and friendly to the scientific community.

To the tourists themselves, Antarctica is often a dream come true: many have saved for the trip of their lifetime and few seem disappointed by their experience. Tour leaders and their staff work hard each voyage and are rewarded by what must surely be record levels of client satisfaction. Tourists enjoy the scenery, the ice, the wildlife (especially penguins, seals and whales), the sense of remoteness and isolation, the foul weather, the occasional evidence of mankind past and present. They react strongly against the squalor of abandoned huts, wind-scattered rubbish tips and derelict navigation beacons that are a legacy of the past half-century of political claims and counter-claims and the thoughtless conduct of scientists. At the end of each voyage Antarctica—the continent with no human population of its own—has gained a further shipload of friends, supporters and advocates.

TOURISTS ASHORE: THE LINDBLAD PATTERN

Under Antarctic Treaty regulations, captains of tour ships and tour operators are provided by their governments with several forms of information and guidance, outlining the ground rules for taking parties ashore and the location and extent of protected areas (which, for practical reasons, though not very good ones, are seldom marked in the field). A strong duty is imposed on them to ensure the good behaviour of both passengers and crew.

Except in areas set aside under Treaty recommendations for protection or scientific research (Specially Protected Areas, SPAs; Sites of Special Scientific Interest, SSSIs) and in the immediate environs of active stations, tour operators are free to land tourists anywhere within the area covered by the Antarctic Treaty (i.e. south of 60°S). In the Antarctic Peninsula and Scotia Arc alone ship-borne tourists are currently landed at over 70 sites; a further 20 sites have been identified in the Ross Sea sector. Popular landing areas may be visited every second or third day throughout summer by successive cruise ships (Stonehouse, 1992; 1993b); some have now been visited regularly for over 30 years.

It is fortunate for the Antarctic environment that, at least from 1966, Antarctic tourism has been dominated by a strong ethic of environmental concern and conservation, based largely on the management concepts of its foremost practitioner and entrepreneur, Lars-Eric Lindblad. Many of today's cruise directors were trained in, and continue to follow, the Lindblad pattern of tourist management. That this ecologically benign pattern of management clearly appeals to most Antarctic tourists is a happy coincidence; like all the best ecotourism, it handsomely rewards the operators who practise it.

The Lindblad pattern was devised for, and works best with, ships of 100 to 140 passengers operating under an experienced captain and cruise leader. Each voyage is treated as an adventure expedition, with shipboard lectures, briefings and one or more daily landings. Lecturing staff are themselves often experienced Antarctic researchers or administrators; landing sites are selected for their historical associations, natural history or scenic beauty. Passengers, before their first landing, are briefed on the requirements of the Antarctic Treaty covering visitors and issued with a set of Treaty-based guidelines that cover their behaviour ashore, possible hazards, the need to avoid interference with wildlife and other points of conduct.

Landed by inflatable boats in parties of 10 to 15 (Figure 12.3), the passengers are helped ashore by experienced handlers and accompanied and supervised by well-informed guides. For safety reasons and to ensure satisfactory guide to passenger ratios, most ships avoid having more than about 100 passengers ashore at a time. Individuals wear gumboots and bright padded jackets, the latter to ensure that they can be seen from a distance. They are usually free to wander from their parties, but required to keep off glaciers, avoid climbing and other hazardous pursuits, and stay within easy reach of the embarkation point.

Passengers ashore are almost invariably well behaved. The author has yet to see one drop litter, knowingly trample vegetation or interfere seriously with wildlife. Those who infringe the generally accepted guidelines are likely

FIGURE 12.3.   Landing a group of passengers through heavy surf: Deception Island,
South Shetland Islands (Bernard Stonehouse)

to be reminded of responsibilities by their guides, or more often by fellow
passengers. The most persistent offenders are keen photographers; those with
the longest lenses seem always to need the closest approach to their subjects
and most often infringe the rule that requires them to stay over five metres
from nesting birds.

Passengers remain ashore for one to three hours, moving within a radius of
a few hundred metres, seeking photo-opportunities and watching wildlife
(Figure 12.4). There may be up to three such landings each day, interspersed
with pre-arranged visits to scientific stations or to abandoned bases, whaling
stations and historic monuments, or hour-long scenic boat tours among icebergs and islands. Evenings before dinner are usually taken up with a recap
session in which the day's events are discussed and plans for the following day
announced. This is often the occasion for cruise leaders and staff to reinforce
the expedition spirit and reiterate the conservation ethic that all the well-
organised tours actively promulgate.

Despite its relative antiquity in a rapidly developing industry, the Lindblad
pattern continues to be favoured, at least in principle, by most operators.
However, dilutions and weaknesses develop as the pattern is applied in a
wider range of ships and circumstances. Its most serious challenge appears in
ships carrying more than 150 passengers, which for economic reasons may
become the majority in the future. The problem is not usually a matter of

FIGURE 12.4. Chinstrap penguins posing for a photographer: Deception Island, South Shetland Islands (Bernard Stonehouse)

numbers ashore. For safety reasons operators of even the largest ships seldom land more than 100 passengers at a time, though there may be domestic problems in entertaining the majority who are waiting eagerly to go ashore, or disappointed on returning to make room for others. With larger, more heterogeneous communities of passengers there is likely to be a wide range of interests, not all of them enthusiastically receptive to the conservation ethic.

There may be several language groups, to be addressed separately; there are often alternative forms of group entertainment, from bingo to dancing troupes that to some degree compete with natural history. Two sittings for dinner make it difficult for all the passengers to meet in one place at one time and to share their experiences each evening with the cruise director and staff. So strongly implanted is the Lindblad pattern that operators on the large ships try to maintain diluted versions of it which barely suit their needs. Alternative methods of managing large numbers of passengers, both ashore and afloat, may have to be found.

TOURISM AND THE ANTARCTIC TREATY SYSTEM

The Antarctic Treaty of 1959, negotiated between the 12 states whose national expeditions had cooperated with conspicuous success in Antarctica during the IGY of 1957–8, forms the basis of continuing international cooperation over all aspects of human usage of the continent, including resource management. From the original Treaty has arisen the Antarctic Treaty System (ATS), a collective name for recommendations to participating governments arising from the biennial Antarctic Treaty Consultative Meetings (ATCMs), plus three instruments dealing with the management of Antarctic resources. Of these, two are in force—the Convention for the Conservation of Antarctic Seals (1972) and the Convention on the Conservation of Antarctic Marine Living Resources (1980). The more recent Convention on the Regulation of Antarctic Mineral Resource Activities (1988), although adopted by the Treaty Parties, is unlikely even to be ratified or come into force.

A primary purpose of the Treaty was to ensure that the level of cooperation in scientific research achieved during the IGY should continue unimpeded by questions of sovereignty, and enhanced by meetings and exchanges of data and views between scientists. Promotion of science and the interests of scientists were, and have continued to be, of paramount interest in Treaty affairs. However, the sound management of Antarctica has also become a function of the Treaty System. Environmental management issues, including the management of tourism, currently take up much of the time and energy of delegates to ATCMs.

Early Treaty deliberations concerning tourism are highlighted in Heap (1990: 2601–2608) and discussed in Stonehouse (1994: 209). Tourist-related issues were first addressed at the fourth ATCM of 1966, when the delegates recognised that '. . . the effects of tourist activities may prejudice the conduct of scientific research, conservation of flora and fauna and the operation of Antarctic stations'. Recommendation IV-27 provided guidelines covering the conditions under which tourist or other non-scientific expeditions might be allowed to visit scientific stations.

Protection of science against tourists continued to feature in later discussions and recommendations. The sixth ATCM, in 1970, noted that increasing numbers of tourists and other visitors not sponsored by Treaty Consultative Parties could exert '. . . lasting and harmful effects on scientific programmes, on the Antarctic environment, particularly in Specially Protected Areas, and on historic monuments'. Two years later the seventh ATCM recommended (VII-4) that governments consider, at the following meeting two years hence '. . . a statement of those accepted practices and relevant provisions about which all visitors to the Treaty Area should be aware, and that governments '. . . consult each other well in advance about the possibility of designating at the eighth ATCM an adequate number of areas of interest to which tourists could be encouraged to go and about the criteria to be used for such areas' (Heap, 1990: 2602).

The eighth ATCM was the first to consider tourism seriously, though still defensively. Delegates acknowledged that tourism was '. . . a natural development in the Area' that required regulation (Recommendation VIII-9). They recognised also a need '. . . to restrict the number of places where large numbers of tourists may land so that the ecological effects may be monitored'. Annex A of VIII-9 presented a 'Statement of accepted principles and the relevant provisions of the Antarctic Treaty' for the guidance of all who visited Antarctica. These included notes on conservation and wildlife protection, restated the 'Agreed Measures for the Conservation of Flora and Fauna' promulgated in an earlier Treaty recommendation (III–VIII of 1964), and listed Special Measures relating to tourists and non-governmental expeditions, concerned mainly with visits to scientific stations. An appended section 'Guidance for visitors to the Antarctic' listed prohibitions covering disturbance of wildlife, litter, use of sporting guns, introduction of alien species, collecting eggs and fossils and avoidance of interference with scientific work or study sites.

Annex B of this same recommendation provided formally for 'Areas of Special Tourist Interest' (ASTIs), the primary purpose of which was to gather tourists together in places where their effects could be monitored. Four years later, at the eleventh ATCM of 1981, the matter was discussed again (Heap, 1990: 2606). Although SSSI, SPAs and Sites of Historic Interest proliferated, no ASTI was ever designated. It is perhaps remarkable that, on a continent devoted to science, opportunities that ASTIs provided for scientific enquiry into the effects of a growing industry were so thoroughly ignored.

At the tenth ATCM of 1979, Recommendation X-8 set out accepted practices for non-governmental expeditions, encouraging commercial operators to carry tour guides. This had, of course, been a key feature of the Lindblad pattern of management for at least 13 years and was the practice of virtually all operators then working in Antarctica. More perceptively, the same recommendation pointed out that commercial overflights were exceeding existing capabilities for air traffic control, communications and search and rescue, and would exceed the capacity for expeditions to respond in case of emergency. This was a timely warning which, sadly, preceded by only a few weeks the Mount Erebus air disaster.

Tourism was discussed only briefly at the four following ATCMs, but was again featured at the fifteenth meeting of 1989. By the end of the 1980s several nations important in Antarctic affairs, notably Australia, France and New Zealand, had rejected the Convention on the Regulation of Antarctic Mineral Resource Activities, mainly on the grounds that it afforded insufficient environmental protection. Instead there came demands, alike from inside and outside the Treaty forum, for a comprehensive treatment of Antarctic conservation issues. To these pressures the Antarctic Treaty delegates responded: the fifteenth ATCM was notable for its emphasis on environmental matters and tourism was again fully addressed.

Refreshingly, the meeting acknowledged that Antarctica should be open to tourism and other non-governmental activities which, it conceded, '. . . could be valuable in broadening public awareness and appreciation of the continent'. Old priorities persisted: the delegates recorded their continuing concern that such activities could have '. . . potentially serious adverse impacts on scientific investigations and the Antarctic environment'. However, need was expressed for a review that would lead '. . . to further measures to regulate tourist and non-governmental activities, in order to reduce or avoid their possible adverse impacts'.

Responsibility for such a review was passed to a special consultative meeting. The Eleventh Antarctic Treaty Special Consultative Meeting, called to deal with environmental protection, was held in Madrid in 1990. From it emerged the comprehensive Protocol on Environmental Protection, the Treaty's current proposals that seek to regulate all human activities in Antarctica, including tourism.

The Madrid Protocol has yet to be ratified by most of the Antarctic Treaty Consultative Parties, but most of the nations involved in Antarctic tourism already act as though it were operational and seek to work within it. The Protocol imposes a 50-year moratorium on mining, provides for a Committee for Environmental Protection and sets out guidelines for all other activities in Antarctica, ranging from recommendations on liability for environmental damage to settlement of disputes. Five comprehensive annexes cover Environmental Impact Assessment, Conservation of Antarctic Flora and Fauna, Waste Disposal and Waste Management, Prevention of Marine Pollution, and Protected Areas. For a discussion of legal aspects of the Protocol, see van Bennekom (1992).

During discussions preceding and during the sixteenth ATCM of 1991, several delegates queried whether a Protocol that applies impartially to scientists and all other visitors would be adequate to deal with tourism. As with seal hunting, fishing and mineral development, tourism involves the use of Antarctic resources on an industrial scale. Its potential for environmental damage might make it seem dangerous enough to merit separate treatment, and the possibility was raised of a fifth annex of special regulations covering tourism. At the seventeenth ATCM in the following year discussions on tourism, including a draft Tourism Annex to the Protocol, were inconclusive. Parties in effect re-affirmed that tourism did not need special treatment: it could be dealt with like all other visitor activities under existing regulations, recommendations and guidelines.

THE PROTOCOL AND TOURIST MANAGEMENT RESEARCH

Despite the enormous amount of data collected by scientists in Antarctica during the past half century, facts useful in Antarctic management issues are sadly lacking. In no field is this more apparent than tourism. Though many assertions have been made both for and against the industry, there have been few systematic attempts to measure Antarctic tourism, to examine it, describe it, assess with any accuracy its environmental impacts and prescribe sensible remedies.

The most thoughtful approach to the problem in recent years has been that of the International Union for the Conservation of Nature and Natural Resources (IUCN). Its report on Antarctic conservation (1991: 70) recommended that controls over the industry be augmented by

- a comprehensive review of tourism issues (including requirements of prior notification and approval of expeditions and tours, codes of conduct, safety standards, insurance, liability guidelines, environmental impact assessments, inspection and reporting procedures, information and education materials)
- promoting interactions between governments, managers of national Antarctic programmes, scientists and tour operators with the intention of developing tour management guidelines
- proactive planning for ASTIs followed by careful monitoring of subsequent impacts
- controlling choice of tourist destinations

The Polar Ecology and Management Group of the Scott Polar Research Institute, University of Cambridge, which began to consider research on Antarctic tourism in 1989, has accepted these points as guidelines in a six-year programme of research into the management of the industry, in particular ship-borne tourism in the Peninsula sector of Antarctica. The programme forms part of a multidisciplinary study of Antarctic management issues; linked research under this heading includes a study of the heavily impacted environment of King George Island, South Shetland Islands (Harris, 1991a; 1991b), where many nations have sited scientific stations, and comparable studies in both the sub-Antarctic and the Arctic. The project is independently funded, based on an accord between British, Argentine and Chilean scientific institutions, and welcomes research workers from other Antarctic Treaty nations.

The main objectives of the programme include

- investigating how parties of tourists are managed, afloat and ashore
- monitoring impacts of tourists on plant and animal communities and other facets of the environment
- assessing impacts of tourists on all recorded landing sites
- evolving and recommending management procedures that minimise undesirable impacts between tourists and the environment
- finding effective ways of controlling tourism within the means, and consistent with the objectives, of the Protocol

Fieldwork on the project began in 1991–2 with a survey of tourist impacts on Half Moon Island, South Shetland Islands, a questionnaire-based survey of tourist attitudes to and expectations from Antarctica, cataloguing all known landing sites in the South American sector of Antarctica and devising a system of assessment for them (Stonehouse, 1992). These studies provided a ground plan for future research, incidentally identifying several sites that appeared to be at risk and which required immediate attention.

The second season's fieldwork, in 1992–3, was based at Cuverville Island, Danco Coast, a small, picturesque island known to be a popular tourist venue, visited chiefly for its penguins and vegetation, but hitherto unmapped and unstudied. During the study period (late November to early March, in which Cuverville received 35 ship visits and over 2000 visitors) the team surveyed the island topographically, botanically and zoologically, to establish baseline studies of penguins, skuas and other breeding bird populations.

Ways in which visiting parties made use of the island's resources were examined and methods were devised to investigate, as unobtrusively as possible, interactions between penguins and visitors. Simultaneously, other landing sites nearby were examined, providing data for a management plan covering a wide area in which tourist activities might be deployed. The team examined the varying degrees to which key aspects of the 'Visitors' Guidelines' were being observed by groups under different operators and continued their questionnaire-based visitor survey on several ships.

The presence of the research group in a small camp provided a focal point of compelling interest to most of the tourists who came ashore. A modest scientific station and resource centre devoted to tourist interests, competing strongly with Cuverville Island's natural attractions, provided an important clue to how tourists might be attracted away from sensitive sites and towards sites where their impacts could be minimised.

Preliminary results suggest that the number of tourists currently deployed, and under the gentle but strict codes of practice prevailing, have very little immediate impact on ecosystems at many of the sites they visit. Impacts of several thousand visitors each year currently seem far lighter than, for example, those of smaller numbers of researchers at permanent scientific stations. However, the research is only just beginning. Tourist visits may yet be found to be harmful at sites of greater sensitivity than those so far examined, and in the course of time may produce harmful long-term environmental effects, for example on penguin colonies, where in the short term they seem harmless. The long-term monitoring that will be needed to detect such effects should start now, and those concerned should make plans to continue for as long as tourism itself continues.

The scientific studies and monitoring will continue on Cuverville Island and at other sites considered to be at risk and the group is equally concerned to propose and test management solutions to some of the environmental problems identified. For example, many sites that are visited by tourists would benefit from careful management over a number of years; under procedures prescribed in the Environmental Protocol, the team is drafting management plans for several of these sites for submission to ATCMs, to test the practicality and usefulness of the measures provided. It may currently be argued that the most effective policing of tourists ashore is done by the tour operators themselves; the team is considering the legal and practical implications of a ship-borne inspectorate, akin to whaling and fisheries inspectorates, that would encourage the operators to maintain high standards of passenger management on their ships.

If numbers increase at even modest rates, by the end of the century we may see 20 000 to 30 000 tourists ashore each season, from two to three times as many ships as we see at present. Will operators still be permitted to land them at any undesignated site? Has the ASTI concept of attractive areas that facilitate handling and monitoring again become relevant? If so, what makes an area attractive? The possibilities of developing park areas are also being investigated, similar in function to Arctic recreational wildlife parks, with research, information and resource centres, in sites where large numbers of tourists can be set ashore with minimal environmental damage. This kind of development could at least provide a solution to the large-ships problem outlined earlier and at best solve the broader problem of catering for much larger numbers of tourists overall. The team is investigating the use as resource centres of some of the disused huts, well-built but falling into disrepair, which have become surplus to the needs of national operations.

SUMMARY AND CONCLUSIONS

Antarctic tourism, which began in 1956, has since developed and expanded: whatever its merits or drawbacks, it is clearly here to stay. No longer is Antarctica exclusively a continent for science; like every other continent it must accept its quota of tourists and those who seek to administer it would be wise to cater for them with good grace and efficiency. Fortunately for the administrators, both the air-borne and ship-borne tourism evolving in Antarctica are environmentally benign. Shipborne passengers are mostly managed according to a pattern developed by Lars-Eric Lindblad, with almost negligible impacts immediately discernible.

Antarctica is managed under the Antarctic Treaty System. The recently developed Environmental Protocol covers all aspects of human activity on the continent and neighbouring islands and provides the legislative framework for effective tourist management. Surprisingly little study has been made of the tourist industry during its period of growth and expansion and the field data and information needed to create effective legislation are lacking. The Scott

Polar Research Institute is leading a six-year programme of research, providing information that will be processed and made available, together with practical management recommendations, for consideration at Antarctic Treaty Consultative Meetings.

ACKNOWLEDGEMENTS

The author thanks colleagues Kim Crosbie, Pamela Davis, Anita Dey, Debra Enzenbacher, Colin Harris, Cora de Leeuw and Amanda Nimon, whose interest and achievements in this research are constantly encouraging. Our first year's fieldwork was funded mainly by the World Wide Fund for Nature, that of our second and third years through the generosity of the Jephcott Charitable Trust. We are also grateful to the Government of Argentina and Instituto Antartico Argentino for logistic support, to Argentine colleagues who shared our field studies and the Government of British Antarctic Territory. John Heap (Director, SPRI), Mike Richardson (UK Foreign and Commonwealth Office) and David Walton (British Antarctic Survey) have been constructive and helpful throughout. We thank Lars-Eric Lindblad, Werner Zehnder and tour operators Ocean Cruise Lines, Saln Lindblad Cruising, Travel Dynamics, Clipper Cruises and others who have assisted with passages for researchers and freight to and from Antarctica.

REFERENCES

Antarctic, 1966, News items from *The Press*, Christchurch, 4 November 1910, **4**(6), 292.

Auburn, F.M., 1983, The Royal Commission on the Mount Erebus air disaster, *Polar Record*, **21**(133), 359–367.

Boswall, J., 1986, Airborne tourism 1982–4: a recent Antarctic development, *Polar Record*, **43**(123), 187–191.

Chippindale, R., 1980, *Aircraft Accident Report No. 79139*, Government Printer, Wellington.

Codling, R.J., 1982, Sea-borne tourism in the Antarctic: an evaluation, *Polar Record*, **21**(130), 39.

Enzenbacher, D.J., 1992, Tourists in Antarctica: numbers and trends, *Polar Record*, **28**(164), 17–22.

Explorers Journal, 1957, First commercial flight to Antarctica, *Explorers Journal*, **35**(1), 18–19.

Harris, C.M., 1991a, Environmental effects of human activities on King George Island, South Shetland Islands, Antarctica, *Polar Record*, **27**(162), 193–204.

Harris, C.M., 1991b, Environmental management on King George Island, South Shetland Islands, Antarctica, *Polar Record*, **27**(163), 313–324.

Heap, J. (ed.), 1990, *Handbook of the Antarctic Treaty System*. Seventh edn, Polar Publications, Cambridge.

IUCN, 1991, *A Strategy for Antarctic Conservation*. International Union for the Conservation of Nature and Natural Resources, Gland and Cambridge.

Reich, R.J., 1980, The development of Antarctic tourism, *Polar Record*, **20**(126), 304–314.

Stonehouse, B., 1965, Too many tourists in Antarctica? *Animals*, **7**(17), 450–453.

Stonehouse, B., 1990, A traveller's code for Antarctic visitors, *Polar Record*, **26**(156), 56–58.

Stonehouse, B., 1992, Monitoring shipborne visitors in Antarctica: a preliminary field study, *Polar Record,* **28**(166), 213–218.

Stonehouse, B., 1993, Shipborne tourists in Antarctica: Scott Polar Research Institute studies, 1992–3, *Polar Record,* **29**(171), 330–332.

Stonehouse, B., 1994, Tourism and the Antarctic Protected Areas, in Lewis, R.I., Walton, D.W.H., and Dingwall, P.R.(Eds), *Improving the Antarctic Protected Areas,* IUCN, Cambridge, 76–83.

Swithinbank, C.W., 1992a, Non-government aircraft in the Antarctic 1990–91, *Polar Record,* **28**(164), 66.

Swithinbank, C.W., 1992b, Non-government aircraft in the Antarctic 1991–92, *Polar Record,* **28**(164), 232.

Swithinbank, C.W., 1993, Airborne tourism in the Antarctic, *Polar Record,* **28**(169), 103–110.

van Bennekom, S., 1992, A new regime to protect the Antarctic environment, *Leiden Journal of International Law,* **5**(1), 33–52.

Index

Index compiled by Liza Weinkove